the Grace of the Ginkgo

michael r hardesty

 OLD STONE PRESS

The Grace of the Ginkgo

Published by Old Stone Press
an imprint of J. H. Clark & Associates, Inc.
Louisville, Kentucky 40207 USA
www.oldstonepress.com

For information about special discounts for bulk purchases or autographed copies of this book, please contact Old Stone Press at john@oldstonepress.com or the author at michael@blackandwhite.com.

The Grace Of The Ginkgo is a work of fiction. Names, characters, businesses, places, events, and incidents contained herein are either the products of the author's imagination or are used in a fictitious context.

The Grace of the Ginkgo
Library of Congress Control Number: 2015919806
ISBN: 978-1-938462-23-8

Published in the United States

For my granddaughter, Sara Beth, whose beautiful countenance as a toddler in the back seat of my car, was the spark that ignited this story. I still consider her smile a measure of my worth.

ALSO BY MICHAEL R. HARDESTY:

Honey Bun And Chip | Laredo Press, 2012
Who Made The Sun, Mommy? | Author House, 2010

Acknowlegdments

To *those early* readers of *The Grace of the Ginkgo*, Martha Hardesty, Kathy Hardesty-Seay, Bill Medley, Mary Jo Roberts, Noel Thomas, and Leta Watson: thank you. Your encouragement and kindness kept me going.

I also wish to express sincere gratitude to my friends and musicians, Pam French and Zachary French, for serving as acoustic compasses through the musical segments contained herein.

Likewise, I'm indebted to Bridget B. Hittepole, MD, whose generous advice and editing helped me to navigate the medical issues contained in this story.

Finally, to my classmates and instructors in Stanford University's Certificate of Writing Program: I'm lucky to have bumped into you guys. Please accept my heartfelt thanks for veering me in a better direction by showing me precisely how much I didn't know about writing fiction.

Chapter One

"What the devil do you mean to sing to me, priest? You are out of tune."
—JEAN PHILIPPE RAMEAU

It wasn't until my junior year of college that I became completely comfortable with my disdain for the concept of a supreme being of any persuasion; God, including Jesus and the Holy Ghost, Allah, the Great Spirit, Shiva, you name him. As an upperclassman at UMass Amherst, I began to pronounce the word atheist with the accent on the second syllable. I rationalized that emphasis focused on the word's meaning, rather than prompting people to reflexively categorize those of us to whom it applied as either weirdos or pitiable sinners. I must admit, however, that I thought my emphasis gave the word a hint of an intellectual ring, a feature I tended to like in a term that described myself.

It was years later, in early March of 1991, when I drove from my home in Boston to visit Billy Hall at a military rehabilitation center in Rochester, NY. Billy was with my son, Patrick, when he was killed in a Gulf War incident. Billy was the only survivor of the four soldiers involved. I needed to hear from him exactly what had happened.

The young GI, whose words came slowly, remained heavily bandaged from the head and facial injuries he had sustained as he related to me that on February 12, Patrick was told by his CO to take three troops with him on a reconnaissance mission to the outskirts of Khafji, a Saudi city that Iraqi troops had attacked and occupied just days earlier.

"We were about ten or twelve miles out of camp," Billy said, "when our APC came across what seemed to be a local Saudi, kicking a young kid who was lying in the road. We jumped out of the vehicle and ran at the guy, yelling for him to stop.

"When we got close, we could see the kid's face was decomposed, that he'd been dead for a while. By the time we realized we'd been set up, the guy had moved close to us. Just as he pulled the cord attached to the pins of the grenades strung across his vest, he yelled, *'Allahu akbar!'* God is great."

Sudden rage in my head and upper torso displaced the sorrow I'd been enduring. My son, murdered by a fucking fanatic in the name of God.

Billy then reactivated my grief. "Patrick moved in front of me, Mr. Foley. That's the only reason I'm alive. He shot the son of a bitch, but that didn't stop the grenades from going off."

Driving back to Boston after visiting with Billy, I was speeding through the darkness of the Berkshire Mountains in western Massachusetts, hearing and rehearing the young soldier's account of my son's murder. I decided to listen to music in an attempt to divert my thoughts from Patrick's death. When I turned on the tape, it was queued to Mozart's "Requiem."

The irony not withstanding, I became enrapt with "Requiem's" fervor, its disquieting motif. The furious music swirled through the car, pressurized my chest, reverberated stereophonically in my head like an hallucinogen. When the liturgical voices of the mixed choir conjoined the instrumentation, they intoned my precise emotions—anguish, despair, fear.

As my headlights sliced through the dense mountain darkness, I gave thought to turning them off, depressing the accelerator, locking my elbows with clinched fists on the steering wheel, and discovering how long it would take to run off the road, plunge into the Berkshire blackness.

While considering the worth of my life at eighty-five miles-per-hour, a thought of my imminent grandchild sparked in my consciousness, enkindled a vivid impression of Patrick's coming daughter. Contemplating her, the only child of my only child, broke the eerie clench of Mozart's death music. I relaxed my arms, decelerated, and lowered the volume of the euphonious music. That incident in the Berkshires was the first time I ever considered killing myself.

Within days, I began to feel a compulsion to be in close proximity to my son's widow, Kathryn, and her coming child, a child a sonogram had shown to be a female. Patrick had met Kathryn Rausch in her hometown of Louisville, KY, while he was stationed at Fort Knox, his first post after graduating from the military academy at West Point. He was buried with full military honors at Zachary Taylor National Cemetery in the northeast section of Louisville, not far from the small, shotgun-style house Kathryn was renting in the Germantown neighborhood of that city. She had moved back to her hometown from Elizabethtown, a small city near Fort Knox where she and Patrick first lived. She wanted to be near her family after he was sent to the Middle East.

I had grown quite fond of Kathryn and when I visited her in Louisville, we always enjoyed sitting on her front-porch swing, talking about Patrick. Against the backdrop of the quaint Germantown house, it was easy for me to envision her as the waiting wife of a Korean Conflict GI in the 1950s. Her blonde hair was loosely curled and she avoided using much makeup, adding to her anachronistic appearance.

One afternoon, I took a Polaroid of her on the swing, attempting to capture her natural elegance and her 1950s ambience. Her face radiated beauty, even in a spontaneous snapshot, and her smile epitomized the wholesome sweetness that I knew had drawn Patrick to her.

During my regular visits to Germantown, Kathryn often mentioned that she saw many of Patrick's traits in my mannerisms, heard his voice in mine.

"David, you always clear your throat before you speak, just the way Patrick did," she'd say, "and you pronounce 'Bahston' exactly as he did."

Being with Kathryn, listening to her speak of her coming daughter, engendered a need within me to be close to her and my imminent granddaughter, Liesl. Kathryn told me she had loved the name Liesl since identifying as a child with the oldest Von Trapp daughter in "The Sound of Music." I knew from phone conversations with Patrick that he, too, was pleased with the name.

Kathryn was, and Liesl would be, spiritual connections to my son. The pain from losing the boy I raised alone from the time he was four, was less unbearable when I was in Kathryn's company. We seemed to help each other circumvent the finality of Patrick's death. It was as if our exchanges allowed him to linger with us.

After one of my visits to Louisville, I was back home having coffee in my kitchen after another lonely dinner and regarding the photo I had taken of Kathryn on her porch swing. The thought of moving to Kentucky ignited in my consciousness. In short order, it was a wildfire. I decided quickly, with confidence, to move to Louisville. Within weeks, I planned and executed an employee stock-option agreement, wherein the forty-four employees of the firm I founded just out of college, Black & White Communications, agreed to purchase one hundred percent of my stock for $2.7 million, to be paid with interest over ten years. I also had a healthy 401k, full equity in my house, and no debt. Finances wouldn't be a problem.

The more I visited Louisville, the more comfortable I became with leaving New England, winding down to the slower, more pleasant pace that city and retirement afforded. In April, I purchased and began moving into a spacious, three-bedroom house in St. Matthews, a one-time outpost of Louisville that had long since been absorbed into the greater metro area.

It was a Cape Cod-style home of gray creek stone with dormer windows set between green shutters. Two park benches sat under four, well-spaced, mature oak trees in the large, flat front yard. A stone walkway began at the side drive and meandered beneath and between the graceful oaks to the wide front porch of 414 Ascension Road.

A spacious back yard was bounded on three sides by a lining of interspersed dogwood trees and nandina bushes. The side driveway ended at a neat, two-car, wooden garage. It was an idyllic setting that Patrick would have loved playing in as a youngster.

A large, magnificent ginkgo tree in the right rear quadrant of the back yard gently dominated the rear landscape. Its just-budding branches spread from the trunk in random and spontaneous fashion, like sporadic, streaming fireworks in a night sky. In late spring, I noticed the ginkgo's leaves were shaped like Far Eastern fans. After reading a bit, I learned what an irony of nature that was, since the ginkgo's origins trace to prehistoric China.

I cherished the routine Kathryn and I had established, dinner at her

Germantown house on Wednesdays and a regular Sunday lunch at Four-fourteen, followed by an afternoon walk through St. Matthews. During the final weeks of her pregnancy, I enjoyed relieving her of the tedium of errands and chores such as grocery shopping. I also began driving her to the obstetrician's office for her late-term visits.

Kathryn often alluded to the fact that she'd been fed Catholicism by her parents from her earliest years, just as I had been by my mother and my teachers.

"Catechism was my first class of the day for eight years of elementary school," she said during one of our Germantown dinners, "but by the time I was an adolescent, I'd become suspicious of Catholic dogma."

She, like Patrick, hadn't become a dyed-in-the-wool atheist, but each had come to realize "faith" wasn't a necessary criterion for happiness, their own in particular.

"How did you handle all that with Patrick when he was young, David? I mean *God* and *church* and *religion*."

My initial chuckle settled into a broad smile as I placed my chin onto the heel of my hand, supported by an elbow propped on her kitchen table. "That would have been a serious issue if Patrick's mother had stayed with us," I said, "since she was a firm believer in the Lord and the hereafter. As it were, I didn't teach him to be anti-religious, but I omitted any god and the accompanying religion from his upbringing. I only remember him broaching the subject once, when he was in the third grade.

"He asked me if we could go to church sometime and I told him yes, we could go that weekend if he'd like. When I asked what gave him the idea, he said, 'Some kids in my class can't believe I don't have to go to church. They said I'm so lucky.'

"I resisted the urge to agree with his classmates, and told him we'd go to Mass at my old parish, Sts. Peter & Paul, on Saturday at five o'clock. I wanted Mass to interrupt an activity-laden Saturday afternoon rather than a dull Sunday morning.

"One of the reasons for selecting 'P&P' was that the parish school had closed due to dwindling enrollment and that assured most attendees would be old. It was also a 'low' Mass with none of the Catholic bells and whistles, no ringing of altar bells, no choir, only two small lighted candles, and an old man assisting the priest instead of two bona fide altar boys.

"Kathryn, it was a stacked deck. Patrick was bored from minute one; no questions, no curiosity, and no interest. We knelt in the pew during the Consecration and the distribution of Holy Communion, about twenty minutes. He kept arching his back and looking at me. I offered him no relief, just sort of shrugged my face.

"'I can see what the guys at school meant by me being lucky,' he said in the car on the way home. He never revisited the idea of a Sunday church pilgrimage."

Relating stories about Patrick to Kathryn seemed to ease the anguish of losing my son, but at the same time, it made me realize how much I missed him.

I had come to think of Kathryn as a daughter as the time neared for the insertion of a third person into our new confederation. Liesl.

Early in the afternoon of July 10, Kathryn phoned her parents and informed them that her water had broken and she needed to get to the hospital. Floyd and Elizabeth Rausch picked their daughter up about fifteen minutes later and drove her to St. Anthony Hospital. They then called me to join them, as had been agreed.

For the first few hours, during her early labor, the Rausches and I were allowed to be with Kathryn in her private room. As her contractions became more frequent and intense, the three of us were asked to move to the maternity waiting room. After a grueling eleven hours of labor, the last few of which were very intense, Kathryn's obstetrician decided a Caesarean delivery was necessary.

When her parents and I were ushered in to see her just before she was wheeled to the operating room, Kathryn was anesthetized, but awake and comfortable. She told us she didn't want to have Liesl delivered via Caesarean because she didn't want to be recovering from her own surgery during the baby's first few days, but when the physicians explained to her that she was too weak to push sufficiently for a vaginal birth, and that Liesl could possibly be harmed in the process, she agreed to the C-section.

Floyd, Elizabeth and I returned to the maternity waiting room where St. Anthony himself hadn't escaped the contagion of cable TV's specialty programming, and the good Franciscan's wall-mounted, thirty-six-inch, plasma hypnotic eye was rerolling its fourth consecutive, fifteen-minute presentation of the previous day's baseball highlights.

I had tried to turn the set off as the Rausches seated themselves, but the power button was locked on. The best I could do was mute the sound, sneak the remote under the cushion of my chair, and sit with my back to the set. I figured that would give me a fighting chance of avoiding TV's unrivaled, visual suction. Comfortably settled in their chairs, Floyd and Elizabeth offered living proof of the tube's power to mesmerize. Despite having told me that they didn't give a hoot about baseball, the whole time they were chatting with me, both were upwardly agaze, double plays and fancy outfield catches reflecting in their glasses. It was one-fifteen in the morning.

Wadded bags of vending machine potato chips, cheese crackers, and miniature donuts, with respective crumbs of yellow, orange, and brown, littered the tops of three brown, Formica drum tables. Months-old issues of *People, Sports Illustrated,* and *Newsweek* lay open on green and brown upholstered chairs, colors selected, no doubt, because they were efficient at masking beverage and food soilages.

I grimaced at the stale smell of the room and hoped Liesl's birth wouldn't be the event I'd always recall, whenever I encountered a similar malodor in the future.

A sad-looking couple, probably in their sixties, with an accompanying five or six-year-old boy, entered the room and positioned themselves needlessly close to Kathryn's parents and me. The boy referred to his two adults as "Mammy" and "Pappy." The young fellow fidgeted in one chair after another and sometimes used the drum tables as drums. While his grandparents were occupied in what I could tell was serious conversation, the boy picked up a cheese cracker remnant from a table. After a furtive glance at Mammy and Pappy, he slipped it into his mouth.

He gawked at me for a minute or two at a time and I tried to out-stare him every time I noticed him doing it. I was winning handily, four stare downs to one.

"Mammy and Pappy have to be the worst names ever for grandparents," I whispered to Floyd and Elizabeth. "What do Madonna's children call you?"

"Mammy and Pappy," Floyd said, not breaking a smile but breaking the vacuum of the overhead TV long enough to see and hear my reaction, an embarrassed smile and a meek, "Oh."

"I was just kidding, David," Floyd said. "They call us Granny and Grandpa."

The boy moved even nearer to the Rausches, unaware I was observing him. I couldn't believe it when he inserted his index finger into his nostril and started "searching." Coming up empty, he switched to his thumb and soon extracted some sort of mushy matter that he eyed with care before rolling it between his thumb and middle finger. I cleared my throat, hoping to get his attention. When the boy *did* look at me, I asked him, "Did you get it?"

Floyd coughed while Elizabeth shifted in her chair, her face reddened with embarrassment. The boy's expression dropped as he retreated to Mammy, climbed onto her lap. He looked at me with defiance and wiped his fingers on her dress. She was talking to Pappy and didn't notice.

A nurse came through one of two doors in the hallway, smiling. "Mr. and Mrs. Fletcher, you have a new granddaughter. Denzil, you have a baby sister."

Denzil looked at his grandparents as they asked perfunctory questions of the nurse. Mammy and Pappy still seemed sad despite the news of their new granddaughter. I figured their sadness was connected to the lack of a father in Denzil's family. Though I didn't believe my sorrow had been as evident as it was in Mammy and Pappy's faces, I was always distressed that Patrick's family didn't include a mother. All at once, I felt sorry for Denzil, and when the young fellow glanced back at me as he was going through the door with his grandparents, I smiled at him, winked. "You'll be a good big brother, Denzil," I said. I was glad to see him return my smile.

I rejoined the conversation with the Rausches, which was basically an exchange of insubstantialities. We just didn't have a lot in common. I hadn't spent a lot of time with them during Patrick's courtship of and marriage to Kathryn, but I was confident I had them correctly categorized as part of the large, unwitting flock. I often wondered how a person of Kathryn's charm and poise could have sprung from such a prosaic union as that of Floyd and Elizabeth.

Elizabeth had suffered a stroke shortly after Patrick and Kathryn were married, leaving her frail and partially paralyzed on the left side of her face. When she needed or wanted to blink, smile, wince or sneeze, only the right side of her face would express those reflexive commands.

Unlike the Rausches, I'd never set foot in St. Anthony Hospital. Floyd and Elizabeth had been in that same waiting room many times, courtesy of their older daughter, Madonna. She and her husband, Michael Maddox, had made the Rausches grandparents seven times in twelve years. I was tempted to ask if daddy Michael had stretch marks from so many pregnancies.

"I remember each of Madonna's births," Floyd said as he stared at the sky through the waiting room's lone window, to which he'd moved after escaping the TV's spell during a station break. "From Magdalene to Maria Noel, I can describe them all."

Fearing an unabridged account of all seven Maddox births was imminent, I suggested, "How about just the first and last ones? Or perhaps just the highlights."

"That's easy, David," Floyd said, missing my sarcasm. "The first one, Magdalene, came in such a rush that Elizabeth and I weren't notified until after she was born. Madonna woke Michael to go to the hospital at four-forty in the morning. Magdalene was born less than two hours later, at six twenty-nine. Can you imagine?"

"Uh, no," I said.

"And Maria Noel is a beautiful story," Elizabeth interjected with the right side of her lips curling to a smile. "Madonna and Michael planned the conception on the anniversary of the Annunciation, March 25. In the last month of her pregnancy, the doctor was predicting December 27 as the birth date, but he, Madonna, and Michael agreed to induce Maria Noel on December 25."

"Are you telling me," I asked, "that your daughter both planned the conception and had her child induced so that she'd arrive on Christmas Day?"

"Yes," Elizabeth said, her half-smile intensifying.

That's the most moronic goddamned thing I've ever heard, is what I thought. "Well, I'll be darned."

At that moment, one of the nurses who had been pushing Kathryn's gurney when she left the labor room, emerged through the two windowless doors in the hall. She approached us with a facial expression worn only by those contemplating something troublesome. Her direful frown was contagious, first infecting me, and then spreading to Floyd and Elizabeth when they saw my expression grow somber.

"She's having some problems," said the nurse. "Dr. Heston will be here in a minute to tell you about it."

"Who's Dr. Heston?" I asked.

"He's the obstetric surgeon," the nurse answered.

"What do you mean, problems?" Elizabeth asked.

"Her uterus isn't contracting properly after all the labor and pushing she endured. That's causing her to lose a lot of blood. She's unconscious, but we're attempting to stabilize her with fluids, then we'll do a CT scan of her brain."

"Unconscious? What?" I yelled with urgency, fearing the nurse's comments might be but a forerunner of worse news to come from this Heston guy.

Soon enough came Dr. Heston, slowly, somberly, through the same doors from which the nurse had bolted. The look on his face was unmistakable. I knew when I saw him that Kathryn was gone. Heston whispered, to Floyd specifically, "I'm Tom Heston, Mr. Rausch. I'm sorry, we lost her. I'm really sorry. We did everything we could, but the bleeding . . . we just couldn't find which vessel was hemorrhaging."

Floyd sank into a chair and bawled into both hands. "Jesus, Jesus, please, not this, not our baby. You can't, we just can't—"

Elizabeth sobbed from the only side of her face that could express grief and pain. I myself wanted to thrash about, to scream as the expatiating pressure sucked the air out of my lungs. I couldn't move, was unable to escape the agonizing pain descending from my head into my chest. I tried to console Floyd and Elizabeth, but all I could manage was to place my hands on their shoulders and whisper, "I'm so sorry."

After an unmeasured time, with my head bent and my fingers clasped across the crown, I asked Heston, "What about the baby?"

"She's fine," he said with a sigh. "Beautifully formed, neurologically sound, perfectly fine."

"Liesl," I whispered. "Where is she, Doctor?"

"She's in the neonatal intensive care unit, only because that's standard procedure when the mother is lost. It's on the third floor."

"I need to see her," I said to Floyd and Elizabeth. As I moved to the elevator bank, I passed an aged nun wearing the traditional brown Franciscan habit. Her lips were silently moving and she had a single bead of her large, dangling, fifteen-mystery rosary entrapped between her right thumb and forefinger.

"The Lord works in mysterious ways," she said to the Rausches.

"He surely does, Sister," I heard Elizabeth say as the elevator door was closing. My anger rippled between floors. The mysterious fucking ways of the Lord, I thought. Jesus Christ, Elizabeth, have you already forgiven the Lord?

When the elevator door slid open and I stepped into the neonatal unit, the quiet but warm demeanor of a young nurse with "Mia" printed on her name badge neutralized my anger. She pointed me to the dispenser of hand sanitizer, gave me a sterile gown to wrap around my clothes.

"I'm Mia Smith," she said. "Who do you wish to visit?"

"Liesl."

"Liesl?"

"Yes, Liesl Foley. I'm her grandfather."

"Ah, Baby Foley," she said. "I'm so sorry about her mother."

I sensed sincerity in her condolence rather than the mere rote of learned protocol.

"Your granddaughter's the most beautiful little girl," Mia said, "but I didn't know she'd been named."

"Well, I suppose she hasn't been, formally," I said.

"I see. Why don't you just sit here in this rocking chair for a moment? I'll be right back."

Mia opened the security door and walked into the adjoining room that had several rows of Plexiglas cribs, each with a bundling of a soft blue or pink blanket covering all but the face of each tiny occupant. Sitting in the rocker, I could see her returning, pushing one of the cribs toward the still-open door, through it.

When she and the rolling crib reached me, Mia stopped, lifted the occupant with great care, arranged the tube and two lines tethering the child to several portable monitors, and placed the bundle into my lap. I trembled for the first time in my life.

Liesl's eyes were like black liquid pools. They and the rest of her face seemed to be frowning at me. She blurred in my vision as tears accumulated in my eyes, tracked down my cheeks, and onto the pink swaddling.

"Liesl," I whispered.

"Liesl is such a beautiful name," Mia said. "Is that what I should put on the birth certificate? What's her middle name?"

"Can it be just Liesl?"

"Yes," she said. "A middle name isn't necessary."

"Her mother and father never got as far as a middle name," I said.

"I'm sorry," Mia said. "And what will Liesl call you?"

"I was going to be 'Poppa.' I suppose none of this should change that."

"You look like a Poppa. Sit here with your granddaughter, please. I need to take care of a few things elsewhere in the unit. Just push this button when you're ready for me to put her back into the crib," Mia said as she left the room.

Liesl and I were alone. For the next hour or so, I marveled at my granddaughter's expressiveness as I sang to her, echoing melodies I had sung to Patrick as a baby, using a pitch deep enough for her to feel the tonal vibration in my chest.

You are my sunshine,
My only sunshine.

You make me happy
When skies are gray.

I refused to think of what lay ahead but allowed myself to immerse in the moment's intensity.

Chapter Two

"The only love affair I have ever had was with music."
— MAURICE RAVEL

After I left the hospital, still before daybreak, I was sitting in my living room, the night's tragedy and the better part of a bottle of Zinfandel affecting my thoughts. Other losses and family failures resurfaced; Patrick's violent death in the Middle East, the inevitable split with his mother, Elaine. I remembered the night in 1971 that our marriage finished disintegrating.

"Where were you tonight?" I asked. "Patrick was asking for you."

Elaine didn't look at me, feigning a preoccupancy with the *Globe's* business section. "Reggie had some clients to dinner and asked if I'd join them afterward for drinks at The Hub in Newton. It just ran a little late, David."

Rather than a satisfied okay, I said, "That's interesting," to make her understand I didn't believe her. When she failed to respond to my response-begging rejoinder, I figured she was fucking somebody. Both of us knew our marriage was falling apart anyway. For the past several months, Elaine's interest in any sexual activity with me had pretty much dried up. Before, even when we had serious marital problems surfacing, she hadn't let any of them interfere with our bedroom life.

If it wasn't for Patrick, I would have already been long-since gone. Elaine was the pampered product of the coupling of a wealthy chemical engineer and his ultra-conservative, socialite wife. She'd been philosophically static during the span of our marriage, while I myself had morphed from a moderate Republican into an unabashed liberal. My conversion accelerated with the television coverage of Chicago policemen beating surrendering protesters with nightsticks outside the 1968 Democratic National Convention and eventually culminated with the Watergate scandal and the subsequent resignation of Richard Nixon.

Slowly, painfully, Elaine and I each realized the other was married to a stranger. Patrick remained our only child and was just shy of five years old when she announced she was leaving me in favor of Reginald Bartholomew, the nouveau-riche, Greenwich, CT hedge fund investment manager, for whom she had worked for a brief time.

Further, she proclaimed, there was no room in her plans for Patrick and she was comfortable he would be "just fine" remaining with me in Boston. Once the divorce was final, Elaine and Bartholomew moved to South Florida, leaving me the delicate, distasteful, and ongoing chore of explaining to Patrick why his mother didn't love us and wasn't coming back.

Still sitting in my darkened living room in Louisville, I noticed the bottle of Zinfandel and remembered Elaine always bitched that I drank too much wine. Fuck her. I finished it off with a couple of gulps straight from the bottle.

The day after Kathryn's death, Floyd and Elizabeth had to tend to the details of her funeral while dealing with what I knew was the unique and hideous grief parents experience when their children die. They only visited Liesl once, coming to the NICU for a brief time during my second encounter with the child in the late morning. They mostly talked between themselves, paying Liesl only perfunctory attention and excluded me from their conversations. They were occupied with arranging a solemn, Saturday Requiem Mass for their daughter at Precious Blood Catholic Church as well as Thursday and Friday evening visitation at O'Bryan Brothers Funeral Home. Kathryn was to be interred on Saturday, next to Patrick's grave at Zachary Taylor National Cemetery.

I spent most of the day at St. Anthony, beginning to assess options for Liesl's immediate and long-term care, once Mia Smith ceded charge of my granddaughter. Liesl slept for long periods at a time so, other than the two fifteen-minute feedings that Mia allowed me to dispense, I had ample time to contemplate options for Liesl's future in the quiet loneliness of the NICU waiting room.

I didn't see many viable choices for Liesl's care. Floyd and Elizabeth had downsized into a modest, two-bedroom condominium. Elizabeth was physically weak and her infirmities would make it impossible for her to deal with the demands of raising a child. Furthermore, I sensed that Floyd not only lacked the propensity to tend a newborn, a toddler, or a preschooler, he lacked the will. I was thankful, I had no idea to whom or what, that the Rausches' situations eliminated them as potential custodians rather than having to voice my objections to such an arrangement.

To place Liesl into the local Catholic adoption process would have been unacceptable to me. I couldn't have borne to have her in the company of strangers, in particular any rigid, pious strangers who met Catholic adoption criteria.

I thought the best option, but by no means an ideal one, would be for Madonna and Michael Maddox to assume responsibility for Liesl and add her to the last spot on what would be an eight-child roster. The Maddoxes, I had to concede, were doing an admirable job of rearing their seven children. All of them, from fourteen-year-old Magdalene to seven-month-old Maria Noel, were delightful young people and positive confirmation of a loving environment.

I did, however, anticipate a few problems to come in the thus far turbulence-free Maddox family. It seemed unreserved parental love and devotion would suffice to get a child from birth to twelve-years-old in reasonably good mental and emotional order, but I believed a more universal perspective, a greater tolerance for "differences" than the Maddox parents possessed, became necessary just about the time puberty arrived in children.

Magdalene, a beautiful and physically developed young teen, was restricted by her parents from dating, other than on those occasions when there was a sanctioned event such as a freshman mixer or a school athletic competition. Madonna and Michael kept her off-limits to any boy who merely wanted to take her to a party, a movie, or a concert. I thought Magdalene just might have been a candidate ripe to reap much subconscious revenge upon her parents for that suppression.

I further believed that twelve-year-old Urban was even more of a prospect to disquiet the Maddox household. He didn't like basketball. He didn't like football. He didn't like soccer. Urban liked ballet. Whereas Madonna glazed over her son's propensity for plies and pirouettes, Michael seemed in total denial.

"He's so young," Michael would say. "He still wants to emulate his older sisters. He'll be blitzing the quarterback or converting a penalty-kick before you know it."

I myself wasn't quite so sure of that.

In addition, Kathryn once confided to me that ten-year-old John Paul had been astute enough to ask his parents why Jesus had to suffer on the cross. "If he was God, why didn't he just say, 'Your original sin is gone?' Why did he have to bleed and die and stuff?" Could John Paul have been exhibiting the beginnings of serious doubt?

The possibilities of coming turmoil within the Maddox enclave, and my cynicism about their Catholic beliefs notwithstanding, a methodical process of elimination was pointing me to the conclusion that their adoption of Liesl would be the least objectionable solution to the problem of finding a home for my granddaughter.

That is unless—

In the early morning hours on the day of Kathryn's interment, I sat in the silence of stygian darkness on the open back porch of Four-fourteen, contemplating the ultimacy of death. The only sound was the wind swirling in the ginkgo tree.

Kathryn's wake and funeral Mass were well attended. She'd been popular at St. Monica Academy, and had accumulated many more friends while attending the University of Kentucky. I had met many of them at her and Patrick's wedding, a mere year-and-a-half ago. Sadly, I encountered most of them again at Patrick's funeral. When I realized both my links to these people had now expired, I felt an extreme desolation in spite of the ostentation of the ritual at Precious Blood.

The Requiem ceremony hadn't changed much since I myself was an altar boy; full choir, pallbearers rolling the casket to the front of the church where a priest, dressed in a black chasuble, walked around it swinging an incense-burning thurible on a chain. Catholics were still serious about spectacle. I was sure Kathryn would've rolled her eyes, shaken her head.

I was desperate to avoid hearing, therefore possibly remembering, the eulogy the Requiem "Celebrant" was about to deliver. Father Funkhauser seemed like a nice enough fellow, but I knew Kathryn would consider his words irrelevant, so I searched for a memory, an experience, that would fit Kathryn's perception of life and death.

Oh my God, yes.

I remembered sitting on a bench between Sts. Peter and Paul Church's parking lot and the parish school's playground when I was thirteen-years-old. As I idly massaged my left earlobe with my thumb and index finger, I felt a tiny nodule on the back of the lobe. I scraped it with my thumbnail, took a look.

There, half under the nail and half not, was the tiniest of circular scabs, not more than an eighth of an inch in diameter and wafer thin. It was dead-skin white, save for a tiny, dark-red nucleus. Once I was satisfied that the remnant of this miniature, unremembered injury was merely natural elimination, I dislodged it from my thumbnail and watched it float to the gravel below.

When it landed, my eyes rested upon it, lost focus. I thought of the admonition of Sts. Peter and Paul's assistant pastor, Father Mulcahy, on Ash Wednesday. "Remember, O man, that thou art dust and to dust thou shalt return." That's just about the only thing I learned in church I had continued believing. Slight motion on the gravel caused my dormant eyes to refocus. I frowned when I saw my circular shed skin in the clutches of a tiny black ant, not much longer than the scab was wide. The insect was holding my ex-part high, high for an ant anyway, and making its way over the dips and rises of the gray gravel to the dirt at the base of a tree, just off the church parking lot.

Another ant of the same size and color was erratically circling the carrier as it lugged its prize. I wasn't sure if the circler was celebrating its co-conspirator's booty, or if it was an interloper, planning to expropriate the windfall.

As the carrier ant took a turn downward off the gravel and onto the dirt, the circler followed. I was curious to see if both insects were headed to the same anthill at the base of the tree, or if the circler would try to abscond with the tiny trophy. If so, would it succeed or fail?

I rose from the bench, pursued the pismires to the anthill, where the one carrying my scab stopped at the top of the granular mound. The trailing ant walked up the tiny hill and disappeared into the hole at the apex. The carrier ant turned and backed in, so that the last thing I saw was my ex-part disappearing into the hole. Such a propitious recycling. There I went, back to dust, no doubt providing provender for an entire colony.

When the Mass was mercifully over and I emerged from the church, the funeral director pointed me to the third limo in line behind the hearse, joining Michael Maddox's parents and some of Kathryn's aunts, uncles, and cousins for the short ride to Zachary Taylor Cemetery. When we arrived, I saw the Rausches disembark from the lead limo. Elizabeth wrapped both her arms around Floyd's left arm as they walked over moist, mid-summer clover, angling their way down a gently sloping hill toward a plateau just below them.

Each of the scores of white marble tombstones was equidistant from the ones next to it, and each was a component of a horizontal, vertical, and diagonal row, like silent soldiers at parade rest. When activated by a shifting vantage point, that perfect symmetry made the small shrines come alive with motion, like spinning spokes of stone.

When our processional reached Kathryn's gravesite, next to Patrick's stone, her coffin was suspended on thick straps over a temporary, artificial grass carpet. Her freshly created pit was purposely hidden by the green faux-turf, but I knew it was there, awaiting its occupant.

I recognized from Patrick's interment, three cemetery workers standing under a nearby tree, expressionless, unobtrusive, no doubt instructed not to make eye contact with members of the funeral party. I knew after that final, quiet ceremony, when the mourners had departed, the crew would swing into action, lower the casket to the bottom of the grave, cover it with the same earth removed to create Kathryn's ultimate resting place, right next to her husband's.

At the end of a brief service, Father Funkhauser approached the Rausches, handing Elizabeth the crucifix that was displayed in the coffin with Kathryn at the funeral home. As people dispersed, Michael and Madonna circulated among them, inviting many, including me, back to

27

their house. I had planned to be at St. Anthony with Liesl, but I didn't want to offend either the Rausches or the Maddoxes and knew if some of Patrick and Kathryn's friends would be there, I'd be in good company.

The gathering was cheerful, reminding me of the Irish wakes my mother used to describe. There was no trace of the sadness of the moment, everyone was upbeat and the mood was that of a celebration rather than a somber commemoration.

When only a few family members remained, I found myself seated in the Maddoxes' living room with Madonna and her parents. Michael was with a few aunts, uncles, and cousins, recounting family history in the living room. The Maddox children were in the basement playroom, except for Maria Noel who was in her mother's lap.

The conversation inevitably turned to alternative prospects for the guardianship of Liesl.

"Elizabeth and I are unable to take this child," Floyd said, surprising no one. "Ten or twenty years ago, yes, but not now."

"Everybody understands that, Daddy," Madonna said, rising from her seat on the couch and depositing Maria Noel in Elizabeth's lap. "We realize you're in no position—" Her voice trailed off and she shook her head slowly. She moved to the center of the room and attention. "Michael and I received some devastating news yesterday. His position at the bank is being eliminated." After a pause, as if to let the news sink in, she continued, "We're just shattered. We have some savings cushion and he'll receive some severance pay, but with our tuition obligations and all—

"In this economy, it might be impossible for Michael to find similar work, and with all the demands and activities of our children, you have to understand that now just isn't the time for us to take another person into our family."

When Madonna paused again, Floyd's eyes had retreated from their usual brightness into a beseeching squint. "I was sure you and Michael would take Liesl," he said, looking at his daughter with an expression somewhere between disappointment and shock.

His facial skin reddened as if he were angry, but his expression betrayed bewilderment. I couldn't be certain if he was distressed because the Maddoxes were facing hard times or because Liesl's future was unresolved. I suspected the latter.

I myself was skeptical of Madonna's reason for not taking Liesl. I remembered Kathryn's dismay with Madonna's criticism of Kathryn's lack of faith, rejection of Catholicism, and the "hardship" it worked on their parents. Kathryn said she could understand her *parents* having a tough time with her "renunciation," but thought her sister, a generation removed, would have at least a sliver of empathy for her feelings.

This made me wonder if Liesl's being the product of two nonbelievers had influenced Madonna's decision to not take her orphaned niece into her family. Surely not. Regardless of what the real rationale was, I felt a surprising surge of relief.

"So what do you think we should do?" I asked. "What would be in Liesl's best interest?"

Madonna replied without hesitation. "She should be placed in St. Cecilia Children's Home and put up for adoption. There are so many worthy Catholic parents trying to find just such a child."

I thought of my first encounter with Liesl, those beautiful, expectant, circumfluent eyes seemingly fixed on mine. Though I was speaking to his daughter, I looked at Floyd. "I understand your decision not to take her, Madonna, but there has to be an answer other than adoption by strangers. To me, that would be letting Patrick and Kathryn down."

I again pictured Liesl in the NICU unit, comfortable against my chest as I breathed my song into her little body. Having decided not to offer my thus far unarticulated solution until I could be alone with Floyd, I was surprised to hear myself say, "Liesl should be with me. I love her. I want her."

"That's out of the question," Madonna said, still on her feet in the center of the room. "She needs a mother and a father."

"I know," I answered, rising from Michael's easy chair from which I'd been listening, "but her mother and father are dead. Furthermore, what's in or out of the question for Liesl isn't for you to decide. That'll be up to Floyd, Elizabeth and me."

Madonna's face contorted, flushed, as she sought the refuge of the couch from which she had sprung moments earlier. "Daddy?"

Floyd chose not to countermand my assertion of who would decide whom would raise Liesl. Instead, he asked with politeness and sincerity, "David, what in heaven makes you think you could care for this little girl? You're all alone."

"Yes, I'm alone," I said with rising confidence. "And she's alone. There's nothing in *heaven* that makes me think I can raise her and meet her needs," I said, casting my eyes upward as I sounded the word heaven. "But here on earth, there is," I continued, pointing an index finger at the floor when I hit the word earth. "I love her and I want to be with her. She's the only person anywhere to whom I'm related, except a remote cousin or two. Liesl and I need each other."

"What about your age?" Elizabeth asked.

"I'm fifty-one, not seventy-one," I responded, looking at Elizabeth, widening my eyes as I did, "and there's not an unhealthy bone in my body. There's no reason to think Liesl wouldn't make it to adulthood before my time runs out. If I croak before she's an adult, *then* you can make her a ward of strangers, or perhaps the Maddoxes' status will have changed by then."

Madonna's voice intensified. "You're just not the—"

"Not the what?" I interrupted, with perfect timing and a sincere frown. "The prototypical Catholic family? Neither were her parents."

Before Madonna could react, Floyd defused the situation's volatility by turning to me and asking, "Where would you plan on living?"

With that question, I sensed a potential ally and moved to the spot in the center of the room Madonna had ceded. "Here, in Louisville," I said. "I wouldn't want to move anywhere else."

Floyd sighed. "Perhaps we should all contemplate this overnight and meet tomorrow morning to continue the discussion. Everyone's exhausted. In the meantime, let me speak to Father Funkhauser."

"I don't believe there's any point to my meeting tomorrow," Madonna said as she moved toward the kitchen. "You know how I feel, and overnight pondering won't change my mind."

"So be it," Floyd said.

Amen sister, I thought, saying nothing.

At nine o'clock the next morning, Floyd phoned me and suggested we meet at the Omelet Express in St. Matthews at about ten-fifteen. He was seated alone in the corner when I arrived.

"Where's Elizabeth?" I asked.

"She isn't feeling so well this morning," Floyd said. "But I'm not too sure she would have come anyway. This is a tough circumstance for her and she doesn't cope well with tension or adversity."

"I'm sorry," I said. "This has been difficult for everyone, but the loss of a son or daughter is cruel. It takes a terrible toll."

"Yes," Floyd said with a sigh, as he motioned for the waitress to fill his coffee cup. "Now we both know that pain."

When the waitress arrived to pour more coffee, Floyd asked her to bring him two slices of unbuttered wheat toast. I myself ordered a peach danish and orange juice.

Floyd complained about the extreme heat and humidity Louisville was experiencing as the waitress brought our orders and refilled his cup. When she was gone, I asked him if he'd talked to Father Funkhauser.

"No, I haven't," he said, looking at his cup. "I figure I pretty much know how he'd feel."

"Really," I said, feeling that Floyd's dismissal of Funkhauser's feelings was a favorable sign.

"I have no doubt the good father would opt for a Catholic adoption," Floyd said.

"Yes, I suppose he would, Floyd."

"Elizabeth and I thought Madonna and Michael would take Liesl in," he continued. "I'm surprised. Madonna knows Elizabeth and I will help them financially."

I could sense Floyd's disappointment with and his embarrassment about the Maddoxes' position. I gave him an honest nod of understanding.

Looking at the overhead fan on the restaurant ceiling, he continued, "I've seen many adoptions, from boyhood playmates to high school

31

chums to relatives of mine and Elizabeth's." He dropped his gaze to meet mine. "A lot of them, it seems, don't work out so well. I'm not sure if it's an underlying sense of rejection in the young person, a lack of preparation on the part of the parents, or what. But my experience is too consistent for me to consider it coincidental. And though there's only been one, so far unproven allegation of abuse at St. Cecilia's, the widespread reporting of such abhorrent behavior in similar places is too great to ignore.

"So you win by default, David. Elizabeth and I have decided not to contest your guardianship of Liesl. There are formalities we'll have to attend to as for her legal adoption, and we want you to keep her in Louisville. Is agreeing to that a problem?"

"Absolutely not, Floyd," I said, trying not to appear as stunned as I was, but quickly realizing my mouth was agape.

"Kathryn accumulated many items for Liesl," Floyd went on. "A crib, some clothes, a little furniture. We want you to have it."

"That's so kind of you, Floyd. I haven't even begun to think of such things. Thank you."

"There's not much else to say at the moment," Floyd said. "I hope everything works out for you and Liesl. The fine young man you raised in Patrick gives me some confidence. I'll be in touch."

As I watched Floyd leave, I was at once surging with excitement, retracting with fear; a symphony in my head, but discordance in the pit of my stomach. I wondered if I'd given enough consideration to all I had volunteered to undertake, if I was truly Liesl's best alternative.

My house was arranged, the rooms and its furniture, to accommodate a single adult, not a family, even a modest two-person family. There were many things I'd need, but for the moment, I felt a joyous urgency to be with Liesl, a pleasant vibration in my chest, not unlike the blended quivering of musical strings in perfectly executed harmony.

When I arrived at the NICU, the attending nurse told me Liesl had been moved to the regular nursery since she'd proven herself to be a robust, healthy four-day-old.

"Oh, I forgot," I said. "Mia told me that was going to happen. Is she here?"

"No, it's her day off," said the nurse.

"I see. Where's the regular nursery?"

"Up one floor."

I made my way back down the corridor to the elevator, but decided to use the stairway up to the fourth floor since all the elevators were stuck in the typical Sunday traffic of a hospital. The fourth-floor nursery had a decidedly different ambiance than the NICU. There were young mothers in new robes and new fathers dressed in beige cotton slacks and short-sleeve, madras shirts. Grandfathers and grandmothers wore their church-going clothes. The grandfathers looked awkward and uncomfortable in their surroundings, unlike their wives who seemed quite at ease. There was much talk and obvious happiness, in sharp contrast to the sobriety and solemnity of the NICU just a floor below.

I waited until an attending nurse noticed me, and widened my eyes so that she realized I needed directing. When she approached, I told her I was looking for Liesl Foley.

"She's being fed just now," the nurse said. "But if you walk through those double doors and down to the viewing window on the right, you'll see a nurse giving her a bottle."

At the nursery's viewing window, there was indeed a nurse in a rocking chair next to Liesl's empty crib. The middle-aged woman was genuinely engaged with her charge and didn't notice me staring at her and her armful. She was smiling and talking to Liesl as the little one accepted the next-best nipple. Liesl seemed to be paying strict attention to her caregiver, her expressive, dark eyes fixed upon those of the nurse.

Doubt and insecurity had never been frequent visitors of mine, but at that particular moment, both had stolen their way into my thinking.

Was I doing the right thing? Was I being selfish? Was I capable? Did a developing female human, as a toddler, a preschooler, an adolescent, a coed, need an older female's guidance to unfold in normal fashion? I wondered.

Liesl finished her meal and the attending nurse stood. She placed the child's head on her shoulder for burping. I took some semblance of solace in that. "At least we have *that* going for us, Liesl," I whispered. "I *do* know how to burp you."

The nurse noticed me and motioned with her expression and an index finger that I should wait for just a moment longer. She placed Liesl into the Plexiglas crib and rolled it up to the window. Liesl was sleeping, her face relaxed and looking unconcerned about my doubts and down-beat potentialities.

Joining me in the viewing area, the nurse inquired, "Are you Mr. Foley?" Before I could respond, she continued, "I'm Velma. Mia Smith told me about you and Liesl. She'll be ready to go home tomorrow. Have you and the family decided where she'll be going?"

"Liesl is coming with me," I said, awaiting the nurse's reaction with some trepidation.

She smiled immediately, with seeming sincerity. "I think that's wonderful, Mr. Foley. She's had an unusual and rough start, but I know you two will be just fine."

To a degree, her tone eased my reservations. "Thank you," I said. "So tomorrow's the day for her to leave here?"

"Well, it would be no problem to keep her here for an extra day if you'd like. No problem at all."

"Things have happened so quickly," I said. "And with the funeral and all—"

"I can only imagine," Velma said, placing her hand on my elbow and not allowing my unfinished sentence to create any awkwardness. "Why don't we say right now that Liesl will stay with us until Tuesday morning?"

"That would be great," I said. "I'll have this afternoon and all day tomorrow to do a bit of planning. I've done none of that so far, and there's a lot to think about. Thank you."

I wanted to stay with Liesl for a while, but since she had just been fed and was asleep, I decided to drive home and concentrate on the things I'd need to buy or get done before her Tuesday morning arrival. If I could spend Sunday afternoon planning, I'd have all day Monday to rearrange some furniture and do some shopping.

As I walked out of the hospital, I noticed the blacktopped parking lot was heavily puddled with steam rising from its surface, and it was littered with leaves and small branches. The flowers in the garden near the hospital entrance were bowing halfway to the ground, like tiny dancers, and some of their colorful petals had dropped atop the red cypress mulch. As I realized I was seeing the remnants of a brief summer squall, the last of its clouds floated from in front of the sun, leaving me awash in shimmering light.

My afternoon of planning turned up a predictable list of items that would be needed right away. Most obvious of these were short-term supplies, diapers, nursing bottle, pacifiers, and, of course, baby formula. I wasn't sure exactly what items Kathryn had, but I assumed they were more likely to be furnishings than supplies.

Thankful, to whom or what I still didn't know, that I didn't have a large desk on the second floor, I managed to move the furniture from my upstairs study into the den on the first floor. The second floor ex-office would make a great bedroom for Liesl, but the walls were painted a nondescript gray, sterile and stark with dark rectangular outlines where I had removed wall frames the previous owner had left. That just wouldn't do. Not even for a day or two should Liesl endure such cold, uninspired color.

I made a trip to the local hardware outlet, where I purchased paintbrushes, a roller and pan, drop cloths, and two gallons of flat, Buttercup Yellow acrylic paint. I first thought of using "Warm Pink" but dismissed that tint as a predictable cliché. Jesus, I wasn't painting Barbie's room.

I spent the rest of the afternoon and evening applying three coats of the fast-drying paint to the walls of Liesl's very first room. Her temporary sleeping quarters would be my bedroom. Buying a changing stand and some benign wall hangings could wait until tomorrow. That night, I rested on my Buttercup Yellow laurels.

The next morning I was at the Mall St. Matthews at nine o'clock, and by eleven-thirty, I'd purchased every item on my must-have list. I decided to drive to St. Anthony and visit Liesl, but I also wanted to see Mia. Arriving just at feeding time for Liesl, I asked the nurse on duty in the nursery if I could do the honors.

I felt a measure of confidence when Liesl seemed as satisfied feeding in my arms as she had been the day before in Velma's. My granddaughter stared at me unabashed, as she sucked on the realistic-looking, latex nipple. I stared back at her, I, too, unabashed.

After finishing the prescribed four ounces of InfaLac, Liesl fell asleep readily. She was out of consciousness as I placed her upright on my shoulder and patted her back. She burped expertly even though she was fast asleep.

After placing her back into her glass crib, I thanked the nurse and made my way down to the third-floor NICU to see Mia. When I arrived, the colorless drear of the unit stoked my emotion, the anguish of losing Kathryn, the fervency of meeting Liesl.

"Mr. Foley, hello," Mia said, her face breaking into a smile.

"I'm taking Liesl home tomorrow," I said. "I wanted to come by and say thanks and goodbye."

"The Rausches told me Liesl was going with you," she said. "I think that's wonderful. You're lucky to have each other. They also told me the circumstances of your son's death. I'm so sorry. Such tragedies you've endured."

"Thank you," I said, her seemingly genuine consolation stoking a warmth in my chest.

"Mr. Foley," she said. "I've been doing some thinking, and I know there are many things you'll need in the way of baby items, maybe even things you might not think about until the need arises. Would you think I was crazy if I said I'd like to have a baby shower for you and Liesl?"

"I beg your pardon?"

"It might sound a bit far-fetched," she continued, "but there'd only be about eight or ten people invited. My husband thinks it's a great idea. What do you say?"

"Eight or ten? None of them would know me or Liesl."

"They're all my friends," she said, "and I've already told several of them about you, namelessly, of course. They'd all like to meet the two of you."

My instinct was to decline, but I didn't want to offend anyone as thoughtful and kind as Mia, so I mustered, "A baby shower? Gosh. Uh, yes. What can I say? I mean, what do I do?"

"Just call me tonight with a list of anyone you want to be invited. Here's my number," she said, handing me a sheet of paper. "Then just show up next Sunday at 428 Mayfair Avenue at noon. Come hungry and ready to play silly games."

In the car driving home, I tried to imagine myself as a guest of honor at a baby shower. It made me realize my life would never be the same with Liesl coming to live with me. I was both surprised and pleased that I didn't care.

Let it come.

I slept only intermittently that night. Awakening at five-thirty a.m., I climbed out of bed to start the first day of my forever-changed life.

I arrived at the St. Anthony discharge office at seven forty-five and was pleased to learn that the attending pediatrician had approved Liesl's dismissal, so I took the stairs up to the nursery. Shortly after I arrived, an orderly rolled a wheelchair off the elevator and announced, "I'm here for Liesl Foley and her mother."

The nurses who had gathered at the station didn't know whether to laugh or not. Humor and sorrow sometimes occupy the same event.

Mia had arranged her schedule to be on duty in the nursery that morning so she could assist me in getting Liesl out of the hospital and into my car. She and I, with Liesl in tow in a pink infant carriage, walked down the hall and stepped onto the elevator. "On what level is your car parked?" she asked.

"P2."

"Okay, you jump off there and we'll meet you at the discharge ramp in the rear of the building," she said.

When I pulled my Civic under the canopied drive-up, I could see Mia with a St. Anthony Nursery-inscribed tote bag in one hand and Liesl's carriage in the other. I stopped the car, jumped out, came around to the passenger side, and opened the front door.

"That won't do, Mr. Foley," Mia chided. "Infants ride in the rear seat these days. Where's her car carrier?"

My first reaction was perplexity, the second was embarrassment, and the third was total, ultimate, mortifying humiliation. "Oh no," I said with a groan, thinking that Mia might just demand that I give Liesl back to the hospital.

It took about forty-five minutes for Mia and me, mostly Mia, to conceive and execute a plan. She knew that the BabySafe Maxx was a top-rated infant car seat and confirmed by phone that the nearest We-R-Babies store had one in stock. I made the trip to pick it up, returned to St. Anthony with Liesl's very own car carrier anchored in my vehicle's middle back seat.

Mia and Liesl were biding time in the first floor lounge when I pulled into the semicircle. I stayed in the driver's seat while Mia placed and secured Liesl into the carriage of the BabySafe Maxx.

"Mia," I said, "please understand that I'm not stupid enough to think that Liesl doesn't need a special contraption. It's just been a crazy couple of days, for everyone."

"I understand," she said, probably overstating her forgiveness and dismissal of the incident. "You'll need to begin to think in a much different way now, Mr. Foley. But I'm sure you'll manage to do that."

Liesl and I made what should have been an eighteen-minute car ride from St. Anthony to our Ascension Road house in about thirty minutes. I refused to venture onto the fifty-five-miles-per-hour Ali Expressway with her on board, and kept the vehicle two-to-five mph under the legal speed limit for the entire, elongated route home. In addition, I constantly glanced into the rearview mirror to make sure none of those goddamned idiot tailgaters were behind us.

It was almost one o'clock when I pulled the car into the driveway at Four-fourteen, fetched Liesl from her back seat carriage and carried her into the house. Mia had fed her during the discharge dilemma, but now she was awake and the four or five straight "short a" sounds she emanated indicated she was expecting her four-ounce portion of InfaLac once again.

I had her lying on her back in my left arm with her body pressed against my chest for support. Even though she was beginning to fuss, she felt natural to me, a perfect fit, but she was becoming more impatient and soon let loose a loud cry of disapproval that turned into three, that turned into a constant, eardrum-piercing cry except when she was forced to stop and laboriously inhale.

Each time, after getting a lung full of air, the cry returned with a louder vengeance. I was at once trying to comfort her while still holding her with only my left arm. With my right hand, I attempted to open a canister of sealed, powdered InfaLac on the kitchen countertop, scoop a measured amount of it into a bottle, add water, attach the nipple, and shake it without further displeasing the screaming contents of my left arm. I failed at all.

After a few minutes and several attempts at this futile manufacturing process, the result was a substantial amount of adjacent but unmixed powdered InfaLac and water on the countertop of operation, the floor, Liesl's white gown, and my pants and shirt. Liesl was still crying out loud.

At the height of my frustration and growing doubt, I remembered Mia's assertion. *You'll need to begin to think in a much different way now.*

She was right.

I needed to plan and thoroughly think through all things related to Liesl. I remembered the carriage in which Mia had brought her down to the discharge ramp as well as the set of pacifiers I purchased Monday.

I took my still-screaming granddaughter out the back door and into the driveway where I opened the car door and procured the transporter. I placed her in it, which immediately alleviated the massive ache in my left arm from having eight pounds of dead weight parked in it for too long a time. Transporting her back into the house with my right hand allowed the pain to subside in my left arm.

When we arrived in Liesl's room on the second floor, I retrieved the set of pacifiers. Back to the kitchen and up onto the countertop went Liesl and the carrier. I unsealed the pacifiers and coaxed her into taking one into her tiny, expectant mouth. She accepted it, secured it, sucked it, and at last quieted.

With the required two hands, I prepared the four-ounce, mid-afternoon meal of InfaLac for my granddaughter with relative ease. Her face was beginning to contort again as the pacifier slipped from her mouth. She was just about to express her opinion of the placebo nipple, when I lifted her out of the carrier, hustled up the stairs, and settled into the rocking chair, newly stationed in our bedroom.

I substituted a different artificial nipple, one that was connected to a bottle and was the means rather than the end. My first solo feeding session in twenty-five years was underway. After a few gulps of InfaLac, Liesl's tiny body inhaled convulsively and exhaled the most genuine sigh I had ever heard. That miniature reflex soothed both of us.

After two ounces, I successfully elicited a quality burp from my granddaughter. After three-and-three-quarters ounces, she was fast asleep. She started a bit as I broke the suction her beautiful, miniature, wet lips had on the nipple, but she quickly returned to peace. Following another trip to my shoulder and another burp, I placed her into the bassinet, turned on the intercom, and left the room, wincing as the door hinge squeaked.

As I was preparing myself an overdue lunch, I saw a delivery truck from Spencer's Florists in the front part of the driveway, its driver walking on the stone walkway toward the front porch. I got to the door just before the deliveryman could ring the bell.

"Mr. Foley?"

"Yes."

"A basket for you, sir."

I carried it into the kitchen and lifted a gladiolus plant from the carrier basket. It was rooted in a blue and pink ceramic pot with an image of a yellow baby duckling in a diaper. I opened the envelope that was attached to a thin wooden plant stake and addressed, "To Liesl and her Poppa." Inside it read, "Much happiness and best of luck to both my new friends! Warmly, Mia."

The balance of week one was a matter of falling into a basic routine dictated by Liesl's feeding times. She was supposed to get, and she always demanded, four ounces of InfaLac every four hours. Give or take fifteen minutes, the assigned times had become midnight, four a.m., eight a.m., noon, four p.m., and eight p.m. She was also in the steady habit of eliminating eight to ten times a day, so my routine was six InfaLac administrations and eight to ten diaper changes per twenty-four hours, two or three of which made our shared bedroom temporarily smell like there were carcasses in it.

On Sunday, the day of the shower, I bedecked Liesl in a yellow dress over a yellow "onesie," both items coming to us from what Kathryn had accumulated. Soon it occurred to me that I hadn't spoken with Mia about what proper attire might be for myself, the only man at a baby shower.

When in doubt, dress "up."

I pulled a dark suit from the closet and fingered through my ties. "Oh my God," I said aloud when I came upon a yellow one that precisely matched Liesl's dress. "Perfect."

Before toting Liesl, her car carrier, and a diaper bag with its paraphernalia to the car, I held my granddaughter in the cradle of my right arm in front of the mirror admiring our matching yellows. "Look at us, girl. Are we a pair or what?" Liesl's eyes were beautiful, but they betrayed indifference to our outfits.

Driving to Mia's house, I wondered if Elizabeth Rausch and Madonna Maddox would be there. As a gesture of good will, I had asked Mia to invite both, half-suspecting that Elizabeth would show, but that Madonna wouldn't. I was surprised when the reverse occurred and Madonna was there while Elizabeth had begged off, pleading a bout with a virus.

Though Liesl and I arrived promptly at the appointed time of noon, the other guests were already there. I was in no way prepared for the fanfare that erupted when the new Foley family walked into the living room.

"Your tie matches her dress," Mia said, as the women crowded around Liesl and me. After introducing us to everyone, Mia rescued me from my awkwardness by extracting a slumbering Liesl from my arms, affording me the opportunity to yield center-stage to my granddaughter.

"Hello, David," came a man's voice from behind. "I'm Mia's husband, Logan. I'm not supposed to be here, but I just had to slip down from upstairs to meet you and Liesl. Mia talks about you two so much, I feel like I know you."

"Mia kept last week's ordeal from completely overwhelming me," I said. "She was a godsend."

"Well, I'm going back to the Sunday paper, David, and leave all this to you."

When I rejoined the sorority of well-dressed, young women, Mia suggested I sit on the couch. As I did so, one of the guests, an attractive woman, earlier introduced to me as Charlotte, expeditiously squeezed in next to me, becoming the fourth person on the three-seated sofa.

Throughout several whimsical games, drinking tea and eating delicious hors d'oeuvres, my hips and leg were in continuous contact with Charlotte's. Feeling her silken softness, breathing a trace of her fragrance, I became aroused, but that cathexis slowly morphed into a throe of loneliness and a need I hadn't contemplated since moving to Kentucky a few months ago, the simple pleasure of a female companion.

The guests, all young, thirtyish women, were fascinated with the Foleys. "I think of Heidi and her grandfather," said one quite seriously.

I couldn't help from smiling, pleased with the analogy.

Liesl slept in the Smiths' first-floor bedroom strapped in her carrier atop a king bed with huge fluffed pillows on either side of her. I myself got in a mini-nap during a word game, when Liesl's midnight and four a.m. feedings caught up with me.

I nodded forward and drooled onto my lap, much the same as I had done more than once as a youngster in school. Unlike my teachers, the guests laughed when they noticed, understanding my drifting off from their own experiences of round-the-clock baby duty. After momentary embarrassment, I too was laughing.

"Sorry," I managed. "Nodding off is one thing, but the drooling—"

I was warmed by the thoughtful gifts for Liesl and me. A gold music box that alternately played "Brahms's Lullaby" and "Rockabye Baby," a copy of the "Big Book of Wonderful Words," and a hand-knitted, pink and blue blanket with "Liesl" stitched in its corner were among my favorites.

The most touching gift, however, came from Madonna, a beautifully illustrated grandfather's diary. "Madonna, I don't know what to say except thank you. I love it and I'll keep it religiously."

"Religiously?" Madonna asked just before she and I burst into laughter at my choice of adverbs.

As the party tapered to a pleasant ending and Madonna was leaving, she paused to thank Mia for "pulling off a great idea." Turning to me, she said, "You're going to do okay, David. If there's anything I can do for you or Liesl, please just ask."

I felt like hugging her, so I did. "You can count on me to tap those reservoirs of experience you have at motherhood, Aunt Madonna."

I thought she hugged me back and I realized a relationship with her would be a valuable asset for both Liesl and me.

Chapter Three

"To play without passion is inexcusable!"

—LUDWIG VAN BEETHOVEN

Days streamed inexorably into weeks, weeks into months. In her first year, Liesl had thin, light-colored hair with the longest, dark eyelashes I'd ever seen. No matter what the shade of her clothes, her supple and flawless skin made it seem like "her color." Many of her clothes were on loan from the Maddoxes and had most recently been modeled by Maria Noel, who was running through early childhood about a size-and-a-half ahead of Liesl, her newest cousin.

I was fortunate in that Liesl kept to a schedule and she was healthy, save for a few bouts with colic and an occasional painful ear infection. She possessed a mild, easy-going disposition, apparently not inheriting any of my grumpy genes. Most fortuitous, however, were her sleep habits. She was ready for bed at seven-thirty each evening, as long as she had a couple of songs sung to her. Her favorite was "Good Night, Irene," even though I had to ad lib most of the lyrics. She slept for close to twelve hours most nights and her naps rounded into two ninety-minute sessions each day. Except for the first few weeks, I never had to deal with the scourge of sleep deprivation.

Mia Smith's shower was the social highlight of Liesl's first and my fifty-second year. Other than a few brief visits with the Rausches and some celebratory events at the Maddoxes, usually religious holidays, our planned contacts with people were fairly limited.

Liesl became mobile on her tummy and knees at eight months and was beginning to take a few steps with some assistance shortly before her first birthday, which we celebrated with Mia and the Rausches. Michael Maddox had been reemployed at another local banking company, so the Maddox family was on vacation in Michigan and couldn't make the party.

Mia gave Liesl a miniature, eleven-piece tea set, the pieces of which, at least for the moment, she used as percussion instruments. Mia also brought an erasable slate for Liesl to begin to make her mark. The Rausches opted for a book from Brooks Sisters Christian Emporium, "Prayers For Young Hearts" by the Right Reverend Jamal Levy.

"The author's title and name seem to have most of the major persuasions covered," I said. Liesl was fascinated with the sheep surrounding the bearded man with the halo in the cover illustration.

"Can you say 'baaah,' Liesl?" I asked. Elizabeth half-grinned; Floyd didn't. Mia continued smiling her sweet smile and kept her eyes focused on Liesl, reacting neither to the book nor to my review of it.

In the fall, Liesl and I were frequent visitors to the library on the weekly Toddlers Day, as well as to a physical activities center called "InFantaCize," where toddlers could exercise by climbing, rolling, jumping, and running on soft cushiony shapes of bright blue, green, red, and yellow. Our favorite haunt, however, was the Seneca Park Tot Lot in St. Matthews where Liesl delighted in sliding, romping and swinging on mini-scaled play equipment.

Like music, Liesl's gentle laughter as she slid down the board or spun on the mechanical merry-go-round was an acoustical feast. Patrick's laughter sounded the same at that age and recalling it never made me sad. I wondered if there was any classical music themed from the chortle of toddlers.

In late September, I was surprised and elated to read in the newspaper that the Louisville Arts Consortium was sponsoring a concert in the Louisville Gardens featuring world-renowned conductor Seiji Ozawa leading the touring Berlin Philharmonic. Ozawa was the music director of the Boston Symphony, and I'd seen that ensemble perform under his direction many times. One of the pieces to be played was Beethoven's "Fifth Symphony."

I'd not been to a classical music concert in my new city, but the combination of the Berlin Philharmonic, Ozawa, and Beethoven's most passionate composition was too much to pass up.

Madonna said Liesl could spend the night with the Maddoxes, so I bought a single ticket and was fortunate to get a seat near the front on the main floor, center stage, no less. When Maestro Ozawa entered, I realized I'd never seen him that proximately. The enthusiastic applause amplified my emotion and damned if my eyes weren't tearing, from excitement, pleasure.

Seiji had long, resilient gray hair. It returned perfectly to place after he jerked his head or ran his fingers through it. It was actually beautiful. As he directed the musicians to attention, he wet his lips with his tongue. He was without a baton, as he often was when conducting. For a moment he was motionless, looking at the players, then his upper body jumped, following both his arms skyward. His hair followed suit. The musicians intoned those initial dramatic eight notes of the Fifth's first movement, notes with which everyone in the civilized world was familiar.

The Maestro's expression moved from fierce to pleading, from insulted, to satisfied. He coaxed his musicians, sometimes with his eyes, sometimes calmly mouthing to them. Other times he pantomimed yelling at them.

I was breathless after the first movement.

On a cold but sunny late October Monday, with small puffs of white clouds asymmetrically dotting an azure sky, Liesl and I had the Tot Lot to ourselves. We were both dressed in layers of pants, shirts, sweaters, hats, and gloves. Liesl never seemed to be uncomfortable in the cold, and I always believed outdoor activity in bright sunshine and cold weather was healthy for people of any age.

After about thirty minutes of our usual park revelry, a young woman and a little boy appeared near the larger swing set on the opposite side of the enclosed activity area. "Poppa," Liesl said, pointing to the young fellow who was now swinging, the woman pushing from behind. Liesl tottered toward them for a closer inspection.

I lagged behind a bit, not wanting to approach the two newcomers before I could sense whether I'd be welcome. Liesl stopped about twelve feet short of the swing sets, glanced back to make sure I was still there, and continued staring at the boy swinging under the woman's power. "What's *your* name?" she asked of Liesl, who didn't respond. I was hoping she'd give the woman the correct answer, but Liesl just kept staring at the heavily bundled swinger.

"I've seen you at the library," the woman said to me. "Are you her grandfather?"

"Liesl," Liesl finally said, one comment and one question late.

The woman and I shared a laugh at that. "I'm David Foley and, yes, I'm Liesl's grandfather," I said, relieved and pleased with her friendliness. Sometimes park moms would shun me, tacitly suggesting I maintain my distance. That always made me feel embarrassed, awkward. I never understood their wariness while I was in the company of Liesl.

"I'm Emily Parker and this is my son, William," the woman said as she gave the boy another push from behind.

"Hi, Emily," I responded, then looking at her son, I said, "Hello, William. You certainly are a good swinger."

With those words, William leaned back, pulled on the swing chains with mitten-covered hands, thrust his legs out straight, and checked to make sure I was still looking at him.

"Oh my," I said. "Look, Liesl. Look at William swing."

"Swing me, Poppa," Liesl ordered. I obliged, sitting her next to William, boosting her into a comfortable rhythm of back and forth, up and down, to and fro.

"I love the name William," I said. "Is he your only child?"

"Yes, he's two-and-a-half."

"Well, now that I know he has no siblings, congratulations on not naming him Kodiak, Studebaker, or Idaho."

Emily laughed. "I know what you mean. As I said, I've seen you and Liesl at the library. Do you watch her on certain days?"

"Actually, I watch her every day. I'm her guardian. Her father was my son and both he and her mother passed unexpectedly."

"I'm sorry. I didn't mean to pry. It's just that I've seen you with her a lot and admired your relationship."

"It's okay," I said, hoping my tone would make her know I wasn't offended. "It was a natural question."

Emily was short, and her bright yellow earmuffs added to her adolescent ambiance. A pageboy coiffure accentuated the youthful sheen of her light brown hair and I could tell it would be soft and smooth to the touch.

Liesl and William frolicked in the Tot Lot for another twenty minutes or so before it was time for lunch. "We're going to eat at El Rascal's," I said. "Would you and William like to join us?"

"We would," Emily responded, "but William has an appointment with his pediatrician at one o'clock, so we'll have to take a rain check."

"I understand," I said. "Perhaps we'll bump into each other again."

"I'll bet we do," Emily said. "I hope so."

She hopes so?

In early November, I noticed the fan-shaped leaves of our ginkgo tree turning from green to a brilliant orange-yellow in just a few days; not the typical deciduous leaf yellow-gold, but a shade containing a puff of saffron. The ginkgo had the most beautifully colored foliage I'd ever seen.

Before its leaves lost their splendid color, while they were still moist, they jettisoned to earth, robust, beautiful, and whole. Lush and waxen, they fell heavily like the first huge, well-spaced raindrops of a coming cloudburst, no wafting, no swirling, straight down and quickly. The ginkgo lost its foliage in less than a day.

Just before Thanksgiving, Liesl and I were returning from a trip to the mall when I noticed an old, black station wagon too quickly approaching in the rear-view mirror. I had my Civic in the right lane of two northbound lanes, cruising about five miles-per-hour over the posted thirty-five-mph limit.

The station wagon was apparently trying to speed around a line of cars in the left lane, when my car came between the aggressive driver and his imbecilic goal of being the first to arrive at the just-turned-red traffic light approximately seventy yards ahead. I'll admit I was enjoying being in his way. The driver began tailgating us and, when I stopped for the red light, I leaned right, turned my head around, and stared at the driver disapprovingly.

The station wagon driver angrily threw his gearshift into park, got out of his car, slammed the door and quickly walked up to my car door. I made sure the doors were locked just before the man attempted to open my door, all this despite the fact that there were at least a dozen cars stopped in one direction or another at the busy intersection.

"Get out of the car," he ordered. "Get out of the goddamned car."

The guy was large and muscular, in jeans and a soiled sweatshirt, his head shaven and shining with his body oil. A spiraling tattoo of barbed wire rose out of the sweatshirt, circled his neck until it met itself back at his throat, and descended back into the sweatshirt.

I stared at the aggressor, and then turned to look at Liesl. She was looking at the man and perplexed, but not outwardly frightened.

"She can't help you," the man said.

He gritted his teeth, drew back his fist, threatening to ram it through the window. I don't know if he just wanted to see me flinch, which I did, or if he changed his mind, but he didn't follow through. I began pressing on the horn.

"Yeah," he said. "Blow your fucking horn, chicken shit." He put both hands on the outside rear-view mirror and twisted it until it was dangling by a cable. He walked back to his car, got in, and executed a U-turn, making oncoming southbound cars squeal to a stop to avoid colliding with his black station wagon.

I looked again at Liesl and she began to cry. "Oh, Liesl, it's okay. Let's go home." My heart was beating like a vigorous jungle drum. I wanted to hold her, comfort her, but decided the best course would be to get home and not pull over at that intersection, accentuating the ugly incident any more than it already was. Liesl cried with intensity the entire four minutes it took to get to Four-Fourteen. It was agonizing to have to wait before responding to her plea for help.

We pulled into the driveway and I unfastened the BabySafe Maxx, hoisted her to my chest as we went inside, and climbed the stairs to her room. I sat with her in the rocker, still pressed to my chest, and inflected a vibrato into my voice so that she could feel it as I hummed.

When she had almost slipped into sleep, I cradled her in my arms and lowered her to my lap, singing "You Are My Sunshine" as the rocker moved up and back, up and back. Every few moments, she inhaled convulsively, then exhaled a long relaxing sigh, her cheeks still wet with tears.

While we were both swaying, both decompressing, I again remembered what Mia Smith told me about having to think differently with a child in my care. I vowed never to make disgusted eye contact again with any driver, no matter how obnoxious the driving or behavior was. I also swore that I'd make sure my granddaughter and I would be protected from any unstable persons who might threaten us in the future.

After about twenty minutes, Liesl was limp, like a rag doll. I placed her into the crib, went downstairs to my office, and went online to search the term "civilian defensive weaponry."

Waiting for a page to download, I remembered when I was a kid and confrontations were almost second nature to me. I winced and closed my eyes, shook my head as I recalled an incident from high school.

I was crouched behind the cafeteria dumpster, sneaking a smoke. When I butted the cigarette and emerged from behind the bin, my pal, Harvey, was walking toward me.

"Hey David, Jason's busting Noah's balls again. The usual suck-asses are egging him on."

Noah was a slow-moving, slow-thinking classmate who was often the butt of jokes, sometimes the victim of bullies, like Jason.

"Where are they?"

"On the ball field," Harvey said.

When Harvey and I reached the field, we could see Noah within a circle composed of Jason and a few of his minions. Noah was frightened and his eyes were glistening. At that point, I'd already committed to hurting Jason.

"What's going on, Jason?"

"Just having some fun with Noah here, Foley. What's it to you?" Jason's feet were apart, his elbows spread with his hands in his back pockets. He was swaying, left and right, head tilted, staring at me.

"Oh shit," I said, looking past him. "Here comes Brother Dom." Jason turned his head to see, and it was probably the instant he realized Brother Dominic wasn't there, that my right foot, with all the force I could muster, reached the spot where his legs came together at the top.

He folded forward, crossing his wrists in front of his gonads as he began to fall. His head made a thumping sound as it whiplashed onto the hard dirt, just after the rest of him hit the ground. Lying there groaning, he farted for several seconds.

"Jesus, David," Harvey said. "I think you kicked the shit out of him."

When the computer page finally loaded, bringing me back to the task at hand, I found a TASER C2 electroshock weapon that fired electrodes on the end of a thin wire projectile. The product information stated that a three-second charge would completely disorient and drop an attacker by overriding the person's muscle-triggering mechanisms, causing pain and muscular spasms.

The manufacturer stated that Kentucky was one of the states in which a TASER wasn't considered a firearm, so it could be legally concealed on one's person or in a car. I filled out the company's background check form, paid the $445.99 delivered price by credit card and my C2 arrived via UPS three days later. Two days after that, the company e-mailed me the activation code for my TASER that had been withheld, pending the results of the background check.

A few heavy, heavy for Louisville anyway, snowfalls and the ensuing three-tiered, carrot-nosed snowmen, along with some backyard sled pulls, saved Liesl's second winter from being mostly uneventful. She and I still frequented the library and InfantaCize and, weather allowing, took long walks through St. Matthews with me pushing my bundled granddaughter in her stroller.

The Christmas season had scant meaning for me, but for Liesl's second Christmas, I rigged a few colored lights on an indoor fern plant and set a gift for her under it. She delighted in helping me tear the wrapping paper off a soft rocking horse, but when I tried to put her onto "Rocky" for a ride, she was frightened and resisted. All she wanted to do was stare at the horse's face and brown button eyes, touch his soft hair, and watch him rock back and forth as I pushed on his hindquarters.

We received an invitation to join the Maddoxes and the Rausches on the Saturday between Christmas and New Year's. Liesl was to bring a less-than-ten-dollar present for the "cherry pie" gift lottery. All the Maddox children, and Liesl by proxy, drew names to determine their respective recipients.

Liesl drew Christian's name, and she liked and understood the idea that she was giving her nine-year-old cousin a gift, in particular, a "Math Wiz" that was nothing more than an oversized calculator with buttons that made noise similar to a touch-tone telephone and had corresponding blinking, colored lights.

The fact that Michael and Madonna had managed to instill proper manners and poise into seven different children amazed me. They each greeted Liesl and me, calling us by name, Uncle David for me, and needed none of the extemporaneous coaching so many parents were required to impart in such situations. The epitome of this extraordinary social grace came during the Cherry Pie exchange, when six-year-old Lourdes looked up at me and said, "I'm glad you and Liesl came today, Uncle David."

When it was Liesl's turn to bestow a gift, she eagerly handed Christian his present and walked back to my chair to stand in the security of a spot between my knees to watch her cousin open her offering.

"Wow!" Christian erupted, his already large eyes widening with excitement. "It's one of those cool calculators. Thank you, Liesl and Uncle David."

I noted Liesl's expression as she noted Christian's expression. I was pleased that *she* was pleased at Christian's excitement.

Lourdes had drawn Liesl's name and handed her a soft package that was wrapped, but unboxed, easily opened. Liesl took her eyes off Christian long enough to peel the wrapping paper off Lourdes' present. It was a small, royal blue sweatshirt that Liesl took one look at before she unceremoniously dropped it to the floor and returned to her mesmerism with Christian and his electronic gizmo.

Embarrassed, I picked the discarded gift off the floor, held it up by its shoulders to examine. The words "Poppa's Girl" were screened across the chest. This time I was the one genuinely thrilled with a gift.

"Thank you, Lourdes," I said to the shy but pleased little Maddox.

"Look Liesl," I said, holding the sweatshirt for her to see the lettering. "It says 'Poppa's Girl'." To my chagrin, Liesl's disinterest was absolute. She was still fixated on Christian and his new prize.

"David," Michael said. "You've done a wonderful job instilling in Liesl the distinctly Christian tenet that it's more blessed to give than to receive."

Everyone laughed except Elizabeth Rausch. Madonna had warned me when she invited us that her mother's cognition was diminishing. Elizabeth had been subdued the entire evening and reflected a definite aura of sadness. I was sorry for her in that she seemed unable to enjoy the company of her charming and engaging grandchildren.

Other than the snowfalls and the Christmas activities, the only interruption to an unremarkable winter season came in mid-February. Despite having for the first time gotten an influenza inoculation on the advice of Liesl's pediatrician, I battled a bad case of a remote strain of that malady for four days. Liesl was inconvenienced, but remarkably, she seemed to understand that Poppa wasn't well and reacted admirably to the sudden inertia.

"Poppa feel better?" she'd ask, the sincerity of which made Poppa feel better.

I'd been told that winter left Kentucky when March left Kentucky and sure enough, April found Liesl and me enjoying the mild weather in Seneca Park at least three days a week. She was approaching two years and was much more nimble and confident with, on, through, and around the steps, slides, tunnels and mini merry-go-round of the Tot Lot.

One particularly balmy afternoon, we were just leaving Seneca when Emily and William Parker entered the Tot Lot.

"Hi there, Emily and William," I said, surprised. "How've you two been?"

"Hello, Mr. Foley," Emily said. "William, do you remember Mr. Foley and Liesl?"

"Hi, Mr. Foley." William said. "Hi," he said, turning to Liesl, impressing me with his manners and presence.

Addressing Emily, I said, "If I'm too old or too fierce for you to call me David, I'll be disappointed."

She blushed, smiled. "Okay, *David*, I think I can do that."

"We were just leaving," I said. "It's nap time for Liesl *and* her Poppa. Maybe we'll see you guys here another day."

"Sure," Emily said. "Now that the weather's broken, we'll be here often. We usually come in the mornings, but William fell asleep in the car coming home from my mother's house and I knew there wouldn't be an afternoon nap."

"Okay," I said. "Some morning soon then. Bye, William."

Riding back to the house, I was surprised at myself for having been so pleased to see Emily. I was also a bit dismayed at the pleasant churning she caused in my thoughts.

I'm too old for her, I thought, as I fingered my chin and took stock of my image in the rearview mirror.

I usually took Liesl everywhere I went, mostly avoiding situations where an accompanying granddaughter would be either inappropriate or no fun for either of us. There were events, however, that needed to transpire without having the pleasure of her company, events such as my first-ever colonoscopy, a day-long venture to Churchill Downs, or the court date of a small-claims suit I filed against a local wear-it-on-its-sleeve, fish-in-the-logo, goddamned Christian window-washing company for damaging four of the twenty-four windows it had half-assed cleaned at Four-fourteen.

On those types of occasions, I needed a dependable babysitter, so while I was losing my rear-end virginity to a physician's probe, losing my virtual shirt at Churchill Downs, or losing my case against "Sparkling Son Window Services" in Small Claims Court, I engaged Samantha McCoy to care for my granddaughter.

Samantha was a fourteen-year-old eighth-grader who lived with her divorced mother, Idelle, just across the street from us in St. Matthews. We first encountered her when she was twelve, on one of our early walks through the neighborhood. The minute I met Samantha, I could tell she was unusual, a bit forward, opinionated, and so seemingly confident that I knew she had to be insecure. Most obvious, however, she was extremely bright. As a merciless teenager, I would have called her a fink, a frump, or worse.

"Are you her *dad*?" she asked on our first meeting as I pushed Liesl's stroller past her house. "You seem kind of old."

"I *am* old," I said with a chuckle, coming to a stop.

"How old are you?" she said, folding her arms and tilting her head.

"Fifty-two."

"Whoa! *Are* you her dad?"

"No, I'm her grandfather."

"I don't have a dad either."

"I'm sorry."

"What's her name?"

"Liesl."

"I've never heard that name. Can I push her sometime?"

"Sure. Maybe the next time we see you, we can ask your mom."

"No, it's okay. As long as I stay on this block, I don't have to ask. I'm twelve."

"I see."

Samantha was lanky, at least five feet eight inches tall, and wore thick-lens glasses. Her hair was frizzy and she had braces on her overly prominent teeth. When not speaking, her mouth remained open. I supposed she breathed through it.

Her posture, I assumed due to self-consciousness about her height, was dreadful. The clothes she wore never seemed to fit, either too large and bulky or, most egregious, too tight. Too tight was the offense of her pullover shirts, in light of the fact that she was coming in need of a bra. I wondered how long it would take her mother to remedy the situation.

Liesl loved Samantha, or "Manta," as she called her, from the day she met her. It was amusing to see her whenever she knew Samantha was coming. She grinned so hard that her eyes shut and her head contracted into her shoulders like a tortoise. I, too, had come to love Samantha. She was truthful, considerate, and she loved to be with Liesl.

Idelle told me that she had helped put Samantha's father through medical school by working a "job-and-a-half," even while she was pregnant. No sooner had Idelle and her surgeon husband moved to Louisville from West Virginia, than did he become entangled with his scheduler, soon after which, he filed for divorce. I was pleased to learn that a local judge had held Dr. McCoy accountable for the financial security of the family he was dumping. Idelle told me she'd been awarded long-term alimony and child-support payments, but that the good Dr. McCoy rarely communicated with his daughter. This called to mind Elaine's brushing off Patrick, who was young enough at four to not have much memory of her by the time he was nine or ten. By the time he was a teenager, Elaine wasn't his mother; she was but a curiosity.

Initially, Idelle made little attempt to conceal her aspiration for me to be the sequel to Dr. McCoy.

"A man in your situation, with a little girl at home and all, should have a woman around to take care of him and his family," she'd say. "And a man like you would have no trouble finding the right woman."

My challenge was to postpone, confuse, and give Idelle the verbal slip, but with a great deal of finesse. As a moral matter, I didn't want to hurt her feelings. As a practical matter, I didn't want to lose Samantha as Liesl's sitter.

"Why, Idelle," I'd say. "You're just trying to make me feel good. You're so sweet."

Before she could tell me how serious she was, I'd pose a subject-changing question. "How's Samantha doing in school this semester?" I'd ask, knowing the answer. "What she accomplishes is such a tribute to you, Idelle. You should be proud."

I was anxious to try my luck at Churchill Downs on the opening day of its annual spring meet, the last Saturday in April. I enjoyed thoroughbred racing and Louisville was certainly a hot spot for that particular activity. I entrusted Liesl's care to Samantha and Idelle on a perfect Kentucky spring day; seventy-two degrees, blue skies and sunshine, interrupted only occasionally by a high-wafting, white puff of cloud.

Opening day at Churchill Downs was the beginning of the inevitable Kentucky palpitation that would crescendo the following Saturday,

Derby Day. The attending ladies bloomed large, colorful hats topping off the latest spring fashions, while most of their accompanying gentlemen were wearing light-shaded suits, many with thoroughbred-themed ties. These colorful people moved and mingled, mixed and merged like the flakes in a pastel kaleidoscope. Gambling and the dangerous contests of equine speed became the centers of attraction every thirty-five or forty minutes. I was mesmerized by this spectacle.

My unsuccessful handicapping notwithstanding, I was happy with the experience as I made my way toward my car before the day's last race, trying to avoid the inevitable exiting traffic jam. As I was leaving the huge Churchill parking lot, I saw him in the rear-view mirror; the tattooed man in the black station wagon. He must have recognized me too, for he was aggressively following my Civic, bumper almost on bumper.

I pulled my car to the curb, hoping the wagon would drive by. It didn't. The man veered his vehicle to the curb just behind my Civic. As he got out of his car, I pulled away, apprehensive as I glanced in the rear-view mirror and saw him get back into his car and continue following. I drove a few blocks to the next red signal, where the black wagon pulled up next to me in the outside lane. I was now hemmed in by a car on each of three sides and a sidewalk crowded with pedestrians on the fourth.

The man exited his car and was quickly at my locked door, once again trying to open it at a crowded intersection.

"That little girl's not with you today," he yelled, dropping his head to the level of my window. "I'm really going to fuck you up." His breath was fogging the glass and his speech was slurred. There were exploding red streaks in his eyes.

I was frightened and thinking this crazy son-of-a-bitch might be stupid enough to kill me, when I remembered the TASER in the Civic's console. As the man stood again, I opened the console and extracted the C2 without him noticing. I dropped my window about four inches, while he banged his fist on the roof of my car and looked around, apparently pleased with the crowd attention he had drawn.

I flipped the safety lock off the C2, aimed at his chest, and squeezed the trigger, holding it for a full five seconds before the automatic shutoff stopped the electric charge. The tattooed man screamed for the last four of those five seconds as he was jolted backward just before collapsing onto the pavement, writhing, slobbering.

I knew I should drive away, but a violent, usually abeyant demon, the same one that made me kick Jason in the balls, was reminding me of the terror this thug had unleashed on Liesl. I got out of my Civic, bent over, and placed my forearms under the incapacitated man's armpits. It was a struggle, every pound of his hefty bulk was dead weight, but I managed to drag him back to his black wagon. I breathed deeply three times, then, using all my strength, I heaved him onto the hood of the station wagon. He was on his back, his feet dangling just off the ground, twitching. An unintended smile crossed my face; the demon again.

I unbuckled the man's belt, ripped open his button and fly, and pulled his pants down to his ankles, exposing threadbare, red jockey shorts and pasty-white, hairy legs. I wrapped the belt twice around his legs just above the ankles, secured it tightly. I noticed his red underpants had a spreading darkening in the front.

"Goddamn, friend, you're pissing in your pretty panties right here in front of all these people."

The demon pushed my face close to the man's face, our noses almost touching. "If you ever bother me or my granddaughter again, you sheep fucker, I'll take those grimy-ass panties off you and stick this TASER about four inches up your butt before I pull the trigger. And if there weren't anyone around today, if I thought I could get away with it, I promise you, I'd kill your worthless ass so that no one would ever have to be afraid of you again. Do you hear me, you piece of shit?"

In a final display of contempt, again heeding the demon, I spat in the man's ugly face. I hustled back to the Civic, jumped in, and drove off, watching the scene in my rearview mirror of the tattooed man lying on the hood of his station wagon, still convulsing, his ugly white legs separating the tattered red jockey shorts from his ankle-high pants.

As I pulled into the driveway at Four-fourteen, my euphoria from teaching a psychopathic bully a well-deserved lesson was beginning to fade. What if that crazy bastard sees me sometime? Or worse, will he come looking for me? Jesus, what about Liesl? I couldn't believe I'd flown off the goddamned handle like that.

After a few deep breaths, I called the McCoys. Idelle said Liesl had just awakened from a nap, and I could come for her any time. I walked over immediately, still replaying the incident. I was unenthusiastic when I saw Liesl and a brief, forced smile quickly gave way to a contemplative frown.

"Is everything okay, David?" Idelle inquired. "You seem a bit distressed."

"Oh, I'm just tired. That and I lost money at the track," I tried to explain.

Liesl would have been content to stay with the McCoys for a while, but it had been a long day for everyone, so she and I headed across the street.

We remained on the front porch, drifting back and forth on the swing until it was time for dinner. After eating, Liesl fell asleep, back on the swing, lying with her head on my lap. My guilt and regret were overwhelming. I knew I'd let Liesl down. At least *she* didn't know it.

As I looked at her, stroked her hair, I was ashamed of my complete lapse in judgment. I contemplated having to live with the fear of retribution and that Liesl, too, was now exposed to the same possibility. I was awake more than I slept that night.

Samantha came over the following morning when she saw Liesl and me on the front porch, once again on the swing. Liesl ran to meet her and the two of them romped in the yard, playing a spontaneous game of tag. I began to browse the Sunday paper but stopped at a headline on page two of the Metro section.

FUGITIVE NABBED NEAR CHURCHILL DOWNS

Louisville Metro Police apprehended a man at a busy intersection near Churchill Downs on Saturday, whom they say is sought by Missouri State Police on charges of assault and armed robbery.

Dexter Meredith, of St. Louis, was taken to the Jefferson County Hall of Justice, where he was detained without bond. He had not been charged with a crime as of Saturday night, but a police spokesperson said Meredith was being held as a fugitive. Meredith was arrested at Taylor Boulevard and Queen Avenue at 4:40 p.m., Saturday, when police came upon a crowd gathered around the suspected fugitive, who was apparently lying atop the hood of his car wearing only his underwear. The police spokesperson refused to comment on that, but several witnesses said Meredith was aggravated and trying to enter a man's car at the intersection, when the man stepped out of the car and dragged a somehow dazed Meredith to his car and lifted him onto its hood before taking Meredith's pants off and driving away.

"This fellow picked the wrong guy to get into a hassle with," said an unidentified bystander at the scene.

Meredith is to appear in Superior Court on Monday at 9:00 a.m.

"Well, I'll be damned."

Chapter Four

"Love cannot express the idea of music, while music may give an idea of love."
— HECTOR BERLIOZ

When *Liesl and* I would visit the Maddoxes and the girls were wearing their pleated plaid uniforms, I sometimes caught myself thinking back to my days at Sts. Peter and Paul Parochial School with its many nuns and two or three priests. Father Mulcahy was assistant pastor and the priest all the boys wanted in the confessional 'box' when it came time to fess up and repent. That was because the penances he assigned were consistently lenient and he never got angry. Sometimes I thought he even dozed while listening to my sin recitations.

As much as I disliked divulging my depravity to anyone, the nuns had me convinced that Confession was the only way to have my mortal sins forgiven and avoid "the loss of Heaven and the pains of Hell," as the often-recited Catholic Act of Contrition articulated. Venial sins needed to be confessed as well, to moderate one's accumulated time in Purgatory.

Thus once a month or so, I would show up at church on a Saturday afternoon, the specified time for Confession, and spill it all. I remember one time in particular, when I was in the fourth grade. "Bless me, Father, for I have sinned. It's been three weeks and four days since my last confession. I was disobedient four times and I was unkind to my friends twice. I lied to my Dad once, and I goosed Melvin Barker two times while we were in the cafeteria line. I also received Holy Communion one time when I wasn't in the state of grace."

"These sins you have confessed are venial, my son. None would have disqualified you from receiving Holy Communion."

"I was about to get to that one, Father."

"I see. Go on, my son."

"Well, you see, there's this girl. She let me see inside her underpants. She didn't take them off or anything; she just let me look down in there."

61

"Anything else?"

"No, she didn't seem to want to see mine, just asked me to look at hers."

"I meant are there any other sins."

"Oh, I see. No, Father, that's it. Uh, oh yeah. For these and all the sins of my past life, I am sorry."

"God bless you, my son. For your penance say three Our Fathers, three Hail Marys, and three Glory Bes."

Man, that was easy, I thought, as I emerged from the darkness of the confessional, but still in the dimness of the Church.

On the Monday morning after Derby Day, more than a week after I had dispatched Dexter Meredith, Liesl and I were back in Seneca Park's Tot Lot testing how many times she could come down the sliding board, semi-circle back to the steps and try it again. She was up to an even dozen with no sign of a let-up. On the thirteenth sequence, we saw Emily and William Parker coming through the gate.

"Willya," said Liesl. "Lemley."

"Close enough," I said.

After a few perfunctory pleasantries, Emily and I were seated next to each other on a bench. Our legs were touching from the sides of our knees to our hips. I could detect her softness, which was pleasant and stirring. While I was trying to gauge her reaction to me, Liesl was on the swing next to William, seemingly trying to gauge his reaction to her. I could tell she was happy in his company, as was I in his mother's.

"I'm glad you were here," Emily said. "I was hoping you would be."

"You were?" I asked, my blood flow quickening.

"Yes," she said, looking into my eyes after flipping her hair back off her forehead with an upward toss of her head. "I thought about you a lot over the winter."

I wanted to reciprocate, but couldn't quite bring myself to lie. "Well, I sure as heck remembered you on occasion," I said, "but, believe me, I'll think of you constantly tonight." She smiled the smile a girl smiles when she's decided to let a fellow have his way.

"Is there a . . . a Mr. Emily?" I inquired.

Her smile broke into a controlled laugh. "No," she said. "William's father was a nice looking, disingenuous fraternity type." With any levity gone, she went on, "I expected and wanted nothing from him when I told him I was pregnant, and nothing is what I got. 'How do you know I'm the father?' were the first words out of his mouth. He lives in New England and isn't a part of our family."

"I see. Do you and William live alone?"

"Yes, but near my mom's house. She watches him when I'm at school or work."

"So you're a student," I said.

"Most of the time, but a waitress when I'm not. I'm close to my master's in psychology."

Her eyes fixated on mine and, after a moment of silence, I mustered the mettle to force the issue. "Am I not too old?"

"Too old for what?" she inquired, most likely knowing the answer to her question, but feigning puzzlement.

"Too old to be your lover," I couldn't believe I heard myself say.
She looked at me with a serious expression for a few seconds before saying, "You're not too old, David. I prefer to lay with a man's intellect rather than his physique. Not that your physique isn't enticing."

I would have smiled were I not embarrassed about the sudden rise beneath my zipper. As I shifted positions, trying to camouflage the bulge, I said, "Then lay with my intellect the next time my baby sitter is available."

"Tell me when," she answered without the least trace of a smile.

"Oh my! Let me get back to you on that after I check the calendar at home," I said.

For the rest of the Tot Lot session, a trace of awkwardness arose between Emily and me; not so for Liesl and William. Liesl was trying to imitate his exploits. When he climbed the sliding board ladder without Emily attending, Liesl wanted to climb the ladder with no assistance from me. When he went down the slide on his tummy, Liesl insisted on giving it a try.

When it was time for the morning's romp to give way to going home, having lunch and taking naps, Emily said, with her eyes widened and playfully beseeching, "Be thinking about a date. Do you have a cell?"

"Oh hi, Idelle, this is David Foley," I said, with as much formality as I could muster. "Is Samantha at home?"

"Hello, David. How are you getting along?" she said, as if she hadn't heard my question.

"Just fine, thank you," I responded, still in my most business-like tone. "Is Samantha there?"

"She's not home from school yet. Can I help you with something?" Idelle asked, perhaps with a trace of the old college try.

"I'm just wondering if there's a night she might be able to sit with Liesl for me. There's a piece of, uh . . . uh, *business* that I need to tend to as soon as Samantha can help me out." I'd forgotten to plan how to word my upcoming, sitter-demanding activity.

"A piece of business?" Idelle asked.

"Yeah, business, uh . . . good business. Will you have Samantha call me when she gets in?"

"Sure," she replied, as I squeezed my eyes shut, raised my shoulders, and gritted my teeth at my clumsiness. "Is that all, David?"

"Yes. Goodbye, Idelle," I said, still holding the mortified pose.

I was hoping Samantha would call me before Emily did, since I wanted to have a firm date and time for her, rather than another "I'll have to get back to you." I didn't want an opportunity like this to unravel.

I'd managed a few dates since taking Liesl in, but those particular women were recently divorced, wore too much perfume, and liked Liesl a little too much before they even met her. I was beginning to wonder if I'd ever have the intimate company of an interesting and attractive woman again.

When the phone rang a few hours later, I was relieved to see "Idelle McCoy" on the caller identification. It was Samantha, who told me she had an Ichthyology Club meeting on Thursday evening, but she'd be available Friday night.

"Friday will be fine. I can see where you wouldn't want to miss an Ichthyology Club meeting," I said with a condescending sigh.

That night I sang Liesl to sleep with a popular song from the 1950s: "He's Got The Whole World In His Hands." She especially liked that one because I always included many of her friends and relatives in the lyrics. "He's got Samantha and her Mommy, in his hands, He's got Christian and Lourdes, in his hands, He's got 'Lemley' and 'Willya,' in his hands, He's got the whole world in his hands." I just loved it that Liesl liked my singing.

After I put Liesl into her crib next to "Bear" and "Lambikins," I crept out of her room, closed the squeaky door. I swore, for about the fortieth time, to lubricate that goddamned hinge the next day, but I always forgot it until the next time I was trying to silently exit Liesl's room.

Just as I settled into my recliner, newspaper in hand, I remembered I didn't have my glasses. My cell phone rang. "Hello?" I said hopefully, unable to make out the name displayed on caller identification.

"David, it's Emily," said the voice I was anxious to hear. "I trust Liesl's asleep."

"Yes, I just now walked out of her room. Uh, how are you?"

"I'm okay," she said. "Did you get a chance to check your calendar? I was hoping to see you sometime soon. "

The pleasure of hearing this young, comely woman uttering that sentence had me, once again, rising to the occasion. "How about Friday night?" I asked as I adjusted my position to accommodate the sudden eminence in my pants.

"Perfect. I was hoping you could work it in this weekend."
Oh yeah, I can work it in, all right, I thought. "How about eight-fifteen?"

"Yes, eight-fifteen. Can you come here? William sleeps like a log. Once he drifts off for the night, he just doesn't wake up. We're in the Highlands area at 1887 Columbia Avenue."

"Great," I said, my blood still surging just below the belt.

I decided to take Liesl shopping Friday morning. We'd been to the Oxmoor Center many times to visit Mickey Mouse at the Disney Store, ride the escalator, and eat lunch at El Rascal's. Today, however, I specifically wanted to visit the JC Penney Men's Department and buy something for myself, new underwear. I suspected the frayed waistbands on my boxers and the timeworn, yellow underarm stains on my more-gray-than-white tee shirts might not pass Emily's inspection.

While at Penney's, I also bought three pairs of over-the-calf argyle socks that were on special; buy two, get one free. I had an affinity for argyle socks. Because they were so out of the mainstream, I figured one had to be pretty cool to wear them. Another reason I liked them was because my ex-wife, Elaine, always hated them.

After the JC Penney expedition, I took Liesl to the Kiddieland section of the shopping center and let her ride the steamboat, the school bus, and the locomotive until she lost interest close to lunchtime. We shared an El Rascal taco salad, both of us sitting in the same side of the booth, on a bench seat of cracked and brittle vinyl, before heading for home and Liesl's nap.

When we arrived at Four-fourteen, Liesl was asleep in the BabySafe Maxx and didn't move a body part when I lifted her out of the car, carried her inside to her crib. She slept for another hour before I heard the sweet echo of the intercom. "Poppa?"

The sound of my granddaughter's voice summoning me after a nap or in the mornings was wonderful, pleasurable from the inside out. I treasured those times, responding to her electronic beckoning and finding such a beautiful little person so genuinely happy to see me. She was always sitting up in her crib, peering through its spindles when I entered the room.

"Oh my. Look at my beautiful granddaughter in her bed. What a big person she is." With that familiar queue, Liesl dropped to her back, raised her arms above her head as far as she could, elongating her little body until she occupied as much space in her crib as possible.

"Wow! Look how big she is. She stretches all the way from here to there," I said, one hand moving to the top of her fingers, the other to the tips of her toes. "What a lucky Poppa I am to have such a big and beautiful granddaughter."

When I would change her diaper after she awakened, I always noticed how beautiful her eyes and facial skin were. I thought it curious that toddlers could look so vibrant and healthy upon awakening. Her complexion was smooth and flawless, the perfect amount of color in her cheeks. Her once-blue irises had begun to turn green, and, instead of looking sleepy, they were like fresh, deep pools, glistening in the center of pristine whiteness. Her hair was light brown and softer than down. I loved feeling it with my hands or face.

"I want a snack," Liesl said, interrupting my admiration. "Ogyurt!"

"Ogyurt it shall be," I imitated, loving the way she mispronounced yogurt. "Samantha is coming over tonight and will be here at bedtime."

Liesl smiled. She never had anything but a positive reaction to "Manta."

Samantha arrived just before eight. Liesl was in her pajamas and looking forward to thirty or forty minutes of frolicking in her basement playroom with her sitter. It was bittersweet for me when Samantha asked Liesl if she wanted "to see Poppa off." Liesl said, "No," which made me understand how content she was in Samantha's charge. Nevertheless, I wouldn't have minded if she might have wanted to see her Poppa to the door as I was leaving.

Emily's Columbia Avenue house was a modest bungalow with a stone coping around a porch that spanned the front of the house. The porch had three white concrete flowerpots atop the coping, each boasting newly planted pink geraniums. Emily was on the porch in a ceiling-suspended swing when I arrived just after dark. She was wearing jeans and a white turtleneck, under a cardigan sweater.

I had stopped on the way for a bouquet of cut flowers and a bottle of wine. She seemed happy with the early yellow crocuses and daffodils, mixed with purple phlox. Flowers always seemed to advance one's cause with women. I was hoping she'd like the Cabernet, as well.

"William's asleep," she said. "I didn't dare tell him you were coming or he would have never gone to bed."

"Liesl is with her usual sitter and perfectly content," I told her as I stared into her brown eyes, hoping to communicate the admiration in which I held her youthful countenance. She wore a trace amount of eye makeup, just enough to accentuate the alluring luminescence of her brown irises.

"May I pop the cork on this wine?" I asked.

"Yes, please. Let me find the corkscrew and a couple of glasses."

As she walked from the swing to the porch door, I furtively admired her shape. Nonetheless, I knew that *she* knew I was assessing her form as she walked. Girls learned that about men and boys at an early age. She had ample and shapely hips, a flat stomach, and full breasts, easily detectable though camouflaged beneath the turtleneck and sweater.

When she came back through the porch door with corkscrew and glasses in hand, she approached the swing and stopped in front of me. Capturing my eyes, she bent over and kissed me with her soft, thick lips. She placed the corkscrew and glasses on a small table aside the swing and sat across my lap, putting a hand on either side of my head, holding it in position while she placed her lips on mine and parted them with her tongue. I was hoping she could feel the bulge beneath her.

As if sensing that she was moving too quickly for her own satisfaction, Emily abruptly stood and said, "Let's have a glass of wine." I realized this relationship was going to consummate, so I was content to let it unfold at her speed.

"How did you wind up as Liesl's guardian?" she asked as she handed me the corkscrew, "if you don't mind me asking."

I recounted Patrick and Kathryn's courtship, marriage, and the birth of Liesl. When I told her about the death of Patrick in Iraq and Kathryn at St. Anthony, Emily's eyes still shone, but they were downcast. I saw sadness in them. I was sure the anguish I felt, when thinking of Patrick and Kathryn, showed, but even unspoken sympathy helped, and I appreciated hers. Not wanting her to feel awkward, I changed subjects, asked how she managed to make ends meet with William occupying so much of her time.

"I make a little waiting tables three nights a week," she explained. "And my mother helps out. Her second husband died and left her a little money. She's very generous to William and me. She owns this house and we live rent-free. May I have a glass of wine?"

I rolled my eyes in mock disgust with myself for not having already poured. As the wine gurgled from bottle to glass, I said, "I didn't discover how much I liked wine until I was about forty."

"I didn't discover that until I was about sixteen," Emily said, making me laugh. "How old *are* you, David? God, I shouldn't have asked that."

"Oh, I don't mind," I said smiling, "as long as you don't care what the answer is."

"I don't."

"I'm fifty-three."

"You sure don't look it."

"I sometimes feel much older," I said, "but then again, sometimes I feel much younger." I set my glass on the coping, took hers, and placed it on the table. With my thumb and extended forefinger, I lifted her chin to the angle where my lips would squarely meet hers. She put one hand high on the inside of my thigh and the other on the back of my head, pressed my lips to hers. Our lips and tongues were wet and sweet with the Cabernet. Our mouths became one, a swirling and sensuous vacuum, offering and accepting, merging utterly.

"Let's go inside," she said.

"Inside," I repeated. Yes, I wanted to be inside.

She took my hand and led me through the porch door into the living room, past a dining area, down a narrow hallway into her bedroom. Next to a double bed, she stopped on a small, plush throw rug, guided my hand under her tops, and placed it on her breast. Softness, I thought, like no other body part.

I kicked off my shoes as she began to remove my shirt and trousers so that I was left only in my snappy new JC Penney outfit of boxers, tee shirt, and over-the-calf argyles. Soon she had me down to just the argyles. She divested her jeans, cardigan sweater, and turtleneck. I wanted to observe her in her underwear for a while, but she took off her panties quickly. As she slipped under the bedcovers, she looked at my argyles and frowned. "You might want to take those off."

"Uh, if it's all the same to you, I think I'll leave them on."

Her frown continued. "Are your feet cold?"

"Not exactly."

"Well, what then?"

"Emily, I think it was precisely at midnight on the day I turned for-ty-five. I looked down, and where I once had clear, smooth toenails, I suddenly had sharp, pointed claw-talons. Trust me, I should wear the socks."

She rolled her eyes but let me keep my socks on, then quickly forgot the issue for about half-an-hour. Afterward, as she was resting atop her guest, contented, still connected, she said after a deep sigh, "That was awesome before the word lost its meaning."

"Yeah, I almost came," I said. She laughed so hard that her midsec-tion contracted causing her to expel my diminishing appendage.

"Oh dear," she said.

Once dressed and back on the porch, we dropped any pretensions we had brought to the engagement. We were much looser in our conver-sation, bantering like old friends. On my way home, I couldn't help from looking at myself in the rearview mirror. You still da' man.

It was ten after eleven when I arrived at Four-fourteen. Samantha told me of her forty-minute romp with Liesl, the fifteen-minute quiet time before going to bed, and Liesl's complete willingness to hit the hay.

"How was your night?" she inquired.

I didn't mention my forty-minute romp with Emily, the fifteen-minute quiet time before going to bed, and Emily's complete willingness to hit the hay. "Quite nice," I answered.

I dismissed Samantha forty-five minutes early with full pay plus tip.

I would have been content to sleep until about nine o'clock the next morning. Instead, I heard the intercom at six-fifteen.

"Poppa?" Liesl was summoning her grandfather to get this day started. Again, "Poppa?"

"Where's Manta?" she asked as I entered her room in my boxers and t-shirt, hair frazzled.

"She went home after you were in bed."

"Call her."

"I can't, Liesl. It's six in the morning. Maybe Samantha can come over this afternoon or sometime tomorrow."

Liesl, as was her wont, accepted the idea that she wasn't going to get her way, and that Samantha wouldn't be coming for a while. I wasn't positive whether her understanding of the concept of doing without was a product of my grand-parenting skill, or if she was merely born with the innate and rare trait of occasional self-denial. I suspected it was more genetic than acquired, but either way, I just *knew* I was responsible for that admirable quality in her.

It took several minutes before the pleasance of the preceding evening's events occurred to me. I wanted to savor my escapade with Emily, but Liesl's early morning requirements made me realize that would have to wait.

After a breakfast of oatmeal, "meat-mo" Liesl called it, a jar of pears and buttered toast, we headed for the supermarket where she loved to ride in the cart and talk to anyone she encountered. "This is my Poppa," she'd say to one woman, "I like meat-mo," to another.

By the time we got home and she awakened from her morning nap, it was close to eleven. I suggested we go to Waterfront Park in downtown Louisville. "Maybe Samantha would like to go," I said, adding to her delight with the idea.

"Call her," she ordered for the second time that day. I dialed the McCoys' number, and thirty minutes later, Samantha was piling into the back seat of my Civic next to the BabySafe Maxx, while Liesl was chattering with anticipation.

Waterfront Park, on the banks of the Ohio River, was a labyrinth of fascinating choices for children who visited. It boasted steps and mazes, slides and swings, steamboats and rockets, water sprays and a wading pool. It also had one of Louisville's many El Rascal restaurant franchises on its grounds.

Though I monitored the activity from the vantage point of a comfortable swing, Samantha took charge of Liesl's entertainment at the park, affording me more time than usual to contemplate my life outside of my granddaughter, and the evening before with Emily was certainly pleasant contemplation. I wondered how *she* felt on that morning after.

After lunch at El Rascal's, it was time to return home. On the way, Liesl had a bowel movement and when the familiar odor reached my nostrils in the front seat, I exclaimed my traditional reaction. "Shoo, doggies! Liesl, do you need a diaper change?"

"No, you do Poppa," she said, rendering all three of the car's occupants weak with laughter.

About halfway home, my cell phone was producing a different type of signal. "Hello?" I answered as I flipped open the device and placed it to my ear. Hearing nothing, "Hello?"

"Maybe that was a text message," Samantha said.

"A what?"

"A text message."

"I've never had one of those. Here, see if you can make anything out of it." I passed the phone underhanded back to Samantha through the opening between the front seats. Pushing a few buttons with her thumbs, she recited, "'Can we do it again tonight? Call me. Anxiously, Emily.'"

"Uh, must've been a wrong number. Give me the phone," I said as I extended my arm over the console and into the back seat.

"It's from someone named Emily Parker," Samantha continued.

"Give me the phone, Samantha!"

"Lemley," Liesl said.

"I don't know any Lemley, I mean Emily," I said.

"Lemley at the pawk," Liesl said, unable to sound the "r" properly. "Lemley and Willya."

"Darn, I'm trying to remember," I prevaricated.

We drove the rest of the distance home with the car windows lowered due to Liesl's bowel movement. We also maintained silence, primarily because Liesl had nodded off, despite the load in her diaper, secondarily, because my thoughts were flush with Emily.

As I eased the car into the driveway, I asked, "Uh, hey Samantha, do you think you could sit for Liesl again tonight?"

"What time would you like me to come over, Mr. Foley?" she asked. I thought I could see a bit of a smirk in the rearview mirror.

"Let's say seven-fifteen, okay?" I said, our eyes meeting in the rearview.

"Sure," she said, with a smug smile.

As Samantha walked toward her house, I unbuckled Liesl's car seat straps and, with my back bent, lifted the twenty-six pounds of dead weight out of the BabySafe Maxx. As I pulled her from the car, before I could straighten my frame, I felt a pain shoot through the small of my back. I froze in position and held my breath, knowing inhaling would be excruciating. I unlocked after a few seconds and was able to straighten, so Liesl's trip from the car to her room was only momentarily interrupted.

After changing her diaper, I placed my still sleeping granddaughter into her bed, straightened myself and admired her innocent countenance. She was lying with her knees tucked under her midsection, elevating her small, round, diapered bottom. She was facing the blinded window with enough light filtering through it to subtly illuminate her face. I thought of Raphael's painted angels.

As I exited the room, the closing door creaked rudely, forcing me to relinquish the image of Liesl. God*damn* that door!

From the kitchen, I dialed Emily's number, reaching only her voice mail. I left a message that I'd be there at seven-thirty unless I heard back from her.

Liesl slept for the next two hours, about forty-five minutes of which, I also napped. I was awakened at quarter after four by the telephone. "Hello?"

"David, this is Idelle McCoy," the familiar nasal voice identified itself including last name, as if there were several other nasal Idelles who called me frequently. "Samantha tells me she's going to sit for Liesl again tonight. I guess you didn't close the deal on that big business last night, huh?"

I knew then that Samantha had told Idelle all about the afternoon's messaging in the car. "That's right Idelle, but I think one more session might get it done. Is that why you called?"

"No," she said, "I just wanted you to know that I'll be out myself until about ten-thirty tonight and wouldn't be here for Samantha and Liesl should they need me."

"I see," I said. "That should be all right, don't you think? Samantha has both our cell numbers."

"Yes," Idelle replied, "I just wanted you to know."

Yeah, I'll bet, I thought. "That's really nice of you, Idelle."

Later that evening, after Liesl had responded "No" once again to Samantha's ". . . see Poppa off?" question, I was excited and driving to Emily's house. I was both singing and envisioning myself as "The Duke of Earl," while squinting, rhythmically nodding my head, and looking at myself in the rear-view mirror. With no warning, the unmistakable feel and sound of oneself breaking wind interrupted my self-admiration. Shit! Am I going to be flatulent?

Emily was again seated on the porch swing when I arrived. "Hi," I said, surprised at and somewhat leery of how fond I was becoming of this young woman.

"I'm glad you got my message and that you could make it."

"Gosh, Emily, the only thing in my way of going anywhere is Samantha not being available. I don't have much of a social calendar."

"Samantha?"

"She's the young teen who lives across the street from us and watches Liesl when I need a sitter. Liesl absolutely loves her and vice versa. I'm lucky to have her."

"Sort of like my mom," Emily said. "William is spending the night with her."

"Really? I guess that means I can make a lot of noise then?"

"As much as you'd like," she said, as she knelt in front of me, flawlessly unzipped my jeans.

After ten or fifteen minutes of what anyone would term serious foreplay, Emily suggested we go inside. By the time we arrived in the bedroom, we were both unclothed, except for another pair of my over-the-calf argyle socks.

"Take them off," she said. "I might like the pain of your claw-talons."

"I don't want to chance it," I replied.

I was just about to shove her onto the bed, take command and mount her, when pain roared into my lower spine, causing me to yell, "My back! I'm frozen. Shit! Oh wait, hold on."

"What's the matter? Are you okay?"

"It's my back. Sometimes it just locks up on me. There, that's a little better. Would you mind getting on top?"

"Not at all," she said with a confident grin. "In fact, I kind of like that you're handicapped. Yes, I'll dominate you."

"Dominate me?" I practically whimpered, a degree of apprehension in my widened eyes, I'm sure.

She stripped off my argyles and, looking at the claw-talons with her eyes widening, said, "Wow, I've never seen any nails that . . . that old."
She pounced on me like a mountain lion atop a helpless prairie horse; total control. All I could do was lie there, as she played me like a slide trombone. She bit me. She scratched me. She bent my appendage so far back I thought it would surely break off, lodging in there. I could only take what she insisted on doing to me and hope her intentions were honorable. Just as her squeals demonstrated she was feeling what every woman wanted to feel . . . I farted. Loudly.

"Oh Emily, I'm sorry."

"It's okay," she said, frowning, pursing her lips and shaking her head tightly. "I was already there."

I was trying to hold the second wind breaker in, but my butt cut it loose. It was a little louder and a lot longer. With that, Emily expelled my appendage and dismounted.

Suffice it to say, the atmosphere the rest of the evening was fairly tense, fraught with embarrassment, mostly mine. We actually talked about the weather and changes to William's nap schedule. Jesus!

In the car on the way home, I was grateful, as always, to whom or to what I hadn't a clue, that my back had unlocked and Emily didn't have to drive me home or call a goddamned ambulance. My unguided gratitude waned severely, however, when I replayed the first fart, then the penile pink slip she gave me after the second. Fuck!

Samantha was asleep on the couch when I arrived at Four-fourteen. I studied her face for a few moments and asked myself; at what age or stage did females morph from the innocence of this child to the savvy and imperious skills of an Emily. I awakened Samantha, gave her a twenty-dollar bill, and watched until she was safely across the street and into her house.

April lapsed into May, and it'd been three weeks since the defecation debacle, as I had come to term it. I was eager to know if there was any interest in me at all still alive with Emily, but I hadn't called her, calculating that she would contact me if she wanted to continue the relationship.

When the end of the school year arrived, Samantha invited me to her eighth-grade graduation Mass at St. Columba Catholic Church. Liesl went too, since her only sitter was graduating from St. Columba and unavailable for duty. As the honored graduates filed down the church's aisle way to "Pomp and Circumstance," Liesl spotted Samantha.

"Manta," she yelled kneeling on the pew between Idelle and me, her head bobbing like a cork in rippling water. Samantha smiled broadly and waved to Liesl. "What's Manta doing, Poppa?"

"She's finishing school, Sweetie." I continued, more to myself than to Liesl. "But more so, she's changing stages. From sweet youth to awkward adolescence."

I glanced at Idelle. She was crying and I took her hand and patted it. Liesl noticed and patted Idelle's thigh, looking at her face with anxiety.

"She's a fine young lady, Idelle," I said. "She'll be an accomplished woman before we know it."

Idelle was silent, but smiled at Liesl through her tears, like the sun occasionally shines while it rains.

The next day, Liesl and I had been invited to a party for the two Maddox children who had late May birthdays, Urban and Christian. On the way to the festivities, a white Cadillac SUV cut into my lane, causing me to brake severely.

"You goddamned butt breath!" I said, reflexively offering the driver the worst insult I could spontaneously conjure.

The SUV continued weaving in and out of traffic until it ran a stoplight a half-block ahead and was gone. I have to watch my language in those situations, I thought. When I glanced back at Liesl, she showed no signs of reacting to, or of even having heard, my poor choice of words.

To get over negative experiences such as rude drivers in gigantic

SUVs, I always adjusted the rear view mirror so that I could observe Liesl's cherubic face. She never noticed that I was staring, so I enjoyed long glimpses of my granddaughter's expressions.

She was always looking out the windows with curiosity, glancing left and right, and on occasion, catching sight of something that demanded her consideration, such as a school bus or a fire engine. Passing fancies such as those caused her to lean forward in her BabySafe Maxx and turn her head to see the object of her attention, until simple physics allowed her to see it no more. When she turned back around, she would soon find some new curiosity to take the place of the departed one.

Liesl was beautiful and had redefined the meaning of love for me. Seeing her in the mirror seemed as if I'd fast-forwarded twenty years or so and was observing an old video of my granddaughter when she was just shy of two years old. That illusion always made it clear to me that those, indeed, were the good old days, even while they were occurring.

When we arrived at the Maddoxes, several of Liesl's cousins, as well as Madonna, came out to greet us in the driveway.

"Goodness," Madonna said. "How big she's gotten, and how beautiful."

"Hello, Madonna," I said, holding Liesl in the cradle of my arm, "and thank you for inviting us. She's been so excited about coming." Liesl leaned away from me, offering herself to Madonna with two extended arms. Madonna took over as Liesl's conveyor, and it was easy to see she was pleased to do so.

The entourage of Maddoxes and Foleys made its way into the house and down to the basement family room where the party was already under way. Space was always at a premium at Maddox functions, with nine immediate family members, the Rausches, and the Foleys, plus Michael's parents, his sister, her husband and their four children.

After the candles on the cake were blown out and tri-flavored Neapolitan ice cream served, it was time for gift opening. Liesl watched the proceedings with restraint, not coveting the presents of her birthday cousins, but enjoying the frolicking. Five-year-old Christian received a "Smurf" bowling ball and ten soft pins, each of which bore the likeness of a fantasy character.

After Christian had fully inspected his new prize, and moved on to open another package, Liesl wanted to see the pin that was a replica of her favorite character, Amy Angel. As she tested Amy's softness with a squeeze, Thomas, the three-year old son of Michael's sister, snatched it from Liesl's hands, almost pulling her off her feet in the process.

"Thomas! Thomas, no," said his embarrassed mother. "Liesl was playing with that."

Liesl, somewhat rattled, looked up at me. My tilted head, shrugged shoulders, pursed lips and wide-eyed expression made her know she should let it go. Her face rallied from a contorted, near crying expression to one of resignation.

Before any of the nineteen merrymakers could utter something clever to say to break the awkward silence, Liesl calmly said to Thomas, "You goddamned butt breath."

One evening shortly thereafter, when Liesl was asleep for the night, I recounted in succulent detail, my last session with Emily, sans the gas passing. I dialed her number.

"Emily, it's David."

"David. Yeah, oh sure, how are you?"

"I'm somewhat anxious, actually. I've been wondering if there's any way I might still occupy some small part of your life."

"David, of course," she responded in a tone that immediately let me know the jig was up. "You always will. Maybe not in the same sense as you have for the last few weeks, but nonetheless—"

"It was the farting, wasn't it?"

"Of course not, silly!"

"Well what then?"

"David, there's this guy. He's an assistant professor of psychology at school. He's moved in with me."

"Moved in with you and William?"

"Yes."

Hearing that scenario propelled me from the fog of phantasm to twenty-twenty clarity with such speed that I didn't have time to properly compress before hitting the hard wall of reality.

How could a man of my age, forget sophistication, think, even for a moment, I was more than a mere anomaly to this young woman? How could I have allowed my ego to inflate to the point that it would puncture so painfully when pierced?

"I see," I finally said. "Well, I hope it works out for you and William."

"Thank you, David," she said. "I knew you'd understand. I'm glad you called, though. Things have been happening so fast. All I have between my master's and me is a thesis. Pollard, the assistant prof I'm living with, has given me the summer to submit it."

"Pollard? Did you say *Pollard*?" I asked. Christ almighty, anyone with that name had to be a dink.

"Yes, David. Pollard," she said, obviously irritated with my sarcastic tone. Then back to normal, "Guess what the title of my thesis is; 'The Sex Life of Demi-centenarians in the Late Twentieth Century.'"

"What?"

"Yes! You're part of it. You're such an interesting dichotomy. On one hand, erections a cat couldn't scratch, all that staying power, not to mention the will to please. On the other hand, argyle socks, claw-talons, a bad back, and occasional tooting during sex. David, you're a psychologist's treasure trove."

Then I heard, "Excuse me a second David, what's that Polly? Oh yeah, for sure.

"Sorry David, I'm back. Pollard says I should find out for my paper if you use an erectile dysfunction product."

Chapter Five

"Sins cannot be undone, only forgiven."

— IGOR STRAVINSKY

As a two-year-old, Liesl was confident, loquacious. The narcissistic, obstinate and hard-to-live-with characteristics that temporarily possess many toddlers of that age, just didn't occur with her. To my best recollection, Patrick never displayed such behavior either, surely proving that I was pulling the correct levers, rather than just being lucky.

One afternoon in the late fall of 1993, I was pushing my grand-daughter in her stroller on the large oval walking path that encompasses several athletic fields as well as the Tot Lot in Seneca Park.

The grass in the park was browning from the nip of nighttime lows, thinning like the follicles on a balding man's head. Yet the muted mix of beiges and browns served as an appropriate carpet for the brilliant red, yellow, and orange tones of nature's furniture, its trees, bushes and brush. Liesl often seemed stoic while observing the park's explosions of color, as if the beauty had narcotized her.

I myself had always found it unnatural to walk an elliptical circuit in any direction other than counter-clockwise. If you were at the side of, and facing a track, when you moved onto it, you would move to the right. This was North America, for Christ's sake, and auto, dog, horse, and human races were without exception traversed in such fashion. Hell, the earth even rotates around the sun that way. *Doesn't it?*

Despite the logic of that physics, or the physics of that logic, it was quite common to encounter walkers moving in a clockwise motion, def-initely against the grain. On that particular day, coming out of turn No. 2, Liesl and I were approaching a 'clockwise' woman and her *three* equal-ly 'clockwise' white poodles taking up the entire width of the walking path.

Move your prissy poodles out of our way, lady, or I'll— is what I thought. "Aw, look at the cute little doggies, Liesl."

"Poppa, they're lambs."

I was wise enough not to debate the point.

Despite Liesl having called their nephew, Thomas, a "goddamned butt breath," the Maddoxes kept us on their invitations list, mostly to parties to celebrate birthdays or holidays, particularly Catholic holy days, such as Christmas and Easter.

Though my acute philosophical differences with Madonna bubbled to the surface on occasion, I was happy that Liesl was able to maintain relationships with her cousins. She needed family other than I, and it seemed Madonna and Michael felt the same way. Theirs were good and decent children, and Liesl benefited from exposure to their pleasant, polite demeanors and wholesome activities.

Liesl's three- and four-year-old periods were filled with much happiness and satisfaction as I watched her burgeon into a thoughtful, kind, and curious young child. She was tall for her age and her hair had darkened to medium brown, a hybrid of her parents' hair colors. Her friendly, smile-induced dimples were definitely in her mother's image, while her prominent cheekbones were an obvious reflection of her father. I loved catching glimpses of both Patrick and Kathryn in Liesl's countenance.

She was they.

Five days before Liesl's fifth birthday, Elizabeth Rausch died uneventfully in her sleep. Early on, Floyd and Elizabeth came to various celebrations and attended Liesl's first two birthday parties, but Elizabeth's advancing dementia made it difficult for Floyd to manage such outings when she would agree to them.

At the end, the only external contact the Rausches had was when a deacon came to administer communion or when the Maddoxes visited, on occasion taking Liesl with them. I was sad for Madonna and wanted to console her. I knew, however, her large family cushioned her sadness.

Having lived with the void of not having parents, Liesl was familiar with the results of death. She was not, however, acquainted with death itself and, in my opinion, certainly wasn't ready to experience a corpse.

I decided not to take her with me to the funeral home. Though I believed death was easy on the dead, a weightless, painless nothingness, a not-uncomfortable black hole, how did one explain that to a five-year-old?

Samantha McCoy, who was now almost seventeen, tended Liesl while I paid respect to Elizabeth, Floyd and the Maddoxes. I was surprised at how Floyd's memory had diminished. Madonna had to slowly explain to her father who I was and even then, I'm not sure Floyd made the connection.

Elizabeth's body had a Catholic rosary intertwined in its folded hands and a brass-plated, equally Catholic crucifix was perched against the silky white lining of the top of the coffin. Heavy facial makeup failed to make Elizabeth look undead.

"She's in heaven now, waiting for me," Floyd told me as we stood together as strangers beside the casket. I didn't begrudge him the comfort of that belief, and felt a sense of shame for my initial categorization of him as an unsophisticated rube. I knew I'd never forget his conciliatory wisdom in the days after Kathryn's death, when he kept the custodianship of Liesl from becoming a bitter family feud and first facilitated my guardianship of her.

I'd always been forthright, albeit economical, with what I told Liesl about her mother and father. When she first asked why she had "no mommy or daddy," I told her, "They died. They're both gone, but they were very brave. Your father was a soldier, trying to make things more peaceful and make people happier. Your mother became very sick just after you were born, but she was trying to make you comfortable and happy." Liesl had allowed me to be sparing when talking about her parents. "I wish I would have known them," she said once. "but I'd still want you to be my Poppa."

With Liesl on the threshold of the age of reason, I was feeling somewhat guilty for not doing much to memorialize and celebrate the lives of Patrick and Kathryn. One hot summer afternoon, while checking the electrical connection of an attic fan above a closet at Four-fourteen, I found the cardboard box of bittersweet photos I had shuffled into that unused space after Kathryn's death.

Yes, I thought, these must come out. It's time for them to be seen and understood by Liesl, remembered and confronted by me. I needed to give Liesl a sense of who her parents were, moreover, who *she* was. I believed sifting the contents of the entire photo box, however, could be overwhelming for her, not to mention myself.

I chose three pictures that had particular emotional triggers for me and, at the same time, were images to which a young girl would naturally be drawn. One was a wedding picture of Patrick and Kathryn with the three parents, smiles and happiness all around. Another was a portrait of Patrick as a West Point cadet with a serious but pleasant expression in his full-dress, gray coat, with tails and ball-shaped brass buttons. He was wearing starched white cross belts with a brass breastplate above a white waist belt.

The last picture was the one I had snapped of Kathryn on the front porch swing of her Germantown house, the one that had catalyzed my move to Louisville. She was wearing one of her simple maternity tops and her beauty and kindness shone.

I bought simple, silver frames to display the three pictures and asked Liesl to help me mount them. She talked about each as we put them under glass, but it was the image of Kathryn on the porch to which Liesl was inextricably drawn.

"Poppa, will I be pretty like Mommy?"

"Oh, Liesl, you already are, but, more important, your Mom was *so* nice and you're nice, just like she was." I tried to keep her from seeing my face contort as I began to cry, so I clutched her to my chest, she standing, I sitting. She could feel me sobbing and she, too, began to cry loudly, her small body convulsing. I didn't think Liesl was crying for her parents, I believed she was distraught that her grandfather was sad.

I chose not to send Liesl to daycare or nursery school, preferring, as I liked to say, to "home preschool" her and delay the start of her formal education until kindergarten, when she would be five. My understanding from the reading I'd done on the subject was that preschool fever in the U.S. wasn't a result of credible educators and behavioralists advocating its necessity or advantages.

Rather, it was a device of convenience for American parents, particularly mothers, who still bore the obligatory brunt of child rearing in this country. Any benefits of formal, early childhood education, were totally unproven, I deduced, except in cases of children from impoverished environments and/or dysfunctional homes.

Furthermore, I was damned determined to delay Liesl's exposure to the deleterious effects of American pop culture and the resulting civil and social "bar lowering" until she was into her sixth year, safely away from the impressionable three and four-year-old periods. I saw anecdotal, but convincing, evidence every day that courtesy was no longer common, consideration of others was no longer important, and that self-centeredness was no longer the exception, but the rule.

I was resolute to insulate my granddaughter from those undesirable realities until I felt she was of the age where she'd be capable of assessing the behavior of others for herself and making decisions, with at least a beginning degree of rationality, as to how *she* wanted to conduct herself. I detested the thought of mass-produced, dumbed-down, proprieties swirling around her until she was mature enough to resist them if she chose.

I used three criteria for selecting a school for Liesl; small class size, a half-day schedule for kindergarten, and a rigorous academic curriculum, but not until the first grade. Thomas Jefferson Preparatory School met all those benchmarks. It was a Kindergarten through grade-12 school, and Liesl would be one of only fourteen students in her morning kindergarten class.

So on August 22, 1996, Liesl and I made the fifteen-minute car trip to TJ Prep. I escorted her into Mrs. Gillespie's AMK class at eight-twenty a.m., and Liesl began her academic career.

I didn't mind finding myself somewhat of a curiosity among the other parents and children, but I wondered if and when such attention would adversely affect Liesl.

"Is that your dad?" a schoolmate asked. Having to answer, "No, he's Poppa, my grandfather," didn't seem to bother Liesl on that day, but I feared the day it might.

Promptly at eight-thirty, Mrs. Gillespie informed the attending adults it was time for the school day to begin and for us to depart. Liesl was at ease with me leaving and seemed quite comfortable with her teacher, who I thought to be about thirty-five, attractive, and very kind of demeanor.

When I reached my car, the same Honda Civic I brought her home from St. Anthony's in some five years ago, I was quietly crying, discomposed by the realization that the moments just passed were transformational for Liesl *and* me. She had just metamorphosed from one stage of life to another, from an unburdened preschooler to a responsibility-laden student. I would never again experience her as she was just previously, except in inadequate and imperfect memory. I couldn't relinquish that cycle without emotion, but I knew I had no choice other than to concede, for that precious period was gone. How many more transformational moments did Liesl and I have left together?

In the early fall of her first grade year, Liesl spent a weekend with the Maddoxes. "We went to the zoo on Saturday morning with Aunt Madonna," she said, back home for Sunday dinner.

"I forgot," I said. "Madonna told me you guys were going to do that. What were your favorite animals?"

"I think I liked the camels best," she said, squinting and tilting her head left. "They seemed like they were sad to me. John Paul said they were stupid looking. I felt sorry for them."

"I wonder what the camels thought of John Paul," I said, more to myself than to Liesl.

"What do you mean, Poppa?"

"Oh, never mind, Sweetie. Just remember that those camels aren't stupid and they are very well taken care of at the zoo. I'm sure they're happy." I could usually make Liesl feel better when she was sad or worried about things like that.

Lourdes Maddox was a second grader at Precious Blood parochial school, preparing to make her First Communion. Liesl wasn't sure exactly what that was, but she knew it was special. Madonna let her see Lourdes' lacy white dress, complete with sheer veil, and when Lourdes

85

showed Liesl the white-beaded rosary she'd been given for the occasion, Liesl decided that she, too, wanted to make her First Communion.

"Lourdes is going to get a First Communion soon, Poppa. Can I get one? Please?"

"Oh dear, why do you want a First Communion, Liesl?" I asked.

"Because you get to wear a white dress and a veil, and Lourdes got these pretty white beads called a rosary," she said, eyes wide with possibility.

After a moment of thought, pursed lips, and slowly nodding, I said, "You know, Liesl, if you want a First Communion, you'll have to change schools, go to Precious Blood instead of TJ Prep."

I was relieved to see Liesl's frown, a tip that she didn't like that idea. "And you know what?" I continued, warming now to the task of sacramental discouragement. "We can get a nice white dress for you without getting a First Communion."

"With a veil?" she asked, excitement building.

"Absolutely, and if you'd like a rosary to play with, we could get one of those too."

"We can? Tomorrow?"

"How about next weekend?" I suggested. "Say, Saturday."

"Will you remember, Poppa?"

"Oh yes, and you can remind me if I don't."

"Okay, Poppa. I don't want to go to Precious Blood. I like my friends at TJ."

"I'll bet you didn't know I had a First Communion, did you?"

"Really, Poppa?"

"Yes, a long time ago, when I was in the first grade, and it wasn't that much fun. I remember thinking after Father Mulcahy mumbled something and put that wafer on my tongue, 'Is that all there is?'"

The guest list for Liesl's eighth birthday party would have included Floyd Rausch, had he any clue as to where he would be going or whom he would be honoring. Like his wife before him, he had fallen victim to dementia, so the invitees were limited to Idelle and Samantha McCoy, who was a recent pre-med graduate from the University of Louisville,

Mia Smith, as well as Madonna, Michael, and the four younger Maddox kids, including the newest addition, Bernadette.

Bernadette was the out-of-wedlock, two-year-old daughter of nineteen-year-old Angela Maddox. I always thought Magdalene would be the one most likely to make premature grandparents of Michael and Madonna, but Angela proved me wrong.

She and "Reckless" Rex Hardaway, a star running back for Louisville high school football power, the Holy Trinity Triplets, conceived Bernadette the summer before Angela's senior year at St. Monica Academy. Rex, who was a year older than Angela, was a prized football signee of the University of Notre Dame.

When his parents learned of the pregnancy, just days before he was to report for preseason practice in South Bend, they met with the Maddoxes and suggested, even offered to pay for, an abortion. The Hardaways wanted a "clean break" from Angela so that Rex could "put this incident behind him." Just before asking the Hardaways to leave, the Maddoxes informed them that there would be no abortion, but that they could consider the meeting the "clean break" they had sought.

So while Angela spent her senior year boarding at Blessed Virgin School for Unwed Mothers in Bardstown, KY, "Reckless" Rex indeed put the incident behind him and plied his trade in the Fighting Irish backfield in the shadow of Touchdown Jesus, I assume with his proud parents in the stands for every game. Bernadette was born on Easter Sunday the following year and Michael and Madonna took her to rear as their own, insisting that Angela continue, as much as possible, with a normal, young-adult life.

At the same time the Maddoxes were coming to terms with Angela's ordeal, twenty-year-old son Urban was coming to terms with his sexuality. While studying ballet at the Interpretive Dance Center in New York City, he decided it was time to "come out."

One day, while Liesl and I were visiting the Maddoxes, Madonna told me of a letter she and Michael received from Urban, informing them of his decision to stop pretending he wasn't something he was. "He wrote he's living with another dancer," Madonna said. "His name is Wolfgang, a German national. Urban's going to bring him home some weekend soon and he's sure we'll just love Wolfie.

"Michael and I weren't exactly clueless to Urban's orientation," Madonna confided. "It would have been difficult to live with a boy for eighteen years and not notice his affinity for dolls and his sisters' clothing, not to mention ballet. But 'don't ask, don't tell' was our operative mode."

I knew how difficult it must have been for the Maddox parents to learn of Urban's partner, but I hoped their innate decency would overcome their lack of understanding.

Not to be outdone by his older siblings, seventeen-year-old John Paul caused a furor in the Maddox household when, in the process of college shopping, he began receiving letters and flyers from such organizations as *Humanists On Campus*, *Free Thinkers of Middle Kentucky University*, and the College of the Bluegrass's chapter of *Secularism Now*.

When asked about the spurt of heathen postal material, John Paul explained to his parents that he must have accidently hit a wrong link on one of the schools' websites and gotten into a broader database of such organizations. But Madonna admitted to me that she had surreptitiously scanned the history of websites accessed on the family computer, and found that someone, presumably John Paul, had been exploring with rigor such organizations on the campuses of schools to which he had applied.

"I don't suppose you had anything to do with that," Madonna said to me during a phone conversation.

"Come on, Madonna. I wouldn't do that," I answered truthfully. "Think about it. Would you ever try to introduce Liesl to Catholicism?"

"Of course not," she answered.

Knowing Madonna, I figured she had her fingers crossed.

The triple blows delivered by Angela, Urban, and John Paul had taken some of the dogmatic starch out of the Maddox parents. I sympathized with Michael and Madonna, hoping they'd prove resilient. Rather than consider Angela, Urban, and John Paul outside their definition of mainstream, perhaps their mainstream would flood its banks and flow over a more inclusive spectrum of humanity.

Family turbulence notwithstanding, any part of the Maddox family was always welcome in our home and I was happy to have six of them for the eighth anniversary of Liesl's birth. The sad part of Liesl's birthdays was that there was never any retelling of the joyful events surrounding her birth. Other than she coming to life, her birth was just dreadful.

When it was time to open her gifts, Liesl left the table, asking us to "Wait a minute, I need to get something from my room." When she came back down the stairs, she was carrying the framed pictures of her mother and father, Kathryn on the porch swing, Patrick in his cadet uniform.

"This makes me feel like they're here for my party," she said. "For the first time."

The table was somber for a moment until Madonna said, "Aw, what a great idea, Liesl," triggering the Maddox kiddos and Liesl to resume their revelry.

I saved my gift for Liesl until last. When the packages of books, clothing, and electronic devices were all opened, I walked over to the laundry room that adjoined the basement family room and fetched my offering, a ten-week-old golden retriever puppy. Liesl's expression exploded with delight when I set him on her lap. The pup immediately began licking her face as she closed her eyes and stretched her neck.

"He'll need lots of care and attention," I said. "But we can do that together."

While Mia, Samantha, and Madonna cleared the tables and rinsed the dishes, I gathered birthday cards, fragments of wrapping paper, ribbons and bows. Liesl and I hugged each guest at the door as they left. When it came turn for me to embrace Michael, I did so enthusiastically, looked him in the eyes, and said so that Madonna could hear, "Your family is truly wonderful, from top to bottom." To lighten up a heavy moment, I added, "But you knew that before I told you, Dad."

Once the guests were gone, Liesl was on the floor with her puppy. He had his front paws on her chest, trying to scale her, so he could get to her face and lick it. Liesl shrieked with happiness as she tried to hold him at bay, but found he wouldn't be denied. She crossed her arms over her face and giggled as the new pooch nosed through an opening in her defenses to get to any remnants of ice cream and cake he could find on her face.

"He'll need a name," I said. "Do you have any ideas?"

"I don't, Poppa," she said, suddenly somber.

The next day in the shade of the ginkgo tree, I threw an old tennis ball to the new retriever pup. He proved to be a born ballplayer.

"Poppa, what's the name you call baseball players who chase the ball?" Liesl asked.

"Fielders," I said smiling, understanding where she was going with the question.

I think I'd like to name him 'Fielder.' What do you think?"

"Fielder," I repeated. "Yes, I like it. Fielder Foley has a nice ring to it."

As it turned out, Fielder Foley never met a ball he didn't like. He always found one of many in the yard or in the house and placed it at the feet of the nearest human. If the person didn't respond, Fielder nudged the ball closer to the negligent individual, and whined with wretchedness until the request could no longer be ignored.

Liesl and Fielder became inseparable. If she weren't in school, she was with him, taking a walk, romping in Seneca Park, or playing catch under the ginkgo tree.

Liesl's first two teachers at TJ Prep always told me she was a delightful child and an earnest student. When she entered the third grade in August of 1999, her teacher was Mrs. van Pelt, a twenty-eight year veteran of the school with a reputation of teacher par excellence.

Liesl loved Mrs. van Pelt and benefited from all the savvy, experience, and knowledge of her teacher. At Thanksgiving, she was cast in the lead role of "Mrs. Moose" in the class production of "A Turkey for Thanksgiving." The role of "Mrs. Moose" was coveted by students and parents alike, and for good reason.

The list of those who had played "Mrs. Moose" or the lead male role, "Mr. Moose," for Mrs. Van Pelt in her twenty-eight productions of "Turkey," included the transplanted junior U.S. Senator from Illinois, a Pulitzer Prize-winning newspaper reporter at the Baltimore Sun, as well as the current Museum of Neoclassic Art's Chief Curator of Photography. If you were cast as Mr. or Mrs. Moose in Mrs. Van Pelt's Thanksgiving play, the offers would no doubt come rolling in.

I myself attended the first and third of three presentations of "A Turkey for Thanksgiving" in the TJ Prep auditorium. Liesl had always been a great pretender, but with a little coaching from Mrs. van Pelt, she reached another echelon. Her dramatic ability surpassed even *my* immodest expectations.

My pride in her performance was tempered a bit, however, when the compliments from the other parents were addressed to "Mr. Foley."

"Mr. Foley, Liesl was wonderful," or "You should pursue performing for Liesl, Mr. Foley," or "Mr. Foley, she's such a natural," were among the platitudes I heard, all of which were appreciated, but made me long to be called "David." I recalled the loneliness of single parenting for Patrick. Perhaps it was the age factor making the isolation seem more acute this time around.

Before TJ Prep's Christmas break, Liesl asked me if it would be okay for Heather Cassidy, a classmate who Liesl had befriended, to spend the night with us sometime over the holidays.

"Of course," I said. "That'll be fun. Just tell Heather to have her mom or dad call me."

I didn't know the Cassidys, but had seen Heather at a few school functions and had briefly spoken with her once. She seemed bright, polished and polite. I knew her father was connected to the Blake Distilleries, a very old and prosperous Louisville spirits company.

Three or four days later, Liesl asked if Mrs. Cassidy had called me about Heather spending the night.

"No Liesl, was I supposed to have gotten a call?" I asked, not looking up from the newspaper spread in front of me.

"Heather told me she was going to ask her mom if she could spend the night," replied Liesl, rubbing Fielder's chest. "Maybe she forgot."

"Would you like me to call the Cassidys to see if we could arrange an overnight this weekend?" I realized the newspaper would have to wait.

"Yes, Poppa, would you?" The excited inflection in her voice tipped

Fielder that something was up.

"Do you know where the TJ phone directory is?" I asked, hoping I wouldn't have to move from the recliner.

While Liesl was opening and slamming drawers looking for the directory, Fielder was following, not taking his eyes off her, hoping with his sincerest expression that she was looking for a tennis ball. Whenever he beseeched her so earnestly, Liesl could never refuse, so after finding the directory, she and Fielder headed outside for a game of fetch.

When I dialed the Cassidys' number, a male voice answered, "Hello," with what sounded like impatience.

"Mr. Cassidy?" I asked.

"This is Mr. Cassidy."

"Oh hi. This is David Foley. I'm Liesl Foley's grandfather. She's a classmate of Heather and I believe the girls have been discussing—"

"Hold on," Mr. Cassidy commanded. "Sheila! Telephone!"

After several seconds, I heard a woman's voice say, "Hello?" followed by the unceremonious click of an extension disconnecting.

"Hi, Mrs. Cassidy," I said, trying keep my reaction to Mr. Cassidy's ugly manner out of my voice. "This is David Foley, Liesl Foley's grandfather? Apparently Heather and Liesl have been talking about Heather spending the night here with Liesl sometime, and I was just calling to see if that would be okay with you. We'd love to have her."

"That's awfully nice of you, Mr. Foley, but I don't know if that would be such a good idea."

"Really?" I said, perplexed.

Would it be okay if Liesl came here for the night?" she asked.

"Well, uh, I suppose," I said, hoping my bewilderment was obvious. "It's just that—"

"Good," she interrupted. "How about New Year's night? I'll be able to be with the girls myself that evening."

"Well, I suppose," I repeated.

"Is your e-mail in the TJ directory?" she asked.

"Yes."

"Good. I'll send you the times and directions, okay?"

I didn't want to say, "I suppose," again, so I merely said, "Okay."

"Great," Mrs. Cassidy said. "Good-bye."

I was still replaying the phone conversation in my mind when Liesl and Fielder came bounding in from the cold. "Did you talk to Heather's mom?" she asked.

"Yes."

"Can she come here, or did her mom ask me to come there?"

"Why yes, she does want you to come to their house," I said, "on New Year's Night. What do you know about that?"

"Heather just told me her mom does that a lot. She's not sure why. It might have something to do with money."

"Money?"

"That's what Heather said," replied Liesl as she and Fielder bounded up the stairs side by side. "I don't know."

I tried to envision the life of a woman like Mrs. Cassidy, with all that wealth, and all that social "responsibility," plus the tribulations of dealing with a husband who was obviously a pompous ass. I digressed to ponder whether he would have been an ass if he were born poor, or if the silver spoon caused it.

Later that evening, after Liesl fell asleep reading on the den divan in her wool pajamas, Fielder followed as I carried her up to her room and placed her on her three-quarter bed. She opened her sleepy eyes as Fielder leaped onto the bed to claim the spot next to her that had become his nighttime lair. He swiveled one-and-a-half times before dropping into a semi-circle with his back in contact with Liesl's legs.

Just as I enjoyed singing Patrick to sleep when he was a boy, I loved to sing to Liesl at bedtime, in spite of the fact that the loss of my son was sometimes particularly painful when I did. Even if Patrick were alive, I'd still have been sad that he was no longer the little guy who used to tell me I was "the best singer ever" every single night.

After meticulously arranging the covers to the precise specifications I knew Liesl liked, I put one hand on Fielder's fur and began to sing Kris Kristofferson's "Bobby McGee."

Well, I pulled my harpoon outta my dirty red bandana,
I was playin' soft while Bobby sang the blues.

93

Windshield wipers slappin' time,
I was holdin' Bobby's hand in mine.
We sang every song that driver knew.

"Is that a sad song, Poppa?" Liesl asked, with her eyes closed.

"Yes, it's about two people who loved each other but Bobby had to leave."

"Why?" she asked.

"The song says Bobby had to go 'looking for a home,' but a song is just a story, like any book you read."

"Good night, Poppa," Liesl said in the tone she only used mere seconds before succumbing to slumber.

"Good night, my precious gift," I said, knowing she wouldn't hear my words.

Liesl and I spent New Year's Eve alone at Four-fourteen, watching the Vienna Philharmonic Orchestra on public television in a concert from the Golden Hall of the Musikverein. Elaine always watched this annual tribute to the musical Strauss family when we were married, and I begrudgingly gave her credit for enhancing my fondness of classical music. When the first faint notes of the violins' tremolo and the horns' softness began to intone the beginning of Strauss's "On the Beautiful Blue Danube," my eyes moistened.

There were a few pieces special to me, "Blue Danube" being one, whose beauty shimmered with sadness. Its beginning always entreated the tragedies of my life to revisit; Elaine abandoning Patrick, Patrick and Kathryn's deaths, Liesl's orphan status.

Yet as the piece progressed, it always made me wish I were a dancer. Johann, Jr. would then be forced to behold me attaining an attitude derrière, peer at me participating in a pas de deux. "Blue Danube" begged for graceful movement.

"What's the matter, Poppa?" Liesl asked, noticing the tears behind my smile and moving toward me.

"It's just the music," I said. "That piece is so beautiful and emotional, it makes me smile and cry at the same time."

94

Liesl sat as close to me on the couch as she could and she, too, began to cry. Perhaps because of the beauty of the music, but I thought more likely, she was afraid her grandfather was sad again.

We awakened early the next morning, Liesl because she was excited about going to Heather's house, I myself because I was still thinking about and drawing the worst possible conclusions as to Sheila Cassidy's hesitancy to allow Heather to spend the night at Four-fourteen. I wondered if she was leery because there was no traditional mother/father/children family structure.

Mrs. Cassidy, no doubt, thought I wasn't a fit guardian. Maybe she wondered if I was a molester, some pedophile that preyed upon young girls. Jesus, that's it, I thought. She's afraid of what I might do to her daughter. Goddamn her. How could *anyone* come to such a stupid conclusion?

I felt like calling her, "I want your uppity, social ass to understand, Madam, that I didn't kidnap Liesl out of some happy home, and I'm not holding her against her will. We inherited each other, and do the best we can."

One of the few things Elaine ever told me with any validity was that I had a tendency to assume *my* interpretation of a situation was the *correct* interpretation of a situation and that those misinterpretations often congealed into reality for me, took on a life of their own. Looking back, that propensity of mine might well have been in play. As often happened when speaking with Liesl, I returned to the calm comfort of her influence and realized my hostilities were probably hyperbole.

"You know," I said. "I think Mrs. Cassidy just plain wants the pleasure of your company, rather than bring Heather to our house and not get to have any fun with you girls."

"But now *you* won't have any fun, Poppa."

"Maybe it'll be our turn next time," I said. "Fielder and I will find something to do."

As dictated, Sheila Cassidy had emailed the directions to the their house and said I should have Liesl there at five-thirty p.m.

So at five-fifteen, Liesl and I and Fielder, who had become a car traveling companion fixture, set out for the Cassidys' house. When we arrived, I was amazed by the imposing size and regality of the residence and its surroundings. The compound was in the elite Glen Vista section of Louisville, sprawling on a hill overlooking the Ohio River. An eight-foot wrought iron fence surrounded the estate with a guard shack next to a gate of equal height across the access road.

"Go right in, Mr. Foley," said the guard, as he electronically parted the gates. "Pull to the front of the house and you'll find adequate parking while you drop Liesl off."

"He knew my name," Liesl said, as I pulled the car through the open gate. When we stopped in front of the house, we dropped all the windows three or four inches and left Fielder in the car while we traversed the stone walk up to the front door of the ante-bellum mansion. A woman answered the door in heels, a short black dress with a white apron, and puffy sleeves.

"You're a Victorian maid," I blurted.

"Sir?" she said, as she frowned, cocked an ear toward me.

"Uh, we're the Foleys," I said.

"Yes, you were expected. Mrs. Cassidy wants me to escort Liesl to Miss Heather's room."

"Is Mrs. Cassidy here?" I said, as I maneuvered past the woman into the foyer.

"Yes," she responded. "Will that be all, sir?"

"Well, actually, I was hoping to meet her," I said.

"I'm afraid that would be impossible at the moment, sir. She's bathing."

"I see. How about Mr. Cassidy?"

"He's out of the country, sir. Will that be all?"

"Well Liesl, I guess this is where I jump off," I said, uncomfortable with not having met Mrs. Cassidy.

Heather scurried into the foyer. "Hi Liesl. Come on up to my room before we have dinner. I have lots of things to show you."

"This is Poppa," Liesl said.

"Hello, Mr. Foley. Thanks for bringing Liesl over."

"You're welcome, Heather," I said.

As I stepped through the door back onto the porch, I turned to say, "Have a good time, ladies," but the Victorian closed the door with a thump of authority just as I was beginning the sentence.

On my way home in the car with Fielder, I again speculated about what Sheila Cassidy and her household must be like, all that money, living like royalty. I couldn't imagine.

Fielder was panting with his snout aimed at me. "Christ almighty, Fielder, your breath is horrible." I dropped the front windows despite the sub-freezing temperature and pushed Fielder away with my right arm.

The next evening, around six, the phone rang and I hurried to answer it. "Mr. Foley, this is Sheila Cassidy. I can't begin to tell you how much fun the girls are having. Would it be possible for Liesl to stay another night with us? We just love her!"

"Well," I said, moving the phone to my other ear. "I suppose. May I speak with her?"

"Certainly." Her voice became muffled, her hand no doubt over the speaker. "Liesl, your father, I mean grandfather, wants to speak with you."

"May I, Poppa, please?" implored Liesl upon taking the phone. "We're having so much fun."

"Well, I suppose," I repeated. "Let me speak to Heather's mom again."

"Thanks, Poppa."

"Yes, Mr. Foley," Sheila said.

"Are you sure it's okay, it wouldn't be any trouble?"

"No trouble at all. I'll bring her to your house at five o'clock tomorrow night. You're in St. Matthews, right?"

"Yes."

"Great, we'll see you then," she said.

Fielder and I passed another uneventful night without the pleasure of Liesl's company. "You're not exactly the mammal I'd choose to be here with me tonight, Fielder," I said. "No offense, but there are some female Homo sapiens in whose company I would be much more interested."

Fielder was lazing on his stomach, his hind legs tucked under his rear end, his head resting on his outstretched front paws. The only reaction he gave to my gentle dig was one uninspired flap of his tail upon hearing his name, coinciding with the upward movement of his disinterested eyes to meet mine.

The doorbell rang at precisely five o'clock the next evening. Fielder barked once and, as usual, easily beat his master to the door. He was wagging his tail feverishly, much too anxious to greet the people on the porch, one of whom his olfactory senses had already informed him was Liesl.

"Mr. Foley," said the woman with Liesl and Heather when I opened the door. "I'm Sheila Cassidy. I'm so happy to meet you."

Sheila was dressed as if she were going to a formal dinner, black satin pants, and a Kelly green designer jacket with a short waist and fur collar. Fielder wasted no time in attempting to scale her. "Oh, oh," she said as Fielder tried in vain to stretch his forty-eight-inch length to access her face that fortunately occupied the top eight inches of her five-feet, six-inch frame.

"I'm sorry," I said. "Neither he nor I are very well schooled in the art of dog behavior."

"It's okay," Sheila said. "I love dogs. What's his name?"

"Fielder," Liesl said. "He likes to play ball."

"Liesl, would you and Heather like to throw a few for Fielder while Mrs. Cassidy and I chat for a moment?"

"Can we, Liesl?" Heather said as she rubbed Fielder's chest.

"Sure," Liesl said, brushing past me to grab a tennis ball out of a canister on a hallway table shelf. "Come on, boy," she implored, as she ran into the front yard, Fielder and Heather in tow.

"Won't you come in, Mrs. Cassidy?" I asked.

"Yes, but just briefly."

Sheila Cassidy's appearance conveyed what I would cynically term neo-American aristocracy. Her countenance was not unlike the Kennedy women, prominent brow, wide-set eyes, green in Sheila's case, over high cheekbones. I suspected the aristocratic conveyance was as much a result of attitude as it was physicality. Her mouth, even when assuming the shape of a smile, betrayed the subtlest hint of a superiority sneer.

Her dark brown, almost black hair would be called bay were it on a real thoroughbred. It began with short bangs covering the top of her ample forehead and ended at the back of her neck stylishly tucked under itself, resting just above the fur collar of the designer jacket. She was probably forty-two to forty-five-years-old, artificially preserved, I thought. That, as opposed to thirty-seven or thirty-eight, and unpreserved. I knew wealthy people could purchase such preservation.

"Mr. Foley, Liesl's the most engaging young lady," she said, breaking a short but awkward initial silence in the foyer. "Heather and I enjoyed her immensely. Someone has done a wonderful job of raising her."

"Thank you," I said, thawing a bit with that compliment. "I'm not sure at all how much I've had to do with her good nature. I'd love it if you'd call me David."

"Only in exchange for you calling me Sheila," she said, tilting her head and widening her eyes coquettishly.

"Sure."

"Your house is charming, David."

"Thank you," I said, casting my eyes around the small entry room. "We're comfortable here. I'm from Boston and this type of place would be out of reach there, so I feel fortunate."

"I hope you weren't offended when I preferred Liesl come to our house rather than Heather coming here," Sheila said, her eyes fixated on mine.

"Well, I—"

Rolling her eyes now, "Our security company recommends that protocol. Now that we're familiar with the Foleys, I'd love for Heather to be able to spend the night here sometime."

"Security?" I probed.

"Yes, you know, with the family business and all," Sheila said with a shrug.

"Do you own the distillery?"

"My husband's grandfather founded it. It's a public company now, but Ansel and his two siblings own a controlling interest. Ansel is the CEO."

"Ansel is your husband?" I was particularly curious to observe Sheila as she spoke of Ansel, but a one-word answer made it impossible to discern her spousal attitude.

"Yes," she said, followed by a quick subject change. "What brought you to Louisville from Boston, David?"

"My son was an army officer and met Liesl's mother here while he was stationed at Fort Knox. He was killed in the Gulf War and I moved here after that to be near Liesl and her mother."

"My God, and Liesl's mother?"

"She died delivering Liesl."

"I'm so sorry," Sheila said. "I can't imagine."

"Neither could have I," I said, more to myself than to her.

"Well again, I must tell you what a wonderful little person she is," she said, taking a step back from me and forcing a smile that I could tell was her attempt to break the somberness of the moment. "You're to be congratulated. I have to be going now, but I do hope you'll encourage Liesl's relationship with Heather. It's great for Heather and I think Liesl had fun this weekend. By the way, you might want to contact a company called 'PetCops' for some training for Fielder. They come to your home and the results are amazing."

"I'll remember that," I said. "I can tell Liesl likes Heather, too. I'm sure we'll run into each other again." Against my better judgment, I was hoping so.

Chapter Six

"If I decide to be an idiot, then I'll be an idiot on my own accord."
— JOHANN SEBASTIAN BACH

Liesl's third-grade curriculum at TJ was demanding and kept her busy. I volunteered regularly at the school, which helped keep me occupied and I liked being involved in her formal education.

I would come into contact with women I considered potential good company on occasion, but most often they proved themselves not to be before I got around to asking them out. The divorced TJ Prep moms seemed to be so singularly focused on remarriage, that they were incapable of providing what I was looking for from women, casual relationships. One, Taffy something-or-other, actually once called me on a weeknight after eleven o'clock, ostensibly just to chitchat.

When the spring broke free of winter's clench, I decided to take Sheila Cassidy's advice and try PetCops for Fielder. His manners weren't getting any better, and his increasing size made his misbehavior all the more intolerable. He was, for the most part, unmanageable when visitors called and so frightened when it stormed, or even with a slight drop in barometric pressure, that he would gnaw through anything separating him from Liesl or me. That included household doors.

When the PetCop arrived for the first session, Liesl was in school. The dog of interest was lazing under the ginkgo tree, but when he saw the "Cop," he grew curious and, after a sniff or two of her calf, promptly demonstrated why her services were so urgently needed. Fielder knew he wasn't tall enough to access the Cop's face while earthbound, so he started leaping off the ground, trying to get a lick of any part of her face, preferably her lips and whatever interesting remnants they might contain.

The woman, a sturdy type who I figured could beat the hell out of Fielder and me at the same time, asked me to hold her clipboard, which I did. The next time he jumped, she snared his collar at his throat with her right hand and held him in mid-air, rotating her wrist so that he could only bare his teeth, not use them. With her arm bent at the elbow, she held his forty-eight pounds off the ground until his hind legs went limp in resignation. I was amazed. So was Fielder.

With her right hand still in place on his neck, the Cop lowered him slowly to the ground. When all four paws were back on earth, she said, "Sit," while firmly pushing his rear end to the ground with her left hand. Fielder seemed stunned. "Now stay," she demanded as she withdrew her right hand from his collar and held the palm and five spread fingers of her left hand about six inches in front of his face.

The Cop looked at me. "See how they succumb when you know how to do it? This boy and I are going to get along just fine."

Fielder remained stationary for all of four or five seconds. Then, I suspected, sensing an over-confident opponent, he leaped at the still-gloating Cop and took the sloppiest, fastest double tongue-stroke of her mouth he could manage.

With both hands over my mouth, I mumbled, "Mother Mary." Fielder must have sensed that in close quarters, he was no match for the Cop, but if he used his speed, he could more than hold his own. He took off running through the yard, forming disrespectful figure eights. As he gained confidence, he began a series of wide-arching circles, each culminating with the full-speed brushing of the Cop's leg. After about four such power statements, he landed in and trampled upon my crocuses, the only flowers in the entire yard having any life at this early stage of spring. He was poised to vault away from any pursuer, front legs spread, head and chest near the ground, butt in the air, his tail slowly swishing. He stared at the Cop and me.

"Shit, Fielder!" I said, upset about the crocuses.

As if on cue, Fielder came erect, raised his tail, squatted his rear end, got a stupid look on his face, and impolitely took a two-portion dump, the results of which lay steaming on my crocuses.

"Hey, that's pretty good, Mr. Foley" said the Cop. "What's your command for getting him out of the flower bed?"

"It's something like, 'Fielder, get your goddamned ass out of my crocuses.'"

Just after school resumed from spring break, Liesl came home after classes and asked if Heather could spend Friday and Saturday night with us at Four-fourteen. That evening, a call came through that the caller identification device flashed as "number unavailable."

"Hi David," Sheila said. "What did you do over spring break?" Before I could answer her, she said, "We were in Portugal and just got back Sunday night."

"We did nothing that exotic," I assured her. "I'm not sure what the highlight was, but the low point was when Fielder was expelled from the PetCops program."

"You're kidding," she said.

"It's okay," I said. "He's just immensely wayward, but we'll manage."

"Heather told me that Liesl invited her to spend the weekend with you guys," she said.

"Yes. We'd love to have her."

"That's so nice of you. May I drop her off around six?"

On Friday evening, when Liesl and I answered the door a little after six, Heather and Sheila were standing on the front porch of Four-fourteen.

"Hello ladies," I said, as Liesl and Heather hugged.

Before Fielder could inflict any damage, Liesl, with an old tennis ball in hand, said, "Come on boy, let's play ball." She and Heather led Fielder to the front yard. The girls were giggling wildly while Fielder stood rigid and motionless, eyes glued on the tennis ball in Liesl's hand. The game was on.

"Are you doing okay, Sheila?"

"I suppose," she responded with a half-shrug. "Sometimes it's a little tough."

"What's a little tough?" I asked, sensing she wanted me to.

"Living in a world where I'm always supposed to be *on* even when I don't feel like being *on*," she said, her fingers pantomiming quotation marks each time she said the word "on."

"Do you mean as the wife of the head of an international corporation?" I asked.

103

"Yes," she said with a sigh that exposed a little societal baggage.

"Would you care to come in?" I asked, gesturing toward the door with an extended arm and upward palm.

"Just for a little while," she replied, the same words the little fourth grade girl used when I asked if I could look down into her underwear.

I held the door, followed her into the foyer, with my eyes dropping to her rear end. She turned abruptly, causing us to collide. We froze, in contact with each other. She looked at my lips, parted hers slightly, and looked into my eyes.

With the girls squealing and Fielder barking in the front yard, a security fell over me that I didn't want to waste on inaction. I threw my arms around her; she did the same, until we were locked in an embrace, each squeezing, striving to absorb the other's body into our own. Our lips and tongues were submitting to each other's without reservation. I pushed my hand up her skirt, moved aside the gusset of her underwear and found her quite open to the whole idea.

"Fuck," she said, abandoning any aristocracy I had perceived. "When? We have to!"

Remembering where we were and the extreme downside of being discovered by the front yard frolickers, I backed away a bit, my bulge not withstanding. "Let me get back to you on that."

"Just promise me you will," she said.

"Oh, you can count on it."

A few minutes later and back on the porch, Sheila waved goodbye to the girls in the yard and the weekend evolved into pleasant, unregimented activities. I was pleased that Liesl and Heather seemed so fond of each other. Heather was refined, yet gracious, seemingly unspoiled by material trappings. When she asked if Liesl and I planned to see the Louisville Ballet's performance of "Swan Lake" later in the spring, it seemed to be genuine interest rather than cultural snobbishness.

"Gosh, I didn't know it was coming," I admitted. "We'll have to check it out."

I thought Heather's urbanity might be a constructive counterweight for Liesl to the sweet, but parochial, influence of the Maddox children.

Saturday and Sunday included a visit to the Museum of Natural History in downtown Louisville, Heather's first ever meal at El Rascal's, an excursion to the Kentucky Horse Park in Lexington, as well as a trip to the lake at Louisville's historic Cave Hill Cemetery, where the ducks and geese competed for the attention and bread crumbs of visiting children.

Sunday evening came too quickly for Heather and Liesl. I grilled dinner in the back yard while they kept Fielder in retriever heaven, taking turns throwing a tennis ball for him. After dinner, with our trio still sitting around the picnic table, Sheila pulled into the driveway.

"Mother, we had the best time," Heather said. "We went to the museum and to the Horse Park. And we ate at El Rascal's in the Mall."

"Which did you like best?" Sheila asked.

"El Rascal's," Heather said unhesitatingly. "We laughed so hard. Mr. Foley is so funny"

"I'll bet he is," Sheila said, looking at me, widening her eyes. "We'll have to go there together sometime, Dear. Thank you David and Liesl for being so welcoming to Heather. I can see she had a good time."

"You're welcome," I said. "She was great company."

Heather and Liesl hugged walking to the car while Sheila told me with serious expression that she hoped to see me sometime soon. I smiled, tilted my head, and nodded. The Cassidys semi-circled the black Mercedes-Benz SUV on the expanded backyard driveway, waved, and were gone.

Liesl's school year was swiftly moving to a crescendo of year-end activities. Sheila called me toward the middle of May, inquiring whether Liesl might like to accompany Heather to Camp Willoughby in Newbury, VT the last week of June and the first week of July.

"Heather went last year and loved it," Sheila said. "Another friend of hers had to cancel, so we can offer that spot to someone else to accept within a week. I made Heather promise she wouldn't mention it to Liesl until I spoke with you. I didn't want her to be disappointed if it wasn't something you'd like for her to do."

"I appreciate that," I said. "I'd be all for it if Liesl wants to give it a try. We've never been away from each other for that long, but I'll talk to her about it this evening."

"When might I see you?" Sheila asked.

"This weekend?" I heard myself offer, feeling the rising reflex just below the waist.

"Yes . . . I think," she said with hesitation, as if she were trying to recall her schedule. "Let me call you Friday afternoon. I believe Ansel's supposed to be out of town."

"Okay," I said.

I tried not to think about Ansel or Heather or how many times Sheila might have put herself in this position.

An Internet search turned up ample information on Camp Willoughby and I quickly ascertained it was a prestigious and exclusive 106-year-old girls camp, mostly for daughters of the wealthy. The facilities were outstanding and the activities looked to be exhilarating. One such was a private tennis lesson from retired pro star, Barbara Conway, another, a forty-five minute hot-air balloon ride with campmates.

It was my week to drive the afternoon "school pool" from TJ, and after I dropped off the three other student-riders, I broached the subject of Camp Willoughby with Liesl.

"That would be great," she said. "Heather always talks about the fun she had there last summer. Does she know I'm going?"

"Well, she knows you might. You can talk to her about it at school tomorrow."

"May I call her tonight, Poppa?"

"Sure," I said, just as I began to feel some trepidation about being separated from Liesl for two whole weeks.

Since Liesl was bent on attending Camp Willoughby with Heather from the moment she heard about it, I filled out the application that Sheila had forwarded to me and made the payment for the two-week tuition.

The weekend tryst with Sheila didn't work out because Ansel unexpectedly arrived home a week early from Versailles, France, the result of acquisition negotiations with a French winery coming to an impasse.

The thought of a man returning to his home, preventing me from a tryst with his wife, produced a pang of short-lived guilt, before I remembered Ansel's phone manners.

"Parents night at Camp Willoughby might be our best bet," Sheila said when she phoned me the day before Ansel's early homecoming. "I'll be on Martha's Vineyard and plan to drive up to camp for a few nights. Could you fly up?"

"You bet."

I made arrangements with Samantha McCoy to tend to Fielder and house sit at Four-fourteen while I spent four late June days in New England visiting Liesl at Camp Willoughby and pursuing other adventures. Samantha had finished her first year of medical school at Johns Hopkins University and was set to spend the summer in Louisville, taking a course during the day at the University of Louisville and working part-time at St. Anthony Hospital.

She had overcome the severe awkwardness she had manifested as an adolescent, and I knew how proud Idelle was of her daughter.

Samantha had foregone the thick glasses for contact lenses, and styled her hair into tightly curled, streaming locks. She had developed perfect posture that well accented her tall, now shapely and lithe frame. Samantha was Andersen's *Ugly Duckling* personified. It was hard to believe she was the same person as the awkward twelve-year-old we met when I first brought Liesl from St. Anthony to St. Matthews.

I felt a twinge of pride and gratification in Samantha's metamorphosis. I thought her relationship with Liesl and me had been a favorable influence, perhaps even somewhat responsible for her blossoming. It also drove a chill into my chest, reminding me of the inevitable changes that were already beginning in my eight-year-old granddaughter. I knew I'd need to learn to cope with Liesl's diminishing dependence upon me.

June was usually a pleasant month weather-wise in Louisville. Most days had highs in the low to mid-eighties, but even when the mercury pushed beyond ninety degrees in late afternoon, the humidity was at reasonable levels and evenings and nights were consistently comfortable.

It was also a month in which Liesl and I shifted schedule gears, and were together for more of the day than the school year availed. She was fun to be around, and I loved the relatively long mornings we spent together, free from the pressure of any bells going off. Sometimes I took her to St. Matthews' public swimming pool, but more often, we took the thirty-minute ride to Deam Lake in Southern Indiana. She liked that because we could take Fielder and he loved to jump into the lake from our rented rowboat. I treasured her giggles when he swam in a wide arc, winding up back at the boat where I got soaked pulling him back on board. Again I realized; these are the good old days.

Liesl was both excited and apprehensive about the two weeks at Camp Willoughby with Heather. It would be her first time to fly.

"I wish you were going to be on the plane with me," she said one evening at Four-fourteen during a dinner at which she hadn't eaten much.

I was confident she had more a case of jitters than serious fear. "It's natural to be a little nervous," I said. "Once you're in the air, I think you'll like it."

When the day arrived to travel to Willoughby, Sheila was already on Martha's Vineyard and Ansel was, as usual, "away on business." I was glad it had fallen to me to take the girls to the airport. Once there, I helped them with checking their luggage and accompanied them to the gate security station. I gave and received an energetic, protracted hug from Liesl. Heather moved to give me a hug that I gladly accepted and returned. I couldn't help but wonder how many times she'd been without a hug due to otherwise occupied parents, though no damage was evident.

"Call me often," I said to Liesl.

"We can only use our cell phones between seven and nine p.m.," Heather said. "Camp rules."

"Okay," I said, pursing my lips and nodding. "I'll make sure my phone is clear during those hours and I'll see you two Thursday night."

On the way home from the airport, my cell phone rang with a call from the 508 area code.

"David, it's Sheila. I just bought a new cell phone here in Massachusetts. Use this number to contact me for the next couple of weeks. I'd prefer there not be a lot of call traffic on my regular phone to and from you while we're up here."

"Are you worried about surveillance," I said, thinking for the first time just how much spy power a man of Ansel Cassidy's wealth could buy.

"I just want to be cautious. What time does your flight get into Burlington Thursday?"

"Actually, I'm coming in Wednesday afternoon," I said.

"Then we'll have an extra night together on Wednesday?"

"I was hoping you'd see it that way," I replied, smiling.

Liesl called me promptly at seven o'clock Sunday evening. "Poppa, you'll never guess who's here."

The first person that came to my mind was Ansel. Just momentarily thinking of that possibility made me nervous.

"Raquel and Sophie," Liesl said.

"What? Raquel and Sophie Burnett, the President's daughters? You're kidding me."

"No Poppa, it's true. Mrs. Burnett came with them but left before dinner. There are two men in suits and sunglasses who always stay close to them."

"I knew it was an exclusive camp," I mumbled, "but—"

"What's that, Poppa? You're breaking up."

On Wednesday, my three-legged flight was routine except that the aircraft for the last leg was a small, uncomfortable, Jetsream 32, a nineteen-seat, twin turboprop, that touched down in Burlington twenty minutes late. After sitting in the terminal for a while, trying to recover the mental and physical equilibrium of which flights on undersized aircraft always stripped me, I rented a car and drove to the historic Church Street Marketplace in Burlington that was tightly lined with hip retail shops catering to tourists. I couldn't resist buying a Martha's Vineyard polo shirt for Liesl, but what really caught my eye was a bright green tee shirt with the words "I did it in Vermont" screened in white across the chest. Perfect for Sheila.

After a walking tour of Church Street, I strolled to Waterfront Park near the Burlington Wharves and marveled at the beauty of the rugged Adirondacks. The rising mountains were streaked with fog, layered in hues of purple just across the glistering surface of Lake Champlain. I always appreciated the humbling perspective mountains gave me.

I left Burlington and drove to Stowe where I checked into the Morning Top Lodge. Following a shower, I phoned Sheila. "Should I come down or can you come up?" I asked.

"I can come up, or I can come down," she said. "I can also come sideways."

Her brazenness made me laugh but it also excited me into feeling the familiar rise to the occasion. Forty-five seconds later, Sheila Cassidy was knocking on the door of opportunity, the door of Room 711 at the Morning Top Lodge in Stowe, VT. As soon as that door was closed, we were locked in an embrace and joined at the mouths. Sheila wrapped her right leg tightly around my hips and pressed me to her. A high slit in her skirt was revealed, disclosing she wasn't wearing underwear.

"Mmmm, what do you think of the Burnett girls being here?" she asked as she palmed the inside of my thigh, moved her hand upward.

"At the moment, I don't give a damn," I said, shoving her onto the bed, advantaging the immediacy her lack of underwear presented me. I pinned her arms above her head with my left arm while unzipping my fly with my right hand. I easily and quickly penetrated, more like fell in, and was "there" in about thirty-five seconds.

"Yeah, that's really something about the Burnetts," I casually took up the subject as if nothing had occurred between her question and my response. "Did you know about it? Oh, I forgot, I have a little token for you."

I disengaged, walked to the dresser, retrieved a small gift bag from the middle drawer, and handed it to her. She pulled out the "I did it in Vermont" T-shirt, laughed.

"You're too much," she said.

And so it went for two-and-a half days in either Room 711 or 428 of the Morning Top Lodge; quick climax, small talk preceding a second, longer session of uninhibited coitus calisthenics, wherein Sheila indeed came up, down and sideways. The only interruption of this routine was Thursday evening's Parents Night at Camp Willoughby and an occasional meal.

When Sheila and Heather and Liesl and I took our assigned seats in the Willoughby dining room at Thursday night's Parents' Dinner, ours was the only table not filled to capacity with diners. There were four unused chairs and place settings opposite us.

Miss McTavish, the camp's director, rose and welcomed the visitors to the dining room, then asked for bowed heads so she could recite a blessing before the meal. I sensed from Liesl's glance toward me that she was afraid I'd make this prayer an issue. Even at eight-years-old, she knew my faults, one of which was that I sometimes wore my atheism like an overly large lapel pin. I tended to dig in my heels and not budge if anyone committed the sin of assuming I was God-fearing. It was practically a point of honor for me.

"Poppa?" Liesl whispered, giving me a beseeching glance.

I literally bit my tongue, figuratively held my nose, and actually bowed my head as Miss McTavish started in. "Dear Lord, thank you for—"

"That wasn't so bad, was it?" Liesl asked me after the prayer.

She's got my number is what I thought. "Only because it was for you." Liesl smiled. So did I.

When the uncomfortable screeching of scooting chairs against the painted concrete floor subsided, there was a commotion at the screened double-door entrance to the dining room.

"My God," Sheila said. "It's the Burnetts."

Liesl and I looked up to see a dead-serious young man in a dark suit and sunglasses leading First Lady Michelle Burnett, Raquel, and Sophie directly toward our table. A couple of reporters, notebooks in hand, and a photographer brought up the rear. The room erupted with applause.

"You don't mind if we sit here, do you?" the man in the suit asked me as he pulled a chair away from the table and seated himself in it, continuing to look at me.

"Suit yourself, T-man" I responded, causing Michelle Burnett to laugh out loud, though the agent didn't.

"You're Mr. Foley," Mrs. Burnett said. "Raquel and Sophie have told me all about you and Liesl. What a touching story."

I felt my eyes moistening at the thought of the First Lady of the United States knowing *my* story. I could only manage, "Thank you, ma'am," the uttering of which made it impossible for me not to conspicuously sob.

Mrs. Burnett took my left hand in both of hers, squeezed it.

"I hope those are happy tears," she said.

I closed my eyes and nodded twice.

"Then come on," she said, "let's eat. I'm hungry." That made everyone within earshot laugh. Liesl put her head on my shoulder, patted my chest.

On Friday morning, I drove back to Burlington for my return flight to Louisville. When I arrived at Four-fourteen, I found sixteen messages in my voice mailbox, an unusually high number.

"I can't believe it, David," said the nasal recording of Idelle McCoy. "You and Liesl and the First Family. I do declare."

"Mr. Foley, this is Mrs. van Pelt. I saw your and Liesl's picture in the paper with the Burnett girls. Wow!"

"David," said the voice of Madonna Maddox. "Michael and I saw you and Liesl on the news this morning. We just can't believe it. Call us when you get back and tell us all about it."

There were twelve similar sentiments. Everyone from my barber to Emily Parker had phoned and left messages. The last one was from Sheila.

"David, I just wanted to tell you how wonderful the last couple of days were. I've decided to come back to Louisville a bit early. Ansel is leaving for South America Wednesday morning, so I'm flying in Wednesday afternoon. Will you have any time to come to the house that night or either of the next two? Call my cell."

"You're buying an out-of-state cell phone to cover our tracks, but you want me to come to your house through a guarded gate where every visitor and car are logged in and out of the grounds?" I demanded into my cell phone, two days later.

"Ansel knows I'm aware he checks the estate visitor traffic periodically. He would never suspect that a visit from the parent of one of Heather's classmates is anything but school or camp business. You'll be a TJ parent, not a corespondent."

"I don't know," I said. "What will the guard think?"

"Who cares what *he* thinks?" Sheila said. "What's he going to do, call the TV stations? Listen, I'll tell him that you're knowledgeable about videography and you're bringing by some tapes of the Burnett family with Heather and me at Camp Willoughby and we're going to duplicate them as gifts for relatives. See you at eight o'clock."

Bringing an empty briefcase with me, I left for the Cassidy compound early, driving out of my way east on U.S. Highway 42 to the beginning of River Road in the suburb of Prospect. I liked to drive west on River Road at twilight, so I could admire the Louisville skyline in the distance. It was modest, but distinct, and the lighting was perfect at that time of night to make the buildings' chromatic colors pop off their canvass, the dark, blue-gray, post-sundown sky. Even the Ohio River, often muddy with stark banks, glistened beautifully with reflected lights at that time of evening.

I found myself calculating the benefits of Louisville as a place to live, attempting to justify remaining there with Liesl. I always came to the same conclusion. Though the reasons for me being there were totally serendipitous, it was a wonderful place to live and raise a child.

I turned left into the sixth-class city of Glen Vista, right onto Indian Woods Trail, right again onto Seneca Way, the only house on which was the Cassidys' mansion.

At the guard shack, the security man slid open the window. "Hello, Mr. Foley," he said. "Come on through, Mrs. Cassidy is expecting you."

I lifted the briefcase off the seat next to me and with my right hand, shook it two or three times with what I realized was a stupid grin on my face. "Hey, thanks. We have to make these tapes, you know." At that moment, I was sure the guard knew what I was really there for, but I quickly dismissed that interpretation of the sentry's knowledge as my routine paranoia. Relax. That guy doesn't know, doesn't care, what's going on. He just wants his shift to end.

After I coasted the car to a stop in what could only be termed a parking lot, I disembarked, reached into the passenger seat, pulled out the black brief case, headed to the imposing front entrance, and rang the bell.

Who should answer my beckon, but the same Victorian-looking maid who had so effectively screened me from Sheila on my first visit.

"Well, hello again," I said, oozing sarcasm. "Do you think tonight I might be allowed an audience with Mrs. Cassidy?"

"By all means, sir," she replied. "She's expecting you."

"Wonderful," I said, squinting and nodding once, condescension still dripping. "Sometimes she's hard to get in to see, isn't she?"

I must have crossed the Victorian's threshold of tolerance. She straightened, put her hands on her hips. "Look, Mr. Foley, or whatever your name is, I just work here and do as I'm told. When she doesn't want to see someone, I'm her gatekeeper. If she wants to see you, I kiss your ass, okay? That's the way it works, pal. I'm just doing my job."

I'm not often speechless, but as the on-again, off-again Victorian led me to what, in a game of Clue, would have been the Conservatory, I indeed was.

"Have a seat, friend," she said. "I'll go get her."

What was I supposed to do? Report the insubordination of this obvious bitch or just forget it? My host's appearance in the Conservatory settled the issue. Sheila was wearing a short, black, strapless sundress, the length of which was hardly enough to cover the parts of her anatomy I wanted to access again. Screw the maid, first things first.

"Hello, David. What's in the briefcase?"

"Nothing," I replied. "Absolutely nothing. I was just hoping the guard and the maid might think it was the video tape."

"You *are* paranoid," she said, shaking her head and sighing. "The help around here isn't quite as interested in what goes on or who visits as you think they are. Come on, let's go upstairs."

She led me out of the Conservatory into a spacious hallway, in which we walked for at least seventy-five feet before coming to an escalator.

Mother Mary, a goddamned escalator, in a house! The moving metal machinery conveyed us to the third floor and a rectangular concourse with a marble floor and a bordering glass railing surrounding an atria. The spectacular opening descended two floors to the entranceway, rose another three to a huge skylight.

"This is where we'll make another memory," Sheila said. "These are all guest bedrooms. I want you to choose any one of the six doorways, each of which enters a distinctively themed boudoir."

"Please," I pleaded, "let's just go to a room you like."

"Okay, Mr. Killjoy," she said, "I like the second one on the right."

She extended her hand and led me past the first door that was inscribed "Purgatory" in a fiery, orange script. The next door had an etched brass plate that read, "Vive le France."

Upon entering, I thought for a moment I was in a Parisian bordello. High-back chairs, ornate candelabras, elaborate mirrors, small sculptures, even tapestry, were all in abundance in her room of choice.

She sat me in an antique, red velvet chaise longue positioned in front of a mirror that stretched from floor to ceiling. "Wait here, I'll be right back." She moved for an anteroom and was out of sight after closing a door behind her.

I wondered what was behind the other five doorways, moreover, what in hell went on in those rooms.

Purgatory? Holy shit!

The anteroom door reopened and Sheila walked in wearing only the "I did it in Vermont" T-shirt I had given her and fishnet tights.

"These have no gusset," she gushed.

Sauntering up to the chaise, she suggested I remove my pants. I quickly obliged, forgetting my funky, over-the-calf argyle socks.

"They don't match," she said.

"What?" Sure enough, when I glanced down, I had on one light tan and brown argyle and one dark blue and gray.

"Very kinky," she said, her eyes wide with delighted rascality.

I had never considered myself the least bit kinky, but if it helped Sheila get where she wanted to be, what the hell. She was on top of me immediately, showing off her lack of a gusset, while staring in the mirror at my disparate argyles.

"They don't *maaaatch!* They don't *maaaatch!* Yes, yes!" she shouted, still staring wildly at my socks in the mirror and digging her fingernails into my chest. I couldn't tell whether she was about to have an orgasm or a nervous breakdown. Then I felt familiar, pleasant, liquid warmth wash over my equipment, soon after which Sheila ceased her snarling and went limp on top of me, save for an occasional reflexive quiver.

"My God," she said. "I have never—"

Bullshit, I thought. "Really?"

"Please," she uttered after a few minutes, "don't move. I'll be right back."

"Where are you going?" I asked, as she disengaged.

"Just sit tight."

My appendage shriveled quickly to the most Lilliputian of sizes in the relative cold after the warmth of her encasement. Oh well, she's seen me at full mast and might even think it's cute at this proportion.

After raising my appendage and its accompanying baggage with my thumb and forefinger to avoid the uncomfortable thigh entrapment of my testicles, I crossed my legs and argyled feet. I locked my fingers atop my head, closed my eyes and began singing, still comfortable on the chaise.

As I walk through this world,
Nothing can stop
the Duke of Earl.

I heard a door to the room open, it not registering in my unwound mind that it wasn't the door through which Sheila had exited.

"Mmmmm. Back for more, are you, my sweet?" I asked, eyes still closed, hands still locked atop my head.

"I'll say," said a voice I recognized but couldn't quite identify. I opened my eyes to see the voice's owner raise her digital camera to where it was aligned precisely between her eyes and my naked body.

"What? Wait! Who is that?" As my eyes began to make out the

short black skirt and round white apron, my immediate response was to cross my hands in front of my overly modest little appendage.

CLICK!

"Oh fuck," I said, a full second after the camera flashed and an equal full second before my hands got in front of my privates.

The bitch-maid from hell hurried out the door. I had a bit of trouble getting out of the chaise to pursue her and by the time I did, she was about seventy-five feet ahead of me, two-stepping down the escalator, onto which I leaped. I was about halfway down those descending metal grates, grasping the moving, black rubber handrails, when I realized I was on an escalator, giving chase through another man's house, wearing only my deodorant and a pair of mismatched, over-the-calf argyle socks, just after having fornicated with said man's wife.

Oh fuck is what I thought and, "Oh fuck," is what I said.

What I beat was faster than a hasty retreat, beginning by reversing path and running upward against the escalator's downward motion, then speeding back over the concourse, my padded, over-the-calf, mismatched argyle socks rapidly landing one in front of the other, with one hand cupped over my flopping little appendage until I was back in the relative safety of the French room, where I continued to both think and mutter, "Oh fuck."

Sheila came back through the door she had exited, surprised to find me dismayed, disheveled and dysfunctional.

"What on earth is wrong?"

"Oh fuck," was all I could manage.

After a few minutes and a glass of brandy Sheila fetched from the room's wet bar, I told her what had happened.

"Damn her," she said. "I should have fired that bitch after the last episode."

"The *last* episode?" I screamed. "*What* last episode?"

I left Sheila's house with little starch left in my posture. I neither waved to nor stopped for the guard at the gate. I felt a slight bit relieved once home, but nevertheless kept repeating, "Oh fuck."

I awakened the next morning not wanting to arise but unable to maintain unconsciousness. I noticed the red light flashing on the telephone beside my bed, signaling a voice mail was unheard and waiting.

"Hi Poppa," began the message that instantly made me wish I was sitting next to the messenger. "This is the most wonderful place. I want to come every summer if I can. I love the riding classes, the hiking, and the campfires. I love everything about Camp Willoughby.

"Raquel and Sophie had to leave after just a week, but Sophie made me promise to write to her. She gave me a post office box number somewhere in Virginia to send her mail. I wrote it down. She made me give her my address. As much as I like it here, I still miss you and Fielder every day, especially at night. But I'll see you both in four days.

"I love you, Poppa."

I played the tape two more times.

Sheila phoned me Saturday morning at nine-thirty. "She called me this morning. All the little twit wants is ten."

"Who called," I asked. "Ten what?"

"Rhonda," came the reply. "The bitch that took your picture. All she wants is ten thousand dollars."

"Oh fuck."

"Damn, David, stop worrying. I keep that much in my regular checking account. The little shit is too stupid to know she could get ten times that amount."

"Are you *crazy*? What are you *talking* about? Do you think she'll just . . . just go away?"

"It's okay, David. My attorney knows how to handle these situations."

"What? What do you mean, '*these* situations?'"

"Don't worry about that. He'll have her sign documents that will make her a felon if she ever discloses anything about Wednesday night or if it can be proven that she has any copies of that photo in her possession or anyone else's possession, that possession gained from her, her agents or her representatives."

"Jesus, Sheila. Do you hang around with lawyers *all* the time?"

"She's going to turn the picture into him by five Monday after-

118

noon."

"Yeah? What's he going to do with it?"

"I don't know, destroy it I suppose."

"Well, I'd like a little more security than that," I said. "I don't want that photo to wind up as the highlight of some lawyer's party or on some goddamned website."

"You *are* paranoid," Sheila said. "Relax."

"Yeah sure, relax. Even though I might wind up on the cover of the *National Inquirer* sitting naked in a chaise longue if your lawyer doesn't pull this off. Oh fuck."

"Goodbye, David," Sheila said with a finality that, frankly, I welcomed.

Liesl arrived home Sunday afternoon and it wasn't until I was squeezing her that I could measure exactly how much I'd missed her. Obviously, she'd missed me too, yet I could sense Camp Willoughby had increased her awareness that there was a life outside Poppa. I knew our relationship was shifting and that the time had come for me to loosen the reins a bit.

After an elongated evening of romping in the yard with Fielder, who also hadn't realized how much he'd missed Liesl until she was throwing the tennis ball for him, she and I talked about the adventures of the past two weeks, hers, not mine. She then calmly informed me that it was time for her to go to bed.

Yes, I was now certain that brief midsummer period was another one of those emotional, bittersweet, transformational times, the fleeting moments during which one realizes a significant change is taking place while it's still happening. Liesl was morphing from one phase to another. There's nothing in life more profound or poignant than to see and experience such transformation in a child, as I had seen in Patrick's abbreviated five or six phases, and as I was seeing now in my granddaughter's life.

At that moment, I also realized there were fewer and fewer stages remaining in *my* life. How many stages did I have left? One? If I had two remaining, I figured the last one would probably be an unpleasant one.

Infirmities? Dementia?

Unlike Fielder, who was curled next to my granddaughter in her bed, I myself was awake more than I slept that night, sitting in the rocker in Liesl's room, watching her sleep, knowing that I had one less stage to burn than I did when summer began.

Chapter Seven

"When I wished to sing of love, it turned to sorrow."
— FRANZ SCHUBERT

Near the end of Liesl's fifth-grade year at TJ, she and I had been invited to an early dinner on a Sunday evening at the Maddoxes' house. After the meal, Liesl and her cousins were in the basement family room where Michael was officiating a rowdy game of "Red Rover." I helped Madonna clear the table, load the washer, and scrub some pots and pans.

When those chores were done, she untied her apron, slipped it over her head and poured coffee at the table for both of us. "David, have you ever had a conversation with Liesl about getting her period?"

I was flummoxed. "Uh . . . darn. You know, I haven't." Upon making that admission, I needed to rationalize my guilt. "You know, she's only ten, Madonna."

"Yes, but she'll be eleven soon, and the average girl begins menstruating at twelve, some earlier. She needs to learn about it now, before it happens."

"I suppose you're right. Is that something maybe *you* could do, Aunt Madonna?" I probed, stroking my chin while focusing upward on one of about two dozen canister lights in the Maddoxes' huge, canary-colored kitchen "I'm not sure if I'd be up to it, or even get the story right, for that matter."

Madonna's face sweetened, she smiled. "I was thinking you might ask. Yes, that would be easier on everybody."

"Thanks, Madonna. I *know* it'd be easier on me."

"It's also probably the appropriate time to have a simple and short conversation about sex and reproduction, don't you think, David?"

I half-nodded. "I suppose, but shouldn't I assume some responsibility here? I know a lot more about sex than I do about preparing for, you know . . . periods and . . . you know," I said, rolling my hand.

"I'll *bet* you do. But if my father or, God forbid, my grandfather had ever started talking to me about intercourse and such—"

"Uh, yeah . . . yeah, I see what you mean. Will you talk to her soon?"

"Sure, the first chance I get to be alone with her. David, I want to tell her that premarital sexual activity is wrong."

I had my elbow on the table, resting my chin in my hand. I stared at my cup, began circling its rim with my index finger.

"I don't know, Madonna."

"Do you want me to tell her it's just fine?"

"Of course not."

"Then she needs to hear that it's wrong."

After a moment's consideration, I looked at Madonna. "How about this? How about telling her she should refrain because of the possibility of pregnancy or disease, you know, make her understand she has a responsibility and what the consequences are. Then, when her hormones are kicking in at twelve or thirteen, when she needs more detail and another talk, you and I can discuss the moral side of it again."

It was Madonna's turn to place her chin on her elbow-braced palm. "Okay, David, I can live with that. And myself, I guess."

I winked as I nodded at her once. I could always count on Madonna.

When Liesl finished middle school at TJ Prep there was little official fanfare. The school administration had always resisted much pomp and circumstance until students had completed the twelfth grade. Nevertheless, at upper school commencement ceremonies, a few lower and middle school students were always recognized, albeit in a low key.

At the 2005 ceremony, Liesl received the Headmaster's Award, which requires, as the Headmaster himself stated, "a combination of academic excellence, athletic achievement and civic contributions." Liesl was an honor student, a starting midfielder and co-captain of the city-champion, eighth-grade field hockey team, vice president of her class, and a volunteer reading tutor of first- and second-graders at Parks Elementary, one of the public system's poorer inner-city schools.

While she was pleased with the recognition and the award, I myself was on fire with pride. As soon as I was outside the commencement auditorium, I cell-phoned Madonna, then Mia, with the news. I aggressive-ly mingled with the crowd, basking in the congratulatory acknowledge-ments I was receiving. When Liesl asked if I would hold the award for her, I carried it with my elbow bent, shamelessly displaying the com-memorative piece against my chest. I made sure it was impossible to en-counter me without noticing the engraved wooden plaque.

I had subscribed to the Louisville Orchestra's classical music series my second year in Kentucky, and when Liesl turned ten-years old, I be-gan taking her to concerts. She, like I as a youngster, was immediately transfixed with hearing and feeling the swirling sounds of symphonic music. It was in our blood, I guessed.

I always purchased tickets for four seats and we enjoyed taking a va-riety of friends or relatives to the concerts with us. Many times it was Madonna or Michael Maddox and one of their children. Other times it would be a couple of Liesl's classmates or a classmate and a parent.

When Liesl wanted Heather Cassidy to join us, the fourth seat al-ways went to another classmate or perhaps Samantha McCoy, never to Sheila. I hoped Liesl would never decipher that social slight of Sheila. Heather remained Liesl's close friend, but for high school, she followed a longstanding Cassidy tradition and enrolled at a boarding school. For Heather, that school was LaFollette Institute For Girls in Richmond, VA.

Liesl had taken piano lessons since the fourth grade, the first three years at TJ, and later with a private instructor, after the music teacher at school told me she thought Liesl had learned about all the teacher could impart and might have talent worthy of a more accomplished instructor. After a year, however, the private teacher informed me that Liesl was a fine student of the piano and was proficient at playing, but not talented enough to pursue music as a field of study at the post-secondary level.

Just before her sophomore year began, Liesl surprised me with a question. "Poppa, would you mind if I put piano on inactive status for a while and started playing violin?" she asked, pantomiming drawing the bow across the strings of an invisible instrument.

"First of all," I said, "no, I wouldn't mind. You know how I feel about the violin."

"Yes, Poppa," Lisa said, starting to roll her eyes before thinking better of it. "'The sweetest, most emotional music emanates from instruments placed under the chin.' I had a feeling my taking up the violin might be okay with you."

"Well it is, but when did it become appealing to *you*? I'm a little surprised."

"Actually, so am I," she said, "but I feel a little stagnant on the piano and I need to make music of *some* kind. I've been thinking about it a lot. I ruled out percussion, woodwinds and brass. There are surely enough guitar players out there today and I refuse to tote around a cello, harp or double bass."

"That's about as deductive as reasoning can get," I said. "Have you looked into renting or purchasing an instrument?"

"Can you help me with that?" she asked.

"I suppose," I said, trying to disguise my absolute delight at this turn of events.

The Orchestra's classical series began in September, and Liesl and I invited Madonna and sixteen-year-old Maria Noel to the season's initial concert. With Liesl beginning to study the violin, it was ironic that world-renowned violinist Avery Carmichel was the guest soloist, and would be playing the violin transcription of the "Chopin Nocturne in C Minor" in front of the Orchestra.

As we and the Maddoxes took our seats, the cacophony of incongruous warm-up notes coming from the stage put me in mind of some early classical music performances my mother took me to see, hear and feel as a tad.

My mother, herself proficient on the piano, obviously wanted to instill an appreciation of symphonic music in me at an early age. She and her sister began taking me to Boston Symphony Orchestra concerts when I was ten years old. I can remember my first concert, an outdoor event at Tanglewood, the summer home of the orchestra in the Berkshire Mountains of western Massachusetts. I was wearing a lightweight suit, the pants of which were shorts. I had on white knee socks, and un-der my coat were suspenders. Between the collar-points of my white shirt hung a bow tie.

I was transfixed, seeing and hearing the tuxedoed musicians warm-ing up, enticing their polished maple and shiny brass instruments to readiness under high-hanging baffles that reminded me of kites, tents and umbrellas. When the warming up abruptly ended, the musicians sat erect and the crowd quieted. After several seconds, the concertmaster walked onto the stage. The audience applauded.

As the first violinist coaxed the principal oboist to intone the tradi-tional tuning "A" note, I asked my mother, "Who's that man?" I was hooked.

Avery Carmichel was younger than most violinists as accomplished as he, and quite handsome. He possessed a stage presence that everyone in the audience seemed to enjoy. Many times, after a soloist finished his or her piece at such performances, the musician was greeted with polite but passive applause. After Mr. Carmichel finished his interpretation of Chopin's short pieces, the ovation was near thunderous. Liesl, Madonna and Maria Noel were on their toes and stretching their necks, straining to see Carmichel as they applauded him with fervor.

The Orchestra had initiated a practice a few years back of hosting a reception for season subscribers in a large private room of the perfor-mance hall after concerts. The players and conductor attended, and sometimes the guest artist would show up, though not always. After Avery Carmichel's performance, Liesl, Maria Noel, and Madonna were bumping into each other and gawking as they entered the reception, try-ing to see if Mr. Carmichel had yet presented himself. He had not.

I always enjoyed mingling with other patrons and chatting with the musicians, most of which were at least visually familiar with Liesl and me. During this evening's performance, I had noticed a French horn player who I'd not seen before. At the reception, she was talking with Arthur Cohen, a fellow TJ Prep parent. Arthur recognized me and in-troduced me to Justine Colgate.

"I'm pleased to meet you, Mr. Foley," she said.

"Thank you, Ms. Colgate, said Mr. Foley," I said, hoping she'd get my convoluted point of wishing she'd call me David.

She did, because she laughed and replied, "Okay, it's Justine, David, said Ms. Colgate."

Arthur assumed a frown of perplexity at this exchange and awkwardly excused himself. "Goodbye Arthur," I said, my eyes affixed to the French horn player's. "Are you merely new to the Orchestra, Justine, or new to Louisville?"

"Both actually. I moved here this past spring from Minneapolis."

"I enjoyed watching you play."

"Well, thank you, David."

"Actually, I enjoyed watching you turn the pages of the sheet music," I said, still shamelessly looking at her eyes.

Justine smiled at the flirtation, looked at the floor. A noticeable hum of activity at the rear entranceway to the reception kept her from having to come up with an artful response. Avery Carmichel had decided to make an appearance at the affair, and it was his entry that was causing the whirr in the rear of the room.

"That's my granddaughter, Liesl, in the blue dress stalking Mr. Carmichel," I said. "I can't imagine why."

That, too, made Justine laugh. "Wasn't he terrific?" she said. "He was so pleasant and considerate in practice. Not all of the big names are."

"I can only imagine. What brought you to Louisville?" I asked, intentionally personalizing the conversation again.

"I just required a change," Justine said with a sigh, making it obvious that a story was there. "I only looked at cities whose orchestras needed a horn player and I didn't commit to coming here until I had landed this chair."

"That's one of the best reasons I've ever heard for one moving to Louisville," I said. "I came here fourteen years ago and still love it. I hope you will too. Well, I'd better go rescue Mr. Carmichel from Liesl. It was a pleasure to meet you, Justine."

"Likewise, David. Maybe next time I'll get to meet your granddaughter, when Avery Carmichel isn't around."

In the car on the way home, my three companions were still abuzz with having met Avery Carmichel.

"Wasn't he wonderful, Uncle David?" asked Maria Noel from the back seat.

"Yes, very talented and charismatic too," I replied, catching her eye in the rearview mirror.

"And so handsome," added Madonna.

"He plays a five million dollar Strad," Liesl said.

"I read that," I said. "Did you tell him you were looking for an instrument?"

"Poppa, you're so silly."

"I wonder where that instrument was while he was at the reception," Madonna mused.

"You can bet it wasn't in the back seat of his car," I said. "I imagine there's a chain-of-custody protocol after each performance."

"Who was the woman you were talking to at the reception, David," Madonna asked. "She's very attractive."

"Her name is Justine Colgate, a new French horn player. Didn't you notice her during the concert?"

"Not with Avery Carmichel up there on stage, I didn't," Madonna said, making the girls giggle.

Madonna became silent, probably thinking about Avery Carmichel, while Liesl and Maria Noel talked quietly about a boy they had noticed in the audience. I myself was contemplating Justine.

Through the years, Liesl and Sophie Burnett occasionally corresponded. Liesl went to Camp Willoughby for four years in a row before opting out the summer she turned thirteen. Sophie never attended again and told Liesl that was because the Secret Service didn't like the idea of the girls repeating many events or trips. A spontaneous itinerary for the protected was always better than a routine itinerary, as far as the protectors were concerned, no matter how short-lived the routine. Sophie's letters came in plain white envelopes with the initials 'SB' hand-written in the upper left corner above a preprinted Post Office box number in Arlington, VA.

"You got a letter from Sophie today," I told Liesl on the way home from school on an early October day.

"I hope she tells me about the academy she's attending in Maryland," Liesl said. "I read in a magazine she doesn't like it much. The article doesn't quote her, but it definitely implies she's unhappy there. I can't imagine going to a school I didn't like. That would be awful."

When we arrived at Four-fourteen after dropping the other "school pool" passengers at their respective homes, there was Fielder in the front yard with a ratty tennis ball in his mouth, tail wagging, waiting for Liesl.

"Just a second, boy," she said as she put her books down. "I'll throw it once, then I need to change clothes so we can play for a while."

"I have to take him to Dr. Mitchell's tomorrow for his checkup," I said. "That's always fun."

After romping with Fielder in the back yard, but before tackling her homework, Liesl went upstairs to practice her violin. I loved hearing her play, though she had disallowed me from her room during violin practice. I assumed she was too self-conscious to have me see and hear her at the same time, and I knew I'd be a distraction if I were proximate, so I contented myself maintaining a distance, as long as she agreed to keep the door open so that I might hear.

The Orchestra had an early October concert scheduled and guest pianist Robert French was to perform Mozart's "Piano Concerto No. 21." Like many music patrons who weren't musicians themselves, my favorite composer was Mozart. Since I'd never heard "No. 21" performed live, I'd been looking forward to this event since it was announced the previous spring. Liesl and I asked Idelle and Samantha McCoy to join us.

I had high hopes for French's interpretation of Mozart's work and I wasn't disappointed. Music had always been singularly emotional for me and the second movement, with its beautiful, intriguing minors, had my eyes moist, albeit unnoticed by my companions.

After the performance, I noticed Justine talking with Robert French at the reception in the lobby. I couldn't help from moving toward the two musicians, hoping to get noticed.

Justine accommodated, introducing me to "Bob" French. Liesl and the McCoys noticed I had him and Justine within my sphere and they moved to join us.

After the introductions, I said, "Bob, I believe the second movement of "No. 21" is the most beautiful music ever composed." Hearing myself sounding a bit haughty, I hastened to add, "Or perhaps I should say the most beautiful music *I've* ever heard." Yes, that was better.

"I can't say I disagree," French said. "I love playing it."

"So David, what do you think is No. 2?" Justine asked. I couldn't tell from her tone or expression how serious she was. Was she setting me up? Would she pounce on an amateurish answer?

I pursed my lips, moved my eyes upward, and flexed my head, as if I were considering different options. After a brief interlude, "'I Know It's Only Rock and Roll'" by Jagger and Richards," I said, proud of my answer and myself.

"And the third most beautiful?" Justine pursued, this time with an impish grin.

With only the briefest pause: "That would be a tie," I said, "between Johann Strauss, Jr.'s 'On the Beautiful Blue Danube' and 'On The Cover of the Rolling Stone,' by Silverstein, but only as performed by Dr. Hook and the Medicine Show."

Justine beamed.

"You know, David," French said, frowning at his glass of red. "I'm not sure of your order, but those four are all in my top ten." Everyone laughed.

For the remainder of the reception, the McCoys and Liesl gravitated to Mr. French, while Justine and I gravitated to each other.

"I don't know much about the French horn," I offered, "but I understand it's one of the most difficult instruments to master."

"Yes, I think that's what drove me to it," Justine said. "Most musicians, however, refer to it as simply the horn, rather than the French horn."

"I didn't realize that, but now that I'm acquainted with a practitioner of that instrument, I'll remember the proper terminology when referring to *the* horn," I said, surrounding the word *the* in two-fingered quotes. "I guess I'd better gather my companions and head for home now. Thank you for introducing me to Bob, Justine, and I really enjoyed spending some time with you."

"I did too, David."

The warmth radiating within my face made me feel like a nescient schoolboy.

Liesl was at school on Monday when I received a call from the vet, Fred Mitchell, who had overseen Fielder's healthcare since he was a pup. The blood test Mitchell had performed showed that the retriever was in the beginning stages of hemangiosarcoma, a terminal cancer, not uncommon in German shepherds and golden retrievers.

"This cancer is in the lining of the blood vessels and spreads rapidly to other organs," the vet said. "Usually, left to run its course, the animal dies from this disease within two or three months."

"Jesus, Fred, he seems healthy as can be. He's active and he eats anything we put in front of him."

"I'm afraid he won't be that way for long, David. Sooner, rather than later, he'll lose his appetite and become weaker. I'm sorry, this is a call I didn't want to make."

After disconnecting with the vet, I returned to the back window of the kitchen. The ginkgo tree was in its golden October splendor. I wished the miniature Oriental fans would cling to their tree for a few more weeks. I knew they wouldn't.

Fielder sensed I was heading to the yard and was at the door in front of me. When I opened it, he rushed into the yard, nose to the ground, zigzagging forward, tail wagging, straining for a scent of one of his tennis balls. It didn't take him long to discover one, promptly picking it up and bringing it to my feet.

I tried to pet him, but he'd have none of that, not while there was a ball in play. I picked up the fuzzy sphere, sent it flying toward the back fence. Fielder was immediately running all out and, leaping athletically, he snared the toss in mid-air on its first hop and headed back to me on the gallop, hoping for a repeat performance. I obliged, again and again.

When the "school pool" mom dropped Liesl off in our driveway, I watched as Fielder rushed out to greet her, picking up another of his many tennis balls en route. Liesl grabbed it when he placed it on the ground and began to run with it. Fielder bounded along next to her, never taking his eyes off the ball, freezing when she stopped, resuming his pace when she started running again. She always giggled when he did that.

"Silly boy."

Finally she heaved it as far as she could and ran for the porch as Fielder fetched her pitch.

"I have to change clothes," she told him. "I'll be right back."

"Hi, Poppa," she said as she came in the back door. "Did you notice the ginkgo today?"

"Yes . . . I did."

I glanced out the back window after Liesl went upstairs. Fielder was entertaining himself by standing under the ginkgo, leaping, then snapping at a few premature leaves descending upon him. I wrestled with myself whether to tell Liesl the bad news immediately or wait for a while. I chose to wait until evening, hoping by then to have come up with some well-measured, appropriate words for my granddaughter.

After dinner, Liesl headed for her room to practice the violin, Fielder in tow. I suspected the violin's sounds weren't pleasant for Fielder, but that he tolerated them just to be proximate to Liesl. When I entered the room while she was still practicing, she knew something was wrong.

"What is it, Poppa?" she said, dropping her bow and instrument to her sides.

"It's Fielder," I said.

Hearing his name, Fielder gave one swish of his tail from his prone position at Liesl's feet.

"It's not good," I continued.

Liesl put her violin on the bed and focused her narrowed, disquieted eyes on mine.

I looked at Fielder, who sat up and cocked his head slightly, inquisitively returning my stare.

"Dr. Mitchell called today and said that Fielder's routine tests indicate he has a dreadful disease, a disease he won't be able to overcome."

131

"What? He's going to die?"

The criticality in Liesl's voice had Fielder up and trying to get his oversized body onto her lap and lick her face.

I looked downward, nodded. "Yes."

Liesl glowered with the same expression she'd wear if she were exploding with anger toward me. Her features contorted, then she sprawled on her bed and began violently shrieking, heaving with each breath, clenched fists pounding the mattress. Her eyes were shut tightly, part of a grimacing face.

I wanted to hold her as tightly as I could, absorb her pain and her body into mine.

"Liesl, you have to sit up now. Please. Sit up and open your eyes." Hearing my voice seemed to ease her back from the brink. My eyes locked onto a photo on the shelves above her desk. It was an image of Liesl holding my gift to her on her eighth birthday, a ten-week-old, as yet unnamed, retriever puppy. I slid my arm across her waist, pulled her onto my lap.

"Open your eyes, sweet girl."

As she did, she thrust her head onto my shoulder, still crying, but softly by then. I stroked her hair, patted her back. "Now take as deep a breath as you can," I said.

Liesl's chest convulsed several times as she inhaled. When she exhaled, I said, "Now a couple more times." She complied and clutched me tightly, recapturing some composure.

"Poppa," she said as she withdrew her embrace, "I need to sit with Fielder." As she dropped to sit on the throw rug, Fielder aggressively licked her face. That made her laugh just as it had when he did it the first time I placed him on her lap. She put both arms around his neck, raised her head, squeezed her eyes shut, and let him lick away.

"Oh Fielder."

Liesl hadn't been trick-or-treating since she was nine years old. When she gave it up at age ten, she told me it was "something for kids." That suited me fine, as I considered the burlesque of Halloween noxious anyway. The narcissistic celebration was a derivative of Christian cultism, yoked inextricably to a Catholic Holy Day of Obligation, specifically All Saints Day. The amassed pap, in the form of candied junk food, was but icing on the cake of evidence that Halloween fed the greed and self-absorption of modern American youngsters.

I had, however, enjoyed the first three of Liesl's costumed Halloweens, beginning when she was four. That first year, she dressed as a ladybug. The second year, she was a strawberry and when she was six, she donned the stripes and stinger of a bumblebee. I had several snapshots of her in those early outfits, each indeed a picture of happiness.

When she was seven, however, Liesl wanted to dress as a witch. Not only was that choice too reflective of the religiosity of Halloween's origin for a curmudgeon like I was, but I knew that selection was the end of an innocent era. My granddaughter was no longer content to be an innocuous insect or a healthy piece of fruit, now she wanted to be a practical monster. Wasn't a witch's purpose to cast spells, haunt people, and make evil potions? I could think of no redeeming qualities in a witch.

"Why do you want to be a monster?" I asked.

"Poppa, you're so silly. A witch isn't a monster. A witch is a person. Sometimes they're even good."

That exposition caused my memory to trip over the red cape of Wendy The Good Little Witch, erstwhile friend of "Casper The Friendly Ghost."

"Would you like to be a good witch?" I inquired.

Liesl sighed with dramatic flair. She was already savvy enough to know that if she agreed to my wishes, then acted sad about it, I'd usually relent to one degree or another. "I *guess*, Poppa."

"Let me show you Wendy," I said.

"Wendy who?" she asked.

I booted the computer, found a website that showed the Casper characters, including Wendy.

"She looks sort of old-fashioned, Poppa. Would I have to wear that red coat and hat?"

"That's a cape and hood, Liesl, and I don't think she's so old-fashioned. What looks so old about Wendy?"

"There's a mark right there that says '1943,'" she said, pointing to the copyright. "Is that the year Wendy was born?

"Well—"

"I wanted to wear *real* witch's clothes. You know, black with a pointed hat. Do I have to wear that red coat and hood, Poppa? I mean *cape* and hood?"

"Oh, Liesl. I guess not."

The next day, she and I found a witch's costume at a store in the St. Matthews Mall featuring a black tattered dress, black pointed shoes and hat, horizontally striped socks, and realistic-looking, stick-on warts for her hands and face. Fielder thought the warts were treats and was intent on munching and licking them.

Liesl was happy. I myself was not. That October marked the beginning of a three-year period during which I took no Halloween photographs of her as a witch, a vampire or, lastly, a zombie.

As a fourteen-year old, Liesl agreed to answer the doorbell and dispense the quarters I secured at the bank to hand out to trick-or-treaters rather than candy. I couldn't have been happier that she was doing the treating instead of me. I wouldn't have to deal with the younger little beggars whose accompanying parents always had to coach them with a "what do you say?" after their offspring ungraciously received their treats. I was also liberated from interacting with the ten-to-thirteen-year olds, who were even stronger representatives of the "dumbing down" of American kids.

It was well after dark and I thought the last of the year's crop of trick-or-treaters had come and gone. I heard laughter on the porch as the doorbell rang. Liesl was upstairs preparing for bed, so I answered the door. There were three teenaged girls on the porch, none with a costume or mask, but all with a horizontal streak of face paint below each eye. I laughed aloud when I noticed their lashes and lips loaded with serious makeup, young girls trying to become women, but still scavenging on Halloween.

One of them said, "Trick or treat" in a tone remarkably similar to that a robber might use in ordering me to "stick 'em up." My inclination was to say and do nothing, just stare at these latecomers. Considering that they might know Liesl, however, I decided to drop a quarter into each of their large paper grocery bags. When the last one stepped forward for her cash, she was talking into a cell phone pressed to her left ear. She didn't acknowledge me in any way, didn't even *look* at me. She merely kept talking into her cell from the left side, while pushing her bag up to me with her right hand.

I put the quarter in my pocket, reached into her bag and helped myself to a handful of candy. "Happy Halloween," I said, closing the door. *"Hey!"*

Autumn had always been my favorite season. Liesl told me once she thought that was because I actually enjoyed being in a melancholy state. By early November, the crescendo of vibrant reds and brilliant yellows of peaking foliage had given way to muted browns and rusty shades of gold. The ginkgo had again shed its yellow leaves before they shriveled.

Fielder's plight made that particular fall all the more plaintive. His health had diminished steadily and, as his veterinarian had foretold, his strength was waning rapidly. Though he could no longer enthusiastically greet Liesl outside after school, he still showed up at the door, trudging from his den bed to the front room when he realized she was being dropped off in the driveway. He sat up unsteadily while his tail swished on the floor like an intermittent windshield wiper.

She'd sit there with him for a half-hour or so every day, stroking his back and scratching his head as he lay content next to her with his eyes closed.

"He's a good dog. What a nice boy."

On the first Monday in November, the weather was broodingly gray due to what seemed like one huge, depressing cloud suspended in the Louisville sky. Liesl came in from school, but Fielder wasn't on the entry rug where he'd been greeting her. She came into the den where I was sitting next to his bed, gently rubbing him.

"He tried to get up to meet you, but he just couldn't," I told her.

"Oh Fielder," she said. He didn't swish his tail at the sound of his name. Liesl looked at me. "It's time, isn't it?"

I nodded. "I'll take him to Dr. Mitchell's tomorrow."

"I want to go with you. May I? I can miss morning classes."

135

"Sure," I said, "we'll go together and lean on each other."

After attending Fielder for another fifteen minutes, Liesl went upstairs to her room. Apparently feeling she couldn't summon the energy required to *practice* her violin, she simply played it, let the music flow, allowing melodic impulse to give voice to her pain. By that time, she was capable of making music without contemplating the mechanics of it and, on that disheartening day, I envisioned my granddaughter in her room *listening* with intensity to the sad music she was making.

The next morning it was drizzling rain when Liesl joined me at the breakfast table. Her eyes were red.

"Poppa, what should we do with Fielder after—" she pursed her lips, swallowed, then rolled her hand.

"I'm sure Dr. Mitchell's office can arrange a funeral and resting place, if that's what you want."

"What do *you* think we should do, Poppa?"

I gritted my teeth, inhaled, and half shrugged. "Oh, it's your decision, Sweetie. It doesn't matter to me as long as you're comfortable with it."

"I don't want a, quote, funeral, and I'd rather *remember* Fielder than visit a grave or something. What would they do if he was a stray?"

"I'm not sure," I said.

"What do you *think* they'd do?"

"Gosh, I suppose there's a sanitation standard. Perhaps placing the body in a plastic bag of some sort, then getting it to the city waste department, but I'm only guessing."

"Do you think Fielder will exist in any form?" she asked, placing her elbow on the table and fingering her forehead.

"No."

"No life after death?" she pressed.

"I don't think so. You know that."

"What about people?" she said, her eyes moistening. "What about my Mom and Dad? Madonna says that peoples' souls live on after they die."

"Oh Liesl, you know what *I* think. What do *you* believe?"

She began a hard cry, the bawling forcing her to bellow the words unevenly. "I don't know, Poppa, but I want my Mom and Dad to *know* me. I want them to *see* me. I want them to know what I'm *doing* and *thinking* and *feeling*. I want Fielder to *be* somewhere, someplace nice, someplace good." She was yelling and her lungs convulsed, stuttered as she inhaled. Before I could tell her to, she breathed deeply a few times, quieted.

At that moment, I almost wished I believed in the hereafter, so I could comfort my granddaughter with the silly notion of life everlasting. I was close to sympathy for faith in the supernatural, just to be able to give Liesl something to cling to. Atheism offered no solace for death, its weightless, painless nothingness. I was helpless to offer consolation and I hated that inadequacy.

It was still raining when I carried Fielder to the car, placed him in the back seat on an old sheet.

"I want to ride in back with him," Liesl said, nearing the car. She scratched Fielder's head with her fingers for the whole trip, and we both remained silent until we were inside the vet's office and Liesl said "Hello" to Mitchell's assistant as I carried her pet into the small building.

The aide led us down the hall to a room where Fielder had been periodically examined or treated, always against his will. I placed him on the cold, hard, stainless steel examining table, then raised him ever so gently as the assistant slipped a soft cover under him. Liesl held her throat letting a nod and her eyes say thank you to the woman.

Fred Mitchell came in, hugged Liesl, shook hands with me. "I'm sorry about this," he said.

The aide retrieved a hypodermic needle, handed it to Mitchell. "He won't be in any pain," he said. "This injection will put him to sleep, then I'll give him a second one. He'll be totally at rest."

Liesl bent over and put her face on Fielder's, dropping tears on him as she did. He managed to lick her cheek.

"Good bye, good boy."

I wept in silence, one hand on Fielder's coat, the other on Liesl's shoulder. Fielder seemed resigned, obedient. I saw Liesl's chest begin to rise and fall. I knew if she spoke, she'd begin to heave and sob again, but she remained silent as the vet slipped the needle into the top of Fielder's right front foot. Ten seconds later, the dog's eyes closed. After a minute, the aide handed the vet another hypodermic and he injected Fielder in the other front foot.

Liesl and I stood together, each with an arm around the other, and a hand on Fielder's body. Minutes later, when she was sure he was gone,

"Let's go, Poppa."

On our way out, Mitchell's assistant handed the retriever's collar and tags to Liesl. She read both sides of the tag, smelled the collar, and pressed it against her chest with both hands, as if she were praying.

"What would you like us to do with his body, Mr. Foley?" the aide asked.

I glanced at Liesl for a sign.

"Could you just dispose of it in the simplest way?" she asked. I nodded my affirmation.

The windshield wipers slapped a sad percussion as the day's drizzle continued in a soft but unrelenting fashion during the trip home. Neither of us said anything until the car was in the driveway.

"You think death is nothingness, don't you, Poppa?"

"Oh, Liesl, I believe it's something to the living, but to the dead person, or any dead creature, I think it's *precisely* nothingness."

"What if you're wrong, Poppa?"

I wiped away the window fog with the back of my hand, gazed out at the bare ginkgo tree as if I might find a worthy answer for my granddaughter among its branches.

"Let's go inside," she said, before I could summon a reply.

She gave me an extended hug in the foyer, climbed the stairs to her room. She began playing her violin, in particular the simple, lingering chords of Samuel Barber's "Adagio For Strings." As she played that aggrieved melody, music fitting for the reflection of tragedy, I wept at death. I knew Liesl, too, was weeping.

Chapter Eight

*"A creative artist works on his next composition
because he was not satisfied with his previous one."*

—Dmitri Shostakovich

The weight of Fielder's absence was palpable, particularly painful for the first weeks after his death, as I continually expected him at my heel when I walked out of the house into the yard.

"I miss Fielder most at nighttime," Liesl said, noting that she was used to sleeping with him semi-circled at her feet.

As the days passed, however, an inevitable routine without Fielder began to take shape at Four-fourteen. I was relieved my granddaughter's pain was subsiding, but I was sad realizing that the unknown aspect in the specter of death intractably disquieted her.

The Louisville Orchestra's third concert of the season was scheduled for the first Saturday in December, and I welcomed the diversion I knew it would provide us. The performance wasn't part of the subscription series, but an extra, entitled "Music of the Eagles." It was billed as a tribute to what I myself considered the premier pop band of the 1970s. The performance would feature three vocalists with whom I wasn't familiar, but I trusted the Orchestra hierarchy to bring in quality musicians and singers, so I purchased four tickets.

When I asked about guests, Liesl surprised me by saying she'd like to invite a boy from school.

"He's so-o-o nice to me," she said, her eyes searching for my reaction. "His name is Joel Reese."

"Well, uh, I *guess* that would be nice," I said, unable to unconditionally endorse the idea. "Who else should we ask?"

"You let me ask Joel, you pick the other person."

"I wonder if Mia would like to go, and if Logan wouldn't mind. Maybe I'll call them."

"Great," Liesl said. "Mr. Smith's cool and Mia will love the concert."

When I phoned the Smiths, I was glad it was Logan who answered instead of Mia. Surely asking Mia to the concert should first be "cleared" through Logan, and it would be awkward to ask Mia if I could speak to Logan, then turn around and ask Logan if I could speak to Mia.

"The Eagles thing?" Logan asked. "Mia just asked me the other night if I'd try to get tickets, but it's sold-out. The short answer is, yes, she'll love it. She's not here right now, but I'll have her call you."

The upcoming concert found my self-esteem with a bit more torque than usual, no doubt pushing close to the limit of Liesl's tolerance. Defensible or not, I had a certain reverence for the music of my "era," music that "has never come close to being equaled, much less transcended," as I had told her, probably too many times. I actually felt a pride of authorship, ownership even, of the Eagles' music.

On the night of the performance, Liesl insisted that I pick up Mia before getting Joel, most likely thinking it was probably a good idea to have a buffer, other than herself, between her date and me. I pointedly called her attention to the inefficient routing of that of pick-up order.

"Poppa, if you think I'd stick Joel in the back seat alone with me up here with you or, worse, I'd get in the back seat with him and have you chauffer us—"

Those scenarios helped the light at least partially break through in my mind. "I suppose I can see some awkwardness in that," I admitted.

After picking up Mia, I drove to Joel's house where he was waiting on a front porch attached to an expansive, contemporary house. It had more glass across the front than any other material.

"I guess the Reeses don't throw many stones," I quipped. Neither Mia nor Liesl laughed, even perfunctorily.

Joel was dressed in jeans with an untucked, plaid shirt hanging below the waistband of a zippered red windbreaker. I rolled my eyes but not so Liesl could see. "Thanks for having me, Mr. Foley," Joel said, as he slid into the back seat next to Liesl. "I really like the Eagles' stuff. I've been listening to 'Hotel California' and 'Desperado' when my parents aren't home."

"You listen to the Eagles when your parents are *gone?*"

"Yeah, they hate the Eagles," he replied.

So your parents are total fucking morons is what I thought. "I'll be darned."

The Kentucky Center's Whitney Hall was filled to capacity. I spotted Justine six rows from the conductor, one of two horns. I wondered if my admiration was obvious as I gazed at her while she and the other musicians warmed up. Her black satin suit was understated but elegant. Suddenly, I felt Liesl staring at me.

"Poppa," she half-whispered, her lips close to my ear. "Did I tell you how handsome you look in your dark suit and turquoise tie? And your eyes are extra bright tonight." Oh my, more music to my ears. I smiled with surprise at her sweet accolade.

About half the audience members looked to be Orchestra regulars, relatively old and dressed up. The other half was relatively young and dressed down, seemingly comprised equally of teenagers, cowboys and cowgirls, and 1960s hippies. I commented about how many of them were chewing gum. "This is a two-hour show," I lamented. "Where do you think most of that gum will wind up?" Liesl didn't answer.

The concertmaster appeared on stage and I was anxious to show the latter demographic half of the audience, proper orchestral protocol. I applauded the first violin a little more quickly, loudly, and a bit longer than usual. I gave the conductor the same bonus treatment when he entered.

When the three pseudo-Eagles took stage, the audience's latter set appeared anxious to show me, and those of my ilk, how to greet three guys who were about to sing to them.

"Yeee-haaa!" yelled a cowgirl.

"Do it!" screamed a hippie-type.

"Are you ready for some Eagles?" asked the apparent lead singer, who wore a ten-gallon hat that obscured every part of his face except for the bottom third, which included the scruffy results of not having shaved in several days.

Half the audience responded, "Yeaaaah!"

"I *said*, are you ready for some Eagles?"

"Yeaaaah!" yelled the same fifty percent, only louder.

I leaned my head toward Liesl. "Low of brow, red of neck."

"Poppa, shush!"

I squirmed at the rebuke and hoped Joel hadn't heard my comment. My suffering soon ended, however, when the Orchestra broke into the distinctive first chords of "New Kid In Town." The three singers, in spite of a lack of charm or stage presence, had the Eagles' musical style and sound imitated perfectly. They sang lifelessly, as if they were merely in someone's basement practicing, but beautifully.

The melding of the soulful music and intelligent lyrics of the Eagles into the orchestra's strings, brass, and woodwinds was an auditory feast, a practical merger of cultures. It fused a facet of contemporary pop culture with a centuries-old aspect of gentility and refinement.

"Those guys were great in spite of themselves," I said on the way to the lobby and the post-concert reception. Since the after-concert event was only for season subscribers, I'm sure Liesl was relieved to know she didn't have to worry about enduring my reaction to any cowboys, cowgirls, or hippies showing up.

Soon, she and Joel had the concertmaster cornered, and I knew she'd be trying to glean as much violin knowledge from him as she could. Which violin do you play? Have you been challenged for your chair? Do you have a day job? Who's your favorite composer?

I myself was anxious to introduce Mia to Justine. I respected Mia's judgment of character. When I spotted Justine, she was talking to a couple that I recognized from many evenings of shared classical concerts. My age-guessing radar had these folks in the seventy-five-to-eighty range. Any andante or adagio movement always found one or both nodding off.

Justine saw me, and her eyes signaled that she would welcome any degree of relief I could offer her from the couples' loquacity. Happy to oblige, I moved toward them.

"David, this is Walter and Charlene," Justine said.

"Hi," I said. "So you guys like the Eagles?"

"Hardly," Walter said. "We got mixed up and thought tonight was the performance of Mussorgsky's 'Pictures at an Exhibition.'"

"Oh dear," I offered, casting a cavalier smile at Justine. "What was your last name again?"

"Mine's Van Winkle and hers is Courtney," Walter said.

"We're not married," Charlene said. "We just live together, sort of shacked up."

Just as that phrase escaped Charlene's mouth, a bit of wine, almost swallowed, escaped Mia's, spraying Walter's tie and the front of his shirt.

"Oh dear," I said again, reaching for the handkerchief I'd forgotten to put into my rear pants pocket. *Shit!*

"Never mind," Walter said, tugging on Charlene's arm. "Good evening."

"Justine, I'm so sorry," Mia said.

"Don't worry, Mia, they won't remember it tomorrow," Justine said.

"I guess eighty is the new seventy-seven," I said.

"Would you excuse me?" Mia asked. "I'd like to hear Liesl picking the concertmaster's brain."

"The concert was super," I said to Justine as Mia slipped away. "Those guys had the Eagles' sound nailed."

"They did," Justine said, "but they were hard to work with. They're imitators, not serious musicians, and they treated us like bit players in a film. They hit on every woman in the orchestra. It was disgusting."

"I thought I might have picked up some patronizing when they kept referring to "*your* Louisville Orchestra," I said, "but the audience loved the performance."

"I suppose," Justine said. "Let's change the subject. Would you care to come to dinner at my place next weekend?"

Oh my God is what I thought. "You bet."

After the reception had wound down, Liesl quietly reminded me while walking to the car, to retrace the less than logistic route we took coming to the concert.

"What did you think of Joel?" Liesl asked after we'd dropped him and Mia off.

"He was nice, what little we talked," I said. "I could tell he likes you. Do you think he enjoyed himself?"

"Yes, for sure. I mean, I think he did, Poppa."

The rest of the trip home was quiet as I myself thought with pleasance about Justine inviting me to dinner at her condo. I was sure Liesl was thinking with similar emotion about Joel. I had seen him stroking her arm above the elbow with the back of his index finger while she was talking to the concertmaster.

Liesl's week at school was uneventful as was my quiet week at home, though I continued to catch myself expecting Fielder to approach me, tennis ball in mouth, looking for a game of catch. Each time I quickly remembered why that wasn't going to happen, the pain of his death stung anew, but its duration was shorter.

As the weekend approached, I found myself hesitant to tell Liesl about my dinner date with Justine. When I tried to analyze that resistance, to find its cause and overcome my reticence, I couldn't explain why it should bother me to tell my granddaughter that I was looking forward to the company of a woman, a woman other than a relative or longtime friend.

I had to tell Liesl about Justine, I certainly wasn't going to start deceiving her at this stage of our relationship, but I wanted to feel good about it, not in any way unenthusiastic or, even worse, ashamed. It was two forty-five in the morning on Friday when, after lying awake for almost two hours, I deduced why I was so averse to discussing my psychosocio appetite with Liesl.

If, when I was fourteen-years-old, my grandmother, Naomi Foley, had told me that she was going on a dinner date with a horn player, I would have been selfishly repulsed. Furthermore, if she had raised me from birth, I would have been jealous of any relationship she might have with an unrelated man.

In the middle of the night, I'd solved the puzzle.

"Well," I muttered to myself, "she'll just have to get over it. I'm not going to let any immature, possessive feelings interfere with my life."

When Liesl arrived home from Friday classes, I met her on the front porch. Using a tone that I'm sure she recognized as my "authoritative" voice, "Liesl, I'm going to dinner tomorrow night with Justine Colgate. Now I know, this might not—"

"That's great, Poppa!"

There were various triggers that would always activate a memory of an incident in my third-grade class at Sts. Peter and Paul school; hearing the word "catechism," the name "Alma," or the term "supreme being" among them.

Sister Jean Alma had told the class to close our catechisms. "Josette, who made us?"

"God made us," Josette correctly responded after rising from her desk, as all the Sisters of Divine Authority expected those called upon to do.

"Good," said the nun. "Charles, Who is God?"

"God is the Supreme Being, instantly perfect—"

"That's *infinitely*, Charles."

"Yes, Sister, infantly perfect, who made all things and keeps them in existence."

"Very slowly, Charles, say in--fin--ite--ly."

"In--fin--ite--ly," Charles repeated.

"Perfect. Jill, why did God make us?"

"God made us to show forth His goodness and to share with us His everlasting happiness in heaven."

"David, what is a supernatural mystery?"

"Uh, is it something we don't know about?" I fumbled.

The nun approached me, shook my shoulder and said, "David, you go down to the office and tell Sister Claude you didn't study your Catechism again."

"Kristie, What is a supernatural mystery?" the nun continued.

I heard Kristie's answer as I sulked and trudged to the door in the back of the room. "A supernatural mystery is a truth that we cannot fully understand, but which we firmly believe because we have God's word for it."

"Excellent, Kristie," said Sister Jean Alma.

On the night of my dinner date with Justine, I drove Liesl, Heather and another classmate to the cinema to see the remake of "King Kong."

Sheila Cassidy was picking them up afterward, and all three girls were spending the night at the Cassidys' house. After dropping the girls off at the theater, I made the trip to downtown Louisville, easing the car to the curb in front of Justine's Metro Condos. After I identified myself to the guard and signed the register, he said, "She's in 708, Mr. Foley. The elevators will be on your left."

Justine opened the door of her unit just before I knocked. "I could hear the elevator door opening," she said. "Come on in. Let me pour you a glass of wine. I have a nice Chardonnay, an Australian Zinfandel, or an Oregon Pinot Noir," she said.

"Is that it?" I asked.

"Well, yes," she answered, an instant before she realized I was being facetious.

"In that case, I suppose I'll settle for the Oregon Pinot."

While Justine was out of the room filling my order, I glanced around her condo. It was furnished and appointed in a tasteful, but contemporary fashion. Sleek, straight-lined, no-frills furniture was efficiently placed in the combination living room/dining room. Modern, American paintings and abstract European posters of muted color hung on the walls. I could see a galley-type kitchen and a study with louvered doors at opposite ends of the living/dining room combination. I wondered as to the location of her bedroom, and what it looked like.

"I confess to this Pinot coming from a previously opened bottle," Justine said as she reappeared with a glass of shimmering wine in each hand.

"Oh, if I had known that—" This time her smile indicated she was onto me.

She guided me to a small, two-seater couch and settled into an upholstered chair just opposite me, a rectangular chrome and glass cocktail table separating us.

"I thought we'd eat in about thirty minutes," she said. "I was hoping to talk for awhile. You're always with your granddaughter. Are grandchildren as wonderful as some friends have told me?"

"Oh yes, that they are. It's a bit different with Liesl and me, I'm her guardian."

"Where are her parents?" Justine inquired.

I told her in one economic sentence the manners in which Patrick and Kathryn had passed. For some reason, I didn't feel the pressure of pain in my chest that recalling those tragedies usually induced.

"I'm sorry," she said with an embarrassed grimace.

With a squint and a subtle nod, I acknowledged her sympathy and let her know that it was okay.

"Did you find the proper change you said you needed here in Louisville?" I asked.

"So far, so good," she said. "I love the people and the chemistry of the orchestra. Actually, I wasn't all that unhappy with the people or the orchestra in Minneapolis, though the weather might have rendered Minnesotans a bit more pessimistic about things in general than Kentuckians seem to be."

"That's funny," I said, smiling. "I've never thought of it in optimistic or pessimistic terms, but that's a very good way to express it. The people are definitely more laid back here than in the north or the east. Just what sort of change did you require, if I may ask."

"I needed to get away from a divorce," she said. "My ex-husband is quite prominent in and around the Twin Cities and I didn't want to fall into the role of Donald Colgate's ex-wife."

"The Donald Colgate of Three-C Company power?"

"Yes," she replied. "He was less than discretely sleeping around and when I confronted him, it was basically 'What would it take to buy me out of this marriage?' Since we have no children and he had moved out, I merely had my lawyer tell his lawyer what that figure was. He surprised us by agreeing quickly and, as they say, the rest is history."

"My goodness," I said. "What was the time frame of that?"

"Nine weeks. I confronted him in early March and I was on my way to Louisville with his check in my pocket on May 7, Derby Day."

She refilled both of our glasses with the red nectar of the Northwest.

"I think the fact that he was a, quote, *devout,* unquote, Catholic, worked to my advantage," she continued. "He didn't want the entire, ugly story aired in the Minneapolis media."

"Are you a Catholic?" I asked.

"No, are you?"

"Hardly," I said, smiling and close to boasting. "I was raised one, but now I'm pretty much a pagan."

"How long have you been a non-believer?" she asked with what seemed genuine interest.

"Since college or thereabouts," I answered.

"Tell me, has that cost you any relationships with relatives or friends? I've had several at least diminish because of my agnosticism."

"I really have no relatives other than Liesl. But there's a degree of tension between me and her very Catholic aunt and her very Catholic family. And yes, I lost a few friends back in Boston over my heathenism. It was mostly my Catholic pals who seemed to dry up. The Protestants forgave me."

"Are you serious?"

"Oh yeah."

"How do you explain that?" she asked.

"Well, I think a lot of Protestants are under the impression that Catholics who've 'fallen away,' I call it 'risen above,' have done so only as reflexive rebellion to the extreme indoctrination we received in parochial schools, mainly in the form of nuns and catechisms. They think if we'd been exposed to softer Episcopalian, Lutheran, Methodist, or Presbyterian Protestant propaganda, we'd still be Christians.

"They just can't believe I made a measured decision to reject the joke of Jesus being the Son of God. They're so cock-sure I'm merely over-reacting to the brainwashing I was given, they don't look at it as a repudiation of what they believe.

"But Catholics' conviction that their way is the *only* way, causes them to take it personally when someone rejects what *they* believe is infallible truth."

I saw a studied frown on Justine's face, indicating to me something less than total agreement with my analysis.

"Sorry," I said, "I'm sounding as presumptuous about Catholics and Protestants as they are about me and those of my ilk."

A buzzer sounded from the kitchen. "Oh-oh," Justine said. "I'm afraid dinner's ready."

"Don't be afraid," I said winking. "I'm hungry."

She laughed, but perfunctorily. "I'd love to continue this conversation. Do you care if I talk with my mouth full?" she asked, proving she could be as facetious as her guest.

She beckoned me to follow her, motioned me to the table. After a bit of hectic activity at the stove and oven, she set a salad bowl and a dinner plate in front of me, the presentation of each worthy of the finest Manhattan restaurants. She sat next to me, on my left.

"Oh my," I said. "What am I about to eat?"

"That's my version of a Kentucky hot brown. I thought I'd go native."

As we ate, drank, and allowed the inevitable, pleasant buzz of fine wine to overtake us, Justine asked, "What made you realize you weren't a believer?"

"Justine, I simply gave it some thought and quickly saw the lack of light." The humor of the short-form answer, perhaps with some help from the Pinot, made her laugh in earnest.

In truth, I loved the question, having often rehearsed its long-form answer. Forcing Justine to "hang" for my response, I patiently finished chewing a piece of the hot brown's turkey. After I'd swallowed with exaggeration, put the linen napkin to my lips, and taken a sip of wine, I said, "I think it was when I realized, or at least when I realized I *couldn't* realize how incredibly vast and how incredibly old the cosmic world is.

"I assume there has to be a cause for any existence, including yours and mine, our planet, our solar system, the cosmos. But the size of the universe is so immeasurable, its age so incomprehensible, that the inhabitants of this tiny planet, revolving around one of a million billion suns, at this particular microscopic place in time, aren't much in the consciousness of any creator, any *God.*"

By then I was in the zone, totally warmed up. "And if, indeed, a creator or supreme entity exists," I condescended, "it's certainly beyond the scope of our understanding and is so removed from us, that it's irrelevant to our existence. Furthermore, to believe that some unstable Jewish peasant roaming a desert in the Middle East just a relative nanosecond ago, was the Son of God, doesn't pass the smile test.

"Sorry, sometimes I pontificate," I said. "Particularly when I'm drinking good wine."

"No, please. I have some of those same feelings," she said, reaching a hand to touch my arm. "It's just that I've never heard it, uh . . . preached so confidently. Sorry, I mean *expressed so cogently*. I insist on thanking you for that, David." Her eyes remained fixed on mine as she rose from the table, gestured for my hand even though neither of us had finished dinner.

She led me into a not surprisingly contemporary bedroom for the tour I'd hoped I'd get, then coerced me onto her king-size Knoll bed before she began showing her gratitude for an extended fifty-minutes, the first five of which she demonstrated how well indeed she had mastered blowing the horn, French or otherwise.

Chapter Nine

*"All one has to do is hit the right keys at the
right time and the instrument plays itself."*

—JOHANN SEBASTIAN BACH

*L*ate in *Liesl's* freshman year at TJ Prep, I was attempting to straighten our bedrooms on a Monday morning so that the housekeepers, on their weekly visit, could at least see the outline of the rooms' furniture for dusting purposes. I was stacking the strewn paper in Liesl's room, when, under a manila folder, I discovered a sheet of paper, disguised as parchment, bearing ink in the form of the Christian Ten Commandments. The script was set in cheesy old-English type, used, no doubt, to give the text an air of antiquity and authority.

"Well goddamn," I exclaimed, as the source of the document occurred to me. "Madonna." Liesl had spent the weekend at the Maddoxes. Just wait till I see her.

It was always hard for me to stay angry with Madonna. She was, after all, the consummate mother and she obviously loved Liesl in the sincerest way, though she did, on occasion, create unnecessary stress for me, such as having to debrief Liesl on the Ten Commandments, albeit in such manner as not to undercut her relationship with her aunt.

Perhaps I could merely do a slight bit of editing of the Roman numeraled edicts. Yeah, that's a great idea, I thought. To edit the Ten Commandments would be fun.

I scanned the imitation parchment onto my computer and then had its contents in a text document, editable as hell. I enjoyed spending the next twenty minutes or so playing God, that is, tweaking Moses' no longer cast-in-stone commandments to my own specs. I was pleased both with the results and myself, as editor.

I. ~~I am the Lord thy God; thou shalt not have strange gods before me.~~

(Forget this one, useless.)

II. **Thou shalt not take the name of the Lord thy God in vain.**
(This one's tolerable, since it means don't use bad words, out loud in the company of others, anyway.)

III. ~~Remember to keep holy the Lord's Day.~~
(Totally useless.)

IV. **Honor thy father and thy mother.**
(Good rule; tied for second-best commandment. Applies to grandfathers too!)

V. **Thou shall not kill.**
(I have to admit, a pretty good commandment, probably the best.)

VI. ~~Thou shalt not commit adultery.~~
(Madonna's mixed-up about this one. Let's strike it and I'll explain later.)

VII. **Thou shalt not steal.**
(Another good rule; tied for second-best commandment.)

VIII. **Thou shalt not bear false witness against thy neighbor.**
(Another good one, it means not to tell lies; fourth-best commandment.)

IX. ~~Thou shalt not covet thy neighbor's wife.~~
(Useless since one can't help what one covets, can one?)

X. ~~Thou shalt not covet thy neighbor's goods.~~
(It's okay to want them, just don't take them.)

When the housekeepers were gone, I printed my edited commandments and placed them on top of a six-inch stack of loose-leaf paper on Liesl's dresser with a sticky-note that read, "Ask me."

She did not.

Time seems to speed through the agreeable stages of life but can slow to a crawl during unpleasant periods. I believe that's why Liesl's high-school years passed so quickly for me. She was a good student and stayed out of trouble, so there were very few negative or profound incidents to slow the flow of time.

One episode she and I will probably never forget, however, occurred in the early spring of 2007, her sophomore year. I received a notice in the mail that I'd been "inducted" into the Black & White "Hall of Fame." The company I had founded as a young man in Boston and sold to facilitate moving to Louisville, had grown to over a hundred employees and someone had the idea to initiate a farcical company "Hall of Fame," using the initial "induction ceremony" as a vehicle for a company reunion on its forty-fourth anniversary.

When I phoned to find out more about the event, I was told that if I were to come, three of the first eight employees of B&W would be there. Two were deceased, one was in Pondville Correctional Center, one couldn't be located, and one declined. I decided to give it a shot. I'd only been back to Boston a few times since I moved to Louisville and this might be a good opportunity to see my hometown, perhaps activate some latent memories.

As I began to consider travel and lodging logistics for the trip, I wondered if such a whirlwind weekend might be of interest to Justine. I'd enjoy showing her some of the venues of my youth and, if the Hall of Fame event turned out to be a bust, her company would ensure the weekend wouldn't be a total loss.

"Sure, I'd love to see a bit of Boston," she responded to my over-the-phone invitation. "Count me in." We wouldn't be able to see a whole lot in such a short time, but I was already anxious to show Justine my old stomping grounds.

I was confident that Liesl was of age to stay by herself in the house, the first time ever, for the brief weekend. I notified Madonna, as well as Idelle, of my plans and Liesl knew both would be available for her in case of any unforeseen event.

I figured the weekend would be a pleasant blur, Justine and I leaving Louisville on Thursday afternoon and returning on Sunday evening. The two places I would have most enjoyed revisiting, however, were closed, Fenway Park and Tanglewood Music Center.

Nevertheless, we enjoyed a cruise on Boston Harbor, walking the history-rich Freedom Trail on Friday, and perusing the paintings and exhibits of the Museum of Fine Arts on Saturday afternoon.

The Saturday night event itself was an expectation-exceeding success. The "Hall of Fame" motif was a spoof, but the event followed serious protocol, formal attire, honorees introduced, ceremonial inductions. There were over two hundred attendees with an entertaining rock band that could play music from all eras.

After my second glass of wine, Justine had no trouble keeping me on the dance floor, even during up-tempo numbers. Any lack of confidence in my dancing ability disappeared altogether at about Cabernet number four.

"Do you think the alcohol actually loosens me up and improves my physical rhythm, or if it just numbs my self-conscious streak," I asked Justine.

"I think it helps your dancing for sure, David," she said, probably lying. "Go for it."

On Sunday morning, before heading to the airport for our return flight, I showed Justine my childhood home and Sts. Peter & Paul's School and Church. I wasn't surprised at how intensely the emotion swelled within me while revisiting those landmarks of my youth. I was blindsided, however, at how overwhelming my distress was at our last stop, the house where Patrick and I lived after Elaine left us.

I recalled how Patrick excelled in his studies, as well as athletically, in elementary school. He was tall, handsome and vigorous. His blue eyes, perhaps Elaine's best contribution to his person, were a surprise to most people after observing his almost black hair and eyebrows. His smile was instantaneous and kind, wholesome.

During high school, in addition to being a National Merit Scholar, Patrick played football in the fall, basketball in the winter, and baseball in the spring for the Kingsmen of Martin Luther King, Jr. Academy for Excellence, located in Cambridge. My biggest pride, however, came from my son's popularity among his classmates and teachers. Everyone liked Patrick.

I wept aloud, remembering Patrick, as Justine and I sat in our window-fogged, rented car in a drizzle across from that simple, dormered Cape Cod house. Justine held my hand, but apparently knew not to say anything.

Before checking out of the hotel, I had called home to inform Liesl we'd managed to change to an earlier flight that would arrive in Louisville at four-fifteen that afternoon rather than the previously planned nine-thirty. Instead of ringing through or dumping me into voice mail, the call was resulting in a frustrating busy signal each time I dialed. I tried again from Logan International, but the busy signal persisted. When it came time to board the flight, I figured I'd just surprise Liesl, maybe take her to dinner.

The flight arrived at the gate ten minutes early and Louisville traffic was never the burden it was in the larger urban areas. Fifteen minutes after dropping Justine at the Metro condos, I pulled into Four-fourteen's drive at four forty-five. I entered the kitchen from the rear porch, called to my granddaughter. "Liesl?" No response came, but I could hear muted music somewhere in the house.

I moved to the bottom of the stairwell and again tried to raise her. "Liesl?" The music was definite now. I recognized the distinct cadence of Maurice Ravel's "Bolero." I smiled, thinking Liesl was probably practicing that piece on her violin in her room. I climbed the stairs with my suitcase and reaching the top landing, was surprised to see the door to her room closed. Though the music was somewhat muffled because of the closed door, I could sense the volume was ungoverned inside the room.

I knocked sharply. "Liesl?" When I opened the door, "Bolero" was at raucous climax. The cadent percussion, brass and woodwinds, particularly that irrepressible English horn, were flooding the small room, overwhelming my auditory system like a seismic wave. The uncontrolled volume blunted my other senses momentarily. When my eyes began again to convey converted light to my brain, what I saw caused the precise physical pain I felt the moment I learned Liesl's mother had died after giving her birth.

On the bed, a boy was half under the covers, spread atop Liesl, thrusting. His skin was white, the back of his torso youthfully muscular. Her eyes were closed. I remained motionless for a moment before backing out the door without turning. As I was closing the door, Liesl's eyes opened and met mine for a splinter of a moment.

I left my bag on the landing, double-stepped down the stairs, hustled through the kitchen and onto the porch. I needed to get away from the house, get away from them. I reached my Civic, and as I backed around to aim it down and out the driveway, the tires screamed like a wounded animal for a single count in reverse, then cried for two or three seconds going forward.

I drove around and through St. Matthews for more than half an hour, but couldn't escape the sounds and image I experienced in Liesl's bedroom. The impact of a head-on car collision couldn't have felt worse.

Quite by chance, I found myself approaching Seneca Park's lighted Tot Lot, an inadvertent, sanative oasis. I pulled the Civic to the side of the road, tires crunching onto the gravel adjacent to the pavement.

Only a sixtyish man and his apparent granddaughter kept me from having the playground and surrounding area to myself. I sat on a bench from which I could see the pair, but was far enough away so as not to impose on them.

I turned my head to an angle that made it appear I wasn't looking at the man and little girl, but my otherwise unnecessary Ray-Bans allowed me to furtively shift my eyes and focus on them.

I hadn't been in the Tot Lot since Liesl was of the age to enjoy sliding boards and jungle gyms. The play equipment looked to be the same as that I once helped her enjoy.

The grandfatherly man was pushing the tyke on a swing. She was too young to hold on safely by herself, so he had to run alongside, awkwardly back and forth, both hands stabilizing her, keeping her safe and happy on the chain-suspended seat while she made the beautiful music of a child chortling with delight.

I remembered executing that very maneuver with Liesl on the swing. I actually became good at it. But now my granddaughter needed a different kind of two-handed stabilizing to keep her safe and happy.

The house was dark when I pulled into the driveway. It was after seven o'clock. I flicked on a couple of lights as I walked into the kitchen. "Liesl?" After a moment, "Liesl honey?"

I heard the words, "Please leave me alone, Poppa," faintly fall from the second floor.

"For how long?"

"I don't know. For now anyway."

I walked up the steps planning to open her bedroom door, but it was locked.

"Poppa, I need to be alone. Go away."

"Okay, Sweetie, I'll be downstairs," I said, realizing how debilitated and ashamed she must have been. "Just know that everything's going to be all right."

I added the last sentence using such tone that I hoped she would know I meant it, know that I was telling her the truth. Everything *would* be all right.

I walked down the stairs, went into my office. The unmistakable gong of my Macintosh coming to life, such an unremarkable but timely and exquisite normalcy, corroborated that life was going to continue, that I was coping and that my granddaughter, too, would cope.

It didn't take long to catch up on a mere weekend's worth of my mail and news. I heard Liesl's door unlocking. From her doorway, she uttered the word I was most needing to hear.

"Poppa?" I remembered similar beckoning she used as a toddler to summon me to her crib upon awakening in the morning or from a nap. I double-stepped up the stairs, found Liesl face down on her bed. It was as if she needed me to be with her, but didn't want to see my eyes or have me see hers. Leaving the lights off, I sat on the side of her bed, placed my hand on her back. I began stroking it in the same gentle pattern I used when she was a tyke, as I'd sing her to sleep.

Then I said just the right thing. "I love you, Liesl."

She sprang to a sitting position, buried her head in my shoulder. "I can't look at you, Poppa."

"You don't have to."

"This is horrible."

"Just stay where you are."

She did, and as we embraced, we rocked slowly, slowly back and forth for a long time.

"Poppa, I—"

"Shhh, be still. We'll talk about things later."

"Dear Poppa."

As my eyes began to adjust to the darkness of the room, the photo on Liesl's desk came into focus. It was the picture of Patrick in his full dress cadet uniform, looking on as his father comforted his daughter.

I was awake in my bed when I heard Liesl's alarm sound on Monday morning. Ordinarily, I would have arisen and helped her in the kitchen as she prepared to leave for school. This morning, however, I stayed in bed until I heard the door close downstairs as she left to walk to the front of the driveway where she'd await the "school pool" car to arrive.

I looked through an opening in my bedroom window curtains to see Liesl sitting on one of the front yard's green park benches. She was wearing her green plaid TJ uniform skirt and white blouse, reading one of her textbooks, no doubt a chore she should have completed the eventful day before.

The debilitating pain I had experienced yesterday was surprisingly gone, morphed to a feeling of profound sadness, not just for myself because I had witnessed Liesl's innocence dissipate in one disconcerting scene, but for her, the incredible humiliation I knew she was suffering.

I almost convinced myself during the day to let the crisis sink in silence under its own weight, scab over, and fade slowly from both our consciousnesses. The incident, and how to handle it with her, was dominating me. By mid-afternoon I'd decided to address it with her sooner rather than later. I needed to lead in this situation, to try and make any possible scars minimal, inconsequential.

That evening after dinner, when she was clearing the dishes from the table after a silent meal, "Liesl, there are only a few points I want to make about what happened yesterday."

She continued with her dishwashing chore, not looking at me.

"Foremost, you need to be extremely careful in those situations," I said. "Sexually transmitted diseases are rampant. They cut across all demographic lines. And pregnancy cuts across lines of *any* sort. Becoming infected or pregnant would change your life forever.

"I know, Poppa. Do we have to—"

"Yes, we do! If you make the decision to engage in that type of activity, particularly at your age, always be certain your partner is a good person, one you trust completely. The others aren't worth it. Boys and men are often cruel; they talk. Sex is often a game to many of them, just a cheap conquest.

"Furthermore, never, *ever*, take the chance of letting me stumble onto you in that situation again. It's too hard on both of us.

"Lastly, know that I love you as much as ever and if your foolish mistake affects our relationship, I'll be devastated."

Liesl said nothing, nor did I expect her to. She still didn't look at me when I left the kitchen quickly and climbed the stairs, in a hurry to get to my room where I remained the rest of the evening.

Floyd Rausch died the ensuing summer, and though Liesl had seldom been with him since she was a toddler, his passing wasn't easy for her. Of the six people from whom she was immediately descended, only her paternal grandparents remained alive, one of them estranged in virtual non-existence. I was always amazed that Liesl was such a positive, well-adjusted young person despite the fact that the cruel umbra of death had robbed her, starting even before she was born, of people who loved her, or would have loved her, people she loved, or would have loved.

One day early in her junior year, Liesl came into the den after she finished her homework and violin practice. "Poppa, did you ever smoke any chronic?"

"Chronic?" I asked without looking away from the book I was reading. "I'm not sure what that is."

"You know," she said, "marijuana."

I bookmarked my page, set the novel aside. "Chronic, huh? That's a great name for it. I knew a lot of people who used it with, shall we say, frequent recurrence."

"Well, did you, Poppa? Did you smoke it?"

"You ask tough questions, Liesl. You always have."

"That's what I thought," she said.

"What do you mean, 'That's what I thought?'"

"I mean, if the answer wasn't 'Yes,' it wouldn't have been such a tough question."

"Jesus," I said.

"Do you ever smoke it now?" she asked.

"Oh my, no," I answered, with intentional speed.

"Tell me about it, Poppa. What's it like?"

"Why do you ask just now?"

"You ask tough questions, too, Poppa."

"Give me a tough answer."

"You know, there are a few guys at school who do it, and they all say how great it is," she said. "What do you think?"

I looked at her for a moment as I searched for a reasonable response. TJ Prep had a substance-awareness program, but it was focused on hard drugs. I had given the subject of discussing pot with Liesl some thought, but since my official position had never crystallized, I hadn't broached the subject with her. Well, the subject had certainly been broached then.

"Frankly, Liesl, I don't believe smoking—what did you call it, chronic?—would be worth your while. I'll admit that some things such as my political position and the entertainment I liked changed during the couple of years that I smoked it in college."

"What do you mean?"

"I mean I was pretty much a self-centered, ungrounded redneck."

"Poppa, you're so silly."

"No, I mean it. I hadn't bothered to absorb a lot of things of value that my parents and teachers were offering. That might have been because I was so sure they had the 'God thing' wrong, that I figured they had everything wrong. At any rate, pot did seem to offer some clarity for me on some important issues, but I really think that was because I was such a narrow-minded rube. Does that make sense?"

"Sort of," Liesl said, folding her arms and frowning, indicating she needed to hear more.

"Let me put the same premise in a different fashion. You, my dear, already have a wonderful perspective on life, your love of the arts and science, your awareness, your innate high-mindedness. Honestly, I don't believe the—quote, *directional push*, unquote—marijuana might have given me would occur with you. You're already on the right track. Pot can't intensify the life of one who is already intense and it won't furnish clarity to one who already sees issues clearly." Again, I asked, "Does that make sense?" a clear indicator I was less than confident in my spiel.

"What made you stop doing it, Poppa?"

Liesl's question allowed me to segue onto the negative factors of using marijuana. I knew stressing the downside would be more effective than the pedestrian attempt I had made to explain and downplay the "high" that reefer produced.

"Well, for one thing, it dawned on me that I was giving a lot of serious thought to a lot of serious topics, but not getting much of anything accomplished. I realized it was stifling my ambition. Once I stopped puffing, my grades improved. Pot doesn't exactly inspire hard work."

"Funny you should mention that," she said. "The guys who are talking it up at school are all nice, but they aren't the most energetic or industrious students."

"I also knew that sucking that smoke down my throat and holding my breath to allow my lungs to filter out the crud in the smoke was bound to be harmful."

"How old did you say you were?" Liesl asked.

"About twenty. It was during my first couple of years of college. Funny, after I quit, the slight changes in my personality and philosophy stayed changed. It was as if the weed had served its purpose for a misguided rube and there was no need to expose myself to the dangers of further use.

"So what are you going to do?" I asked.

"I think I'll pass."

"I believe that's a wise decision. Will you tell me if you ever change your mind?"

"Yes, Poppa," she said as she turned to leave. "And thanks, I knew you'd have an opinion."

"By the way, Liesl," I called to her as she reached the top of the steps, "a good red wine has a somewhat similar effect, and taken in moderation, has none of the downside health issues."

Liesl smiled.

I myself rejoined the novel.

Liesl's graduation from TJ Prep was one of those transformational incidents that always impassioned me. If there were but a single demarcational line drawn through a person's lifespan, it would be bordered on one side by turning eighteen years old and on the other by high school graduation. That thin stripe of time was the most reliable and predictable indicator that a childhood had been ceded and adulthood attained. An individual never stops changing and learning, but the mental, physical, and socio-psychological framework of one's persona were firmly imbued, cured to near rigidity, as that singular space in time was attained.

Liesl had grant and scholarship offers from a number of colleges and universities. For a while, she talked frequently about Stanford University near Palo Alto, California. The lure of Boston, the city of her father and grandfather's roots, had her seriously pondering Wellesley College and Boston University. She even entertained the idea of studying abroad. Her consideration of those coastal colleges and distant destinations had me dreading the possibility of separation from my only close blood relative.

I was more relieved than happy when she decided to attend Indiana University in Bloomington, just ninety miles from Louisville. She told me she was unsure of a field of study, but was impressed with IU's reputation for rigorous academic demands and felt its undergraduate program would be a solid platform from which to pursue further education or occupational opportunities. I myself didn't care what field of study she pursued or what star she chased, as long as she chased it just an hour-and-a-half up the road.

Liesl found a summer job with Louisville's Farnsley Women's Center, a well-respected organization that primarily assisted abused women and their children. The Center offered victims of domestic violence food, shelter, and counseling. For the most part, the job was running errands, but it exposed her to the issues of working full time as well as to the reality of families within which brutality existed.

When the end of summer approached, I suppose I shouldn't have been shocked at the sentimentality I experienced the day I drove Liesl to Bloomington to begin her college career. After the work of moving her belongings into the residence hall, I realized there was nothing else she needed from me at that moment in time, and that there would be less and less she needed from me going forward.

My eyes moistened as I was hugging her goodbye.

"Come on, Poppa, I'm coming home in ten days."

"I know, I know. I just need to do this," I said, by then sobbing. By the time I was off-campus, I was wailing and bawling with more volume than I thought myself capable. I was relieved to be able to really "cut loose," since no one could see or hear me.

During her freshman year, Liesl routinely spent a weekend a month at Four-fourteen. On occasion, I drove to Bloomington, where I was always grateful, still not having figured out to whom or what, for a Saturday afternoon and a Sunday brunch in Liesl's company. I was savvy enough to not infringe on the social life of an eighteen-year-old coed, leaving my granddaughter's Saturday night activity strictly in her control. There weren't many things that hadn't changed in the years since I was a student, but I was sure Saturday nights remained the buttress of social activity on campus.

During the arts season in Louisville, I continued to subscribe to the ballet, the orchestra, and the touring Broadway musical series, but had dropped my allotment of tickets from four, to a set of two. Those evenings of live entertainment were the mainstay of my social life, and I anticipated and enjoyed them immensely. My guest list hadn't expanded, still including Madonna or sometimes Michael Maddox, Idelle or Samantha McCoy. The person I escorted to events most often, however, was Justine, that is to performances other than those of the Orchestra, for which she still played horn.

I prized her company, but our relationship had become more a loving federation than a romantic liaison. I enjoyed her innate sophistication, considered her an archetype of refinement, an area in which I myself was sometimes deficient.

After the "music lesson," of my first carnal knowledge of Justine, subsequent sexual activity was producing diminishing returns for both of us and eventually started to interfere with our genuine mutual fondness. Moreover, Justine confided to me that she was beginning to suffer increasing vaginal atrophy that had begun when she became premenopausal.

By that time, ironically, I had started to become comfortable with the fact that my sexual activity was relegating to a diversion of mere secondary importance.

"Jesus, Justine. You're becoming hard where you should be soft and I'm getting soft where I should be hard."

"Does that mean we can become better friends?" she asked.

"Yes, as long as you understand that I love you."

"I love you too, David."

"Thank you for making me know that," I told her. "It keeps me happy and content with my new role of delayed empty-nester. Since I have a few years on you, I can tutor you in the proper art of aging. You, in turn, my cultured one, can help refine and polish my minuscule aesthetic and cultural assets."

"Tutor me in the art of aging?"

"Yes, that'll mostly be keeping you from making some of the same dumb mistakes I made."

"David, I do indeed love you, but you're really full of shit."

It was no surprise to me that Liesl was excelling in her studies at IU. Moreover, I could see that she was excelling at life, only now as an adult.

Each of us had found a comfortable niche in spite of the absence of the other. A comfortable niche's downside, at least for me, was that it made time lapse more quickly.

Liesl was home for the summer after her junior year in Bloomington and, for the fourth straight year, had secured a summer job as an intern at the Farnsley Women's Center. She related to me stories of some of those families, without using names, and they were tragic. The cruelty of the abusers was difficult to listen to, much less be around. I didn't know how she did it.

She would be turning twenty-one in July. "I don't want a party," she answered, when I asked how she'd like to celebrate. "Could we just go somewhere and have dinner with a friend or two?"

"Sure. You know what might be nice is to each ask someone and catch the touring Broadway production of "Fiddler On The Roof." I can trade in my two tickets for four together, if you'd like to do that."

"I love that play," she said with eyes adrift, shaking her head slowly, like one just coming to realize that time and time periods melt away too quickly. "I'll bet I was only about ten when we saw it. I remember crying at the end. Yeah, that would be fun," she concluded, eyes now engaged, head nodding.

"I think I'll ask Justine," I said. "Who would you like to ask?"

"Well, there's this guy at school; he's on campus this summer and I'll bet he'd come down for the show and my twenty-first if I asked him. We've never actually dated, we just get along well. He's *soooo* nice, Poppa. I know you'll like Alan."

"I'll tell you what," I said, "I can get tickets for any night that weekend, so give him his choice of Friday, Saturday or Sunday evening. That should make it easy for him to accept."

"Great," Liesl said. "I'll call him right now so you can get the tickets swapped. Thanks, Poppa, this'll be such a nice birthday. Going to the theater with you will be just like when I was a kid."

"What's this fellow's name again?" I asked.

"Alan. Alan Martin," she said running up the stairs, not turning around.

When Liesl informed me that she'd talked to Alan, she said, "Saturday would be the easiest night for him. Is it okay if he stays here with us that night?"

"Sure," I said. "He can sleep with me in my bed."

"Poppa, you're so silly."

"You don't think he'd like that?"

"Poppa."

"Maybe not," I said. "Perhaps we should settle him on the pullout bed in the den."

"He'll be here mid-afternoon on Saturday," she said.

"Would you like to have dinner after the show?" I asked.

"For sure. I always like to have some casual time after a performance just to kind of review it. Do you have a place in mind?"

Well, it's *your* birthday, but I was thinking we might go to El Rascal's."

"Poppa, that's so sweet. Yes, El Rascal's."

Liesl verged toward me, put her arms around my torso. "I love you Poppa."

"I know that," I said, stroking her hair. "Thank you for always making me know that."

Chapter Ten

"Some people come into our lives, leave footprints
on our hearts, and we are never the same."

—Franz Schubert

It was three-thirty Saturday afternoon when Alan Martin popped out of his modest sedan in the driveway at Four-Fourteen. Liesl and I were both on the front porch awaiting him. He was about six feet tall, thin, but muscular. His short-sleeve, button down, oxford cloth shirt was neatly tucked into his jeans and surprisingly unruffled considering the heat of the season and that its wearer had just pulled in from a road trip.

Alan's hair was light brown and long enough on top to have some blonde sun streaking. His tan was uniform and prominent white teeth practically gleamed against his browned facial skin. His eyes were green, their sclera clear and moist.

The enthusiasm with which Liesl greeted Alan was not lost on me. It seemed obvious he wasn't merely a 'bill-filler' for the weekend. She offered him an extended embrace that he definitely returned.

Well I'll be damned was what I thought. "Hello, Alan. I'm happy you could make it."

"Mr. Foley, at last," he said. "You're all Liesl talks about sometimes. She's had me just dying to meet you, sir."

"That's interesting, Alan. You've been pretty much a well kept secret," I said, moving my eyes from him to Liesl as I finished the sentence.

"Poppa, you're so silly."

Ignoring my small provocation, Alan said, as he surveyed the grounds of the house, "This is such a lovely layout, Mr. Foley."

Patronizing bastard was what I thought. "Thanks, Alan."

"Alan is a landscape architect," Liesl said. "At least on paper. He'll get his masters in December"

"That is if all goes well," Alan added, "including a successful thesis."

167

I could just hear the gardening lessons to come. "Oh boy," I said. "All at once I'm insecure about our external scenery."

"There's certainly no need for insecurity," he said. "Your yard is beautiful. The privacy from the intermittent dogwoods and nandinas is nice, and I love the spontaneity of the annuals set about the lot. I'm sure you have dazzling color all season. But I think my favorite is that gorgeous ginkgo tree. I'll bet it's stunning in autumn."

All trees are stunning in autumn, Father Nature, was what I thought. "Yes, the ginkgo is beautiful in fall. Have you ever been around one when its leaves drop?"

"No, actually, I haven't."

"I'll tell you about that sometime."

"Let's go in, Alan," Liesl said, "before Poppa has you mowing the lawn."

"Yes, of course," I agreed. "Let's get you settled and comfortable. We'll need to be leaving for the show in about an hour-and-a-half. Liesl, why don't you show Alan his quarters and familiarize him with the house while I jump into the shower?"

"Sure, Poppa."

Standing in the steaming shower, I couldn't explain the distinctive pang I felt after realizing this young fellow commanded such a measure of my granddaughter's affection. I didn't even know him, and I didn't like not liking him. Nonetheless I didn't.

The unfamiliar emotional discomfort I was experiencing failed to recede after an otherwise refreshing shower. Why would Liesl not have mentioned this guy to me if she were as attached to him as it seemed? I couldn't quite pinpoint what was spurring my distress. Was I experiencing some sort of ridiculous man-thing envy? Surely not. I just would have expected to be the first to know about her feelings for him, even before *he* knew of them. Is that too much too ask?

"Yes it is, numb nuts," I uttered the answer to my unuttered question as I shaved.

I always wore a suit and tie when I attended an evening play or an orchestra concert at the Kentucky Center and usually asked Liesl, "If one doesn't wear a coat and tie to a classical music concert or Broadway

168

play, when *does* one dress up? Besides, when one is seventy-one, one needs all the aesthetic help one can get."

"You sure say 'one' a lot when you're pontificating, Poppa," she used to respond.

She and I were waiting for Alan on the front porch. "I hope he isn't planning on wearing jeans or something," I said. "I'll have to speak up about that."

"Poppa, don't you dare," Liesl said, face tightening and as stern as I'd ever seen it. "The younger guys dress very casually these days. Alan won't be the only—"

Alan opened the screen door and walked onto the porch, wearing a dark, three-piece suit and a solid blue silk tie that even I had to admit was tasteful and elegant. Liesl couldn't keep a laugh from escaping.

"What's so funny?" Alan wanted to know.

"Poppa's always funny," Liesl said, grinning at me.

Though Alan's tie hung properly, breaking just over his belt, I saw its less-than-perfectly constructed knot as an opportunity.

"Here, your knot isn't quite right, Alan. Let me work with it a minute," I said, grabbing the tie with both hands.

"*Poppa!*" Liesl protested.

"It's okay, Sweetie. It just needs a little tweaking." After a jerk to unloosen the knot, I indented the tie with my thumb just below the knot, producing a perfect dimple under the half-Windsor when I recinched it.

"Now you're ready, young fellow."

Alan managed a smile, a very tight one. "Uh, thanks," he said, looking at Liesl as if to say, "What the—"

I could see Liesl peripherally and knew not to look at her, frozen in place, no doubt staring at me with extreme displeasure.

"Say Alan, do you mind driving?" I asked.

"Well, okay," he said, still looking at Liesl.

"Great. Liesl, you want to get in the back?"

I got out of the car when we reached Justine's condo. Before I got to the guard station, she was already walking toward me. I kissed her on the cheek, much the way a man would kiss his sister, and opened the door for her. Liesl had moved to the front seat. I started to complain about the need to stretch my stiff knee in the front seat, but decided not to force the seating arrangement issue.

After introductions, Justine said, "I'll bet I've seen 'Fiddler' three or four times, and I like it more each time I see it."

"I've only seen it once," Liesl said. "Poppa and I went when I was about ten. I just loved it."

"Have you seen it, Alan?" I asked.

"Actually, I haven't. It's one of the reasons I wanted to come to Louisville."

"What were some of the other reasons?" I prodded.

"*Poppa*," Liesl admonished.

"*David*," Justine followed.

Alternately looking at me in the rear-view mirror and watching the road as he drove, Alan said, "Why, the extreme pleasure of your company, the honor of meeting you, sir." His voice was inflected with parody, obviously trying to make me, Liesl and Justine laugh. He succeeded on all counts.

I was always excited when my guests and I took our seats in a performance hall before a theatrical production. The audience would be buzzing with anticipation, the atmosphere practically crackling as curtain time approached. The curtain itself was an icon of promise, an insinuation that there was something special behind it. I relished the moment when the house lights slowly dimmed, calling the audience to a state of heed.

Toward the end of the first act, when Tevye began to sing the evocative "Sunrise, Sunset," I felt an ardency within me. I'd seen "Fiddler" with Liesl the child, but the poignant relevance of the lyrics had escaped me then, as I enjoyed the luxury of the company of a dependent, ten-year-old loved one. Now the loved one was a twenty-one-year-old, independent woman who was sitting next to another man, a man, I suspected, she loved.

Tevye and Golde showed no mercy.

Is this the little girl I carried?
Is this the little boy at play?
I don't remember growing older.
When did they?

I was grateful, still drawing a blank as to whom or what, that there was another song, the vivacious "Bottle Dance," before intermission, offering me a chance to recompose. Only Justine seemed to notice I was wiping my eyes. She wrapped my left hand in both of hers.

At dinner later that night, on the riverfront patio of El Rascal's, I proposed a toast Tevye had taught me. "Here's to our prosperity, our good health and happiness. And most important, to life, to life."

"Mr. Foley, this was such a perfect weekend," Alan said as he placed his overnight bag into the trunk of his car the next afternoon. He needed to get back to Bloomington to prepare for a summer class the next morning. "I loved being with you and Liesl, meeting Justine, and just enjoying your hospitality. I don't think I'll ever forget the emotion and the enjoyment of "Fiddler," and El Rascal's was a wonderful ending."

"The only downside to El Rascal's," I said, "is the total lack of stature of its wine list. But your company more than made up for that. I hope you'll come back sometime."

"I can't wait," Alan said

"Forgive me," I said, "but I need to get a few things done inside. Liesl, can you properly see Mr. Martin off without me?"

"I'll try, Poppa," she said smiling.

As I walked into the house, "So long, Alan."

"Goodbye, sir."

I walked through the kitchen, into the dining room where a curtained, open window allowed me to see them and overhear their conversation. "I'll be back on campus in late August," Liesl said. "Will I see you then?"

"Yes," Alan said. "As much as you'd like."

Liesl grinned and bowed her head, but Alan put his unclenched fist under her chin and pushed it upward. He placed his lips upon hers and pressed her form to his.

"Liesl, I'm afraid I've become quite fond of you."

"I'm fond of you too, Alan, but I'm not afraid."

Alan had been gone about ten minutes when I emerged from the kitchen, joined Liesl on the back porch where she was in the rocking chair.

"What did you have to get done inside, Poppa?"

"I just wanted to give you some privacy to see your friend off."

"You don't like him, do you, Poppa?"

The question made me ashamed. "It's not that, Liesl. I'm just disappointed that you hadn't told me about him, that I wasn't the second person to know how you felt about him."

"Poppa, you *were* the second person. I didn't know how I felt about him myself until he pulled into the driveway yesterday afternoon. It just washed over me all at once. Even when I invited him to come down, he was just a nice guy I enjoyed being with. But when I saw him get out of the car, I just—"

"Shhh, say no more," I said when I saw Liesl's eyes were tearing. "I'm sorry for my boorish behavior. I know that any guy you have affection for is going to be a decent person, someone I'll like too."

"I want you to like him, Poppa."

"I understand, Liesl. Sit here in the swing with me."

She did, no doubt knowing that intensely emotional minutes would follow. Neither of us spoke for a while. Finally I asked, "Have I ever talked to you about transformational moments?"

One evening in mid-August, Liesl and I were on the front porch after dinner as she related an incident that occurred at the Farnsley Center that day. She was working with a young mother and her three-year-old daughter, both victims of a drunken brute, whose first name of Nestor slipped from Liesl before she remembered she shouldn't have named him.

From Liesl's account, the guy had shown up at the Center, demanding to see his wife. When the receptionist told him she couldn't disclose whether the woman was even there or not, and she couldn't have unexpected visitors if she was, he became belligerent and loud. The Center had a twenty-four-hour security person and, when he was signaled there was trouble in the lobby, he came immediately and confronted the man.

"I happened to be passing through the lobby with the three-year-old just as the security officer was trying to reason with the guy," Liesl said. "When he saw the child, he called to her. She cringed, wrapped her arms around my leg and hid her face in my skirt. She was terrified.

"This enraged him even more and he began shouting that anyone who tried to turn his daughter against him would end up being sorry for it. He pointed at me and yelled, 'That includes you, sister.'

"The police had been summoned and when they arrived, his demeanor changed from boisterous outrage to a quiet sullenness, but he kept looking at me. The policemen escorted him out of the building and into their car. I assumed they arrested him, but I don't know."

"Jesus, Liesl," I said. "I don't like the idea of some crazy, violent person threatening you. You have to take something like that seriously."

"I know, Poppa, but he doesn't know my name and I'm safe while I'm at the Center."

"He could probably beat it out of his wife if he wanted to," I responded.

"All she knows me by is 'Liesl'. We don't use last names."
Later that night, in the darkness of my bedroom, I was restless in bed, uneasy that this guy Nestor had threatened Liesl. When I forged an image of him in my mind, it was the image of the Missouri thug I TASERed near Churchill Downs years ago.

Liesl left Louisville for Bloomington and her senior year at IU on August 22. She was majoring in psychology, despite my admonitions that particular field would demand graduate school.

"You'll get all the jobs you want at non-profit organizations, like the Farnsley Women's Center, working for a pittance."

"Or I could go to graduate school in another field," Liesl responded. "An undergrad degree in psychology from IU is considered quite an adequate foundation for admission into most graduate schools and programs." Her widened eyes and tilted head were tacitly asking if I had any more stupid analyses.

Duly admonished, "I'm sorry, Liesl. I keep forgetting you're old enough to know what you're doing and are managing your affairs quite nicely."

In mid-November, Liesl called me from Bloomington to ask if it would be all right if she went home with Alan to Chicago for the Thanksgiving holidays. "But, of course, I'll be home for Christmas," she said.

"Well, I suppose," I said, "though I'm not sure what *I'll* do for dinner that day."

"The Maddoxes always ask us Poppa. It won't be any different this year, just tell them I'll be in Chicago, but that you'd love to come."

Indeed, I was invited and accepted the invitation to the Maddoxes for the traditional Thanksgiving celebration that included a new attendee that year, Urban's partner, Wolfgang Krause. Urban and "Wolfie" had moved to Providence, RI after finishing their terms at the Interpretive Dance Center. They were both dancing for the Festival Ballet of Providence and Urban was teaching dance part time at Brown University. They had a few days off for the holiday break and decided to come to Louisville for some family time.

"We got to see the boys in "Don Quixote" in September," Michael said. "Wolfie danced the part of Basilio."

During the meal and post-dinner bantering, Wolfgang and Urban's affection was subtle, but discernable. The gentle, knowing expression each wore when staring as the other spoke was unmistakable. It was heartwarming for me to see that Madonna and Michael's love of Urban wasn't conditional, that it had trumped any dogmatic religious tripe that condemned homosexuals as sinners.

Liesl called me the Saturday after, relaying what a nice time she was having and how lovely Alan's parents were. "I can tell they like me," she said.

"Do they know you're an atheist?" I asked.

"No, Poppa, it didn't come up. What kind of question is that?"

"I'm just saying that people tend to turn a little cold when they find

174

out someone's a heathen, that's all."

"I believe you sometimes overstate the negativity, Poppa, and I don't think anyone's ever actually referred to us as 'heathens' except you on occasion. Listen, would it be okay if Alan spent some time with us in Louisville over Christmas? Maybe three or four nights?"

"Three or four *nights*?" I wailed.

"Yes. Alan has Louisville on a short list of places where he might want to relocate after he finishes school and I'd like him to get a sense of the city. It won't be until *after* Christmas, maybe on the twenty-seventh or somewhere around there."

"He's thinking about relocating *here*? Damn, Liesl, four or five days are almost a week. That's a long time for—"

"Not four or five, Poppa, *three or four*. Look, should I tell him yes or no?"

No, is what I thought. "Yes, of course."

"Thanks, Poppa. I'll call you in a couple of days. Love you."

"I'll make sure the den is spiffy," I said with sarcasm, but only to the dial tone that resulted from Liesl's quick disconnection.

Liesl finished her penultimate, undergraduate semester on December 17 and drove home that same day in the ragtag, twelve-year-old, 175,000-mile BMW 2002 that had tumbled down the IU student roster, from graduating seniors to underclassmen, four times. That night, she and I sat in front of the fireplace. I led the conversation that went directly to Alan.

"Where does Alan come down on religiosity?" I inquired.

"I think he believes that if you go back far enough," Liesl said, "you'd run into some type of creator or cause, but that it's so far removed from us that it's irrelevant."

"And his parents?"

"He says his parents are serious Episcopalians."

"Ah, Episcopalians," I said, sounding like a prosecutor who had just discovered incriminating evidence. "The bloody Church of England."

"Alan's parents are prudent enough to respect his right to his own way of thought, Poppa."

Again, properly admonished, I tried to diffuse the situation by waxing humorous. "Sorry, Liesl. Not being with you on a daily basis has allowed a degree of righteousness to accumulate in my otherwise benign person. Thanks for the nudge back toward forbearance and please forgive me that trespass."

"You should have been a writer, Poppa," she said as she kissed me on the cheek.

"I know."

Liesl informed me a few days later, "Alan has decided to come the day after Christmas and stay for three nights. We have no firm itinerary, maybe one night with Heather and some of my other high school friends, but that's as far as our planning has gone. We'd like to do something with you, too."

"I don't believe there're any shows or performances that close to Christmas," I said. "Let's just play it by ear. Maybe you can squeeze me in when nothing else is going on."

Liesl and I observed Christmas much as we had since she was a tot. "We did it this way on our very first Christmas," I said, proud of our tradition. I always hung a few colored lights on the indoor fern plant and set a wrapped present for her under it. The only difference was that, by then, she would place a gift for me beneath our understated "tree."

I wanted to open my gift first. Liesl obliged. It was small, with white tissue paper wrapping around a box measuring only about one inch by two by six.

"Can you guess?" she asked.

"I haven't a notion."

The content of the package was totally exposed before I realized what it was, a gold penlight with "Poppa" engraved on the barrel.

"I always see you trying to catch enough light from the stage to read the program during a play or concert," she explained. "I know you like to know exactly where the performance is at any given moment."

"How perfect," I said. "It's one of those things I would never remember to buy for myself. The only time I think about it is during a performance when I sorely wish I had one."

My gift for Liesl was flat and about ten inches by eight. It was wrapped in the same paper I'd used for about the last ten years, a lifelike image of a red-collared golden retriever repeating at six-inch intervals across a solid, Christmas-green background.

She opened the paper to reveal a spiral-bound wall calendar. The bottom pages displayed the days of a particular month under one of eleven photos of her and me through the years, chronologically arranged. The January photo was of us at the baby shower at Mia Smith's house, with my yellow tie matching Liesl's dress. Each ensuing image was about two years further along in time, culminating with a candid shot of Liesl and Alan walking from the driveway across the back yard on his last visit. Liesl reacted as if it was a big deal that I chose a picture of her with Alan for the final image. I was hoping she'd see it that way.

There were occasional other interlopers in the pictures, Michael and Madonna in one, Heather Cassidy in another, Fielder in one too. But for December's final photo to be of her and Alan, well—

"It's so sentimental, Poppa. I love it."

Alan planned to arrive at Four-fourteen on December 26, and when Liesl greeted him, she was reserved, no doubt so that I wouldn't feel any degree of distress from a display of affection. That made me rightfully embarrassed. Alan had placed his luggage in the den and the three of us were settled in the kitchen, when he said, "My professor called this morning to say he liked my paper and that I could consider myself a Master of Landscape Architecture."

"Alan, that's great," Liesl said. I said the same thing, but with a bit less exuberance and whereas Liesl gave him a big hug, I myself merely smiled tightly, nodded economically.

"What will you do now?" I asked.

"Well, my professor said that I could continue this coming semester as a graduate assistant. That gets me to the first of May. After that, I don't know. I'd like to have my own company eventually. I've worked in both residential and commercial landscaping and like them both. The commercial side is more lucrative, but to augment that with some up-scale residential work would be the ideal situation."

"I would think residential landscaping would be easier to break into," I said.

"You're probably right. Residential is mostly what I've done in Bloomington. But I worked for a firm in Chicago for a couple of summers and got to be pretty good friends with the owner's son who also worked there between semesters. The size of those projects made the fees immense and the work long term."

"Well, it's fun to do that dreaming and planning," I said. "You have four months to do that, doing the, uh, spade work, if you will.

"Spade work," I repeated. "You know Spade Work or SpadeWorx, one word with two capitals and ending with an X, could be a great name for a landscaping company," I continued, summoning my marketing communications savvy.

"Yeah," Alan agreed. "It just might."

"I smell a royalty," I said.

Liesl and Alan stayed busy for the next three days, visiting with several of her home-for-the-holidays college friends. All they managed to work me into was a hasty lunch at El Rascal's sandwiched between some ice-skating and a mid-afternoon gathering at Heather Cassidy's house.

"Mr. Foley, have you ever seen the escalator in the Cassidys' house?" Alan asked, when he and Liesl returned to Four-fourteen that evening. "I couldn't believe it. That and the six guest bedrooms, all with a name."

Yes, actually I ran down that escalator stark naked once after screwing Heather's mother in the 'Vive le France' room, is what I thought. "No I haven't, Alan, but Liesl's told me about their house."

Alan wound up extending his stay with us until New Year's Eve. He had again invited Liesl to Chicago for a visit with him and his parents for several days before the spring semester started in mid-January. I wasn't exactly enamored with her for agreeing to go, even though I was thawing a bit to Alan.

"You're starting to spend as much time in Chicago with the Episcopalians as you are at home."

"Poppa, you're so silly."

The icy weeks of early second semester in Bloomington quickly melted into late March and spring break. Liesl called me a week before classes recessed.

"Would it be okay if I go to the Bahamas with Alan and some other friends over the break? We'll be coming through Louisville on the way back, so we could spend the weekend after the trip with you."

"Gosh Liesl, I was hoping we could spend your last spring break together, you know, maybe reenacting some of the 'good old days.'"

"We'll have the whole summer to do that, Poppa. I've sort of committed."

"Sort of?"

"Come on, Poppa, you know. Everyone will be disappointed if I don't go."

"Not quite everyone."

"Poppa."

"Sure, it's okay," I said, practically wallowing. "At least you threw me a bone with the post-Bahamas mini-visit to St. Matthews."

"Right. Alan and I will get back on Saturday the fourth of April."

"You *and* Alan?"

"Poppa, of course."

Since Liesl's stays at Four-fourteen had become fewer and further between, I'd been spending more time with Justine. I often found myself trying to define my relationship with her, but it was like nothing I'd experienced. We weren't in love, but certainly loved each other. Maybe that was what it was like to have an opposite-sex best friend. No, it was more than that. At any rate, I was lucky to have her.

When Alan and Liesl arrived in Louisville after the tropical spring venture, I had the Sunday night planned for them to see the Broadway production of "Jesus Christ Superstar" with Justine and me.

"I've always wanted to see that," Alan said. "Have you seen it, Liesl?"

"No, Poppa thought I was too young at age thirteen to see it."

"Well, you were borderline in age, so I merely played it safe," I said.

"You always played it safe, Poppa. Thanks."

I smiled. A thank-you from Liesl always made me happy.

I'd made reservations after the show at the Three Sixty Restaurant, a turntable venue atop the Jefferson House Hotel, that rotated 360 degrees every ninety minutes, offering a spectacular view of the mile-wide, evening beauty of the shimmering Ohio River. The food and service never quite matched the vista, but the visual opulence always made the evening worthwhile.

"That play was so intense," Alan said as we were seated in the restaurant after the show. "The music was so original and the troupe was truly 'Broadway' in its talent. I wonder how my parents would react to it."

"Most of a Christian ilk probably wouldn't care for it," I said. "It's certainly irreverent to a degree, but as a whole, the story holds fairly true to the yarn of Jesus Christ. It also delineates the good guys from the bad guys quite well, so, other than the irreverence, I myself can't figure why Episcopalians might be offended."

"Don't you believe Jesus existed?" Alan asked.

"You might have just opened the gate," Justine said, at which comment, Liesl half-laughed, uneasily.

"Justine and my beloved granddaughter are afraid of me taking this opportunity to mount the soapbox and pontificate, Alan," I said. "Fear not, ladies. I shall be most economical of answer. Yes, I believe Jesus probably existed. There's too much hubbub written about him to believe otherwise, but he was most likely a deranged nomadic wanderer who was lynched for running around the countryside, adversely affected by desert heat, claiming to be the son of God."

"That's pretty much my take too," Alan said, effectively disarming me and pumping a stream of tension-relief around the table.

"Alan, let's go up the stairs to the Widow's Walk," Liesl urged, "and look again at the river side of the city."

"Where's the Widow's Walk?" he asked.

"Right there," Liesl said, pointing to a narrow, spiral stairwell. "Come on. Will you excuse us?"

"Of course," Justine said, as I remained silent, still surprised at Alan having agreed with my Jesus spiel.

When Liesl and Alan disappeared up the stairwell, feet last, Justine said, "They're such a striking couple, David. They seem very much in love to me."

"I'm thinking he's probably just a passing fancy," I interjected. "Liesl's still so young."

"I don't know about that," Justine said looking at the stairway from which they'd just disappeared. "They look like they're intimate to me. I'm sorry, I just stupidly said out loud what I was thinking."

"It's okay," I said. "You're the only person who could say that without pissing me off."

Justine said nothing, tipping me that she still believed I was wrong in my assessment.

The next morning, I awoke early and got a breakfast organized so that when Alan and Liesl arose, I could expeditiously get the omelets, grits, and biscuits heated and servable with but a few minutes' notice. As I worked in the kitchen, I pondered the pleasure of doing something nice for Liesl, even with Alan around.

She emerged from her room, still capable of looking beautiful upon awakening, just as she had as a toddler. When I thought of what I experienced when catching myself in the mirror in the mornings, I was even more impressed with the beauty of just-arisen youth.

Alan traipsed out of the den yawning. I had to admit that he, too, in his youth, was beautiful.

"Good morning," he said, smiling at his host and hostess. "What a memory last night will be."

"That sounds like something Poppa would say," Liesl said.

"That's not all bad is it?" Alan said, winking at Liesl, but making sure I saw.

When the much-appreciated breakfast was over, I asked, "Have you given any more thought to your business plans, Alan?"

"A little, I think this would be a great place to get started."

"Do you mean *Louisville*?"

"Yes," he said, looking at Liesl as he answered, suggesting that the two youngsters had talked previously about that subject.

He continued. "Louisville seems to be such a vibrant community. It has small-town charm, but a lot of big-city amenities too. I think I might want to come here and start a landscape architecture business. How could I have a better venue than a community that embraced Frederick Olmstead?"

Olmstead was the designer of five of Louisville's parks as well as the tree-lined, beautiful parkways that led to and from them.

"That was over a century ago," I countered, but immediately regretted that I'd wasted some precious ammo by batting away an obviously facetious comment.

"I was just kind of—"Alan started to respond, before I talked over him.

"The business climate here is . . . well . . . stagnant. And every pickup truck in town has one of those cheap grated metal trailers with a riding mower in tow. The competition would be fierce."

"Really?" said Alan. "I saw some data that claimed Louisville is a great incubator for new business, that start-ups are supported by the municipal government *and* the business community." He finished this statement looking at Liesl as if he was soliciting her approval of his performance.

"Oh sure," I said. "You're reading the local chamber of commerce's propaganda. What would you expect them to say? 'Don't come here, you'll fail?'"

"We'll have to talk about this some more, Mr. Foley. You know I respect your opinion."

"If you boys are finished talking business," Liesl said, humorlessly, "I'd like to take a walk through the neighborhood with anyone similarly disposed."

Alan was. I myself was not.

After the stroll through St. Matthews, it was time for Liesl and Alan to return to Bloomington, their classes and job respectively.

"Graduation is May 4, Poppa," Liesl said. "Don't forget."

"The day after Derby Day," I said. "I'll be there."

Three days before IU's commencement, I bought Liesl's graduation gift, a new Honda Civic to replace the clunker BMW.

I was on hand at Churchill Downs on May 3, as Sun Button ran down 32-1 long shot Parkway Sam in the final strides to collect first-place money in the Kentucky Derby. Sun Button's improbable victory, at 12-1 odds, availed me the bittersweet dilemma of having to sign an Internal Revenue Service form before collecting $12,640.20 for correctly predicting the trifecta, the first three finishers of the race in order. That paid for most of Liesl's car.

I made but one stop on the way home from the racetrack that evening, at Estate Liquors in the heart of St. Matthews, where I treated myself to a one hundred ten dollar bottle of 2005 Burgundy in celebration of my good fortune.

The next morning, I was up early and on the road to Bloomington in Liesl's new Civic just before nine o'clock. Still full of myself from the twelve thousand dollar-plus piece of Derby handicapping, I broke into my signature cover of "Duke Of Earl." I wondered how many other seventy-two-year-olds were alive enough, much less cool enough, to be belting out a rendition of the Gene Chandler classic.

The graduation ceremony was to start at two p.m. Alan and I met just outside of Assembly Hall at one-thirty. The sheer number of graduates prevented baccalaureate honorees from walking across the stage individually, but emotion of the convocation was intense and, as with other such transformational moments, my sentiments were not unexpressed.

As the doctoral candidates were introduced, Alan apparently noticed moisture in my eyes when I spotted my granddaughter in a shimmering ocean of black gowns and red stoles. He surprised me by draping his arm around my shoulder, saying, "You can be so proud, Mr. Foley. Liesl is a gem, a finished product, and she loves you so much."

What a sweet thing to say, young fellow, is what I thought. "I *am* proud, Alan, but it hurts so good."

After the ceremony, Alan and I walked out of Assembly Hall into the bright, early May sunshine, both looking to find Liesl amid the now moving sea of black gowns and red stoles. She saw us first and ran to us, greeting me, then Alan.

Alan offered to drive us to dinner, but I insisted that he first take us to the local Big Boy drive-in restaurant's parking lot. I was even specific enough to tell him into which parking spot to pull his car, right next to a shiny new Honda Civic with temporary Kentucky tags.

She loved it!

Chapter Eleven

*"Music should strike fire from the heart of man,
and bring tears from the eyes of woman."*

— LUDWIG VAN BEETHOVEN

I *drove the old* Beamer back to Louisville after an early dinner with Liesl and Alan. She needed to spend another night or two in Bloomington wrapping up her college career before joining me at home. Alan had a few duties remaining at IU as well, then was going to spend a couple of days in Chicago, but he was planning on coming to Louisville for a while after that.

Liesl arrived at Four-fourteen on Tuesday. "I'm not going to do much of anything the rest of this week," she told me. "On Monday, I'll start looking for a job. The Farnsley Center has an opening for a full-time counselor."

"Just prop your feet up and rest on your laurels for a few days," I said. "Can we talk about the Center before you decide? I worry about that place." She didn't answer. I was sure she knew I admired the work the Center did, it was just the exposure to some violent people, including that goddamned Nestor guy, that gave me pause.

We asked Madonna and Michael Maddox to meet us at El Rascal's on Thursday night for a modest family get-together. The Maddoxes were empty nesters except for their sixteen-year-old granddaughter, Bernadette, who accompanied them that evening. Bernadette was the precise image of her mother, Angela, and I awkwardly referred to her as Angela a few times during the meal. Liesl nudged my knee each time I committed that error.

"What's the plan, Liesl?" Michael asked, as he gathered the menus to hand to the waiter after we had ordered.

"Right now, it's just to find a job so I can start thinking about what I want to do in the long-term. I have no idea what that is."

"Well, at twenty-one, you have the luxury of not having to be in a

185

hurry to sort it out," Madonna said, blotting a drop of wayward red wine on her blouse.

"Bernadette, you're a rising junior?" Liesl asked.

"Yes."

"So this is the year you'll probably start looking at colleges. Have you given it any thought?"

"Not a whole lot. But I think I might like IU."

"I loved it," Liesl said, "but it's a huge place. You just have to be ready to deal with that enormity." Liesl made a face after sipping the Sangria she ordered as an experiment. "Whoo, way too sweet!"

During dinner, it was established that Liesl and Bernadette were officially first cousins, once removed, that the Maddoxes had offspring in the four corners of the country, Urban in Rhode Island, Magdalene in southern California, Christian in Washington state and John Paul in Florida, and that Fielder was "the absolute best dog ever."

On our way home, Liesl said, "It's ironic that Bernadette and I were both raised by grandparents. Was there ever any thought given to the Maddoxes taking me in?"

I weighed my words carefully, took my time answering. I'd never been sure if economics or religious politics were the reason the Maddoxes didn't adopt Liesl, but I needed to make sure I said nothing to undercut Liesl's relationship with Madonna and her family.

"Yes, that was considered, but it just wasn't the right time for the Maddoxes to assume the responsibility. Michael had recently lost his job and your mother's death was extremely hard on Madonna," I rationalized.

"No doubt, I'd be a Catholic if that had happened," Liesl said.

"Oh, I don't know, John Paul certainly isn't Catholic, despite the intense indoctrination. Maybe you wouldn't be either."

"Hey, look at the full moon," Liesl said, as it escaped briefly from behind some clouds it had pearlized.

Alan planned to arrive in Louisville from Chicago on Friday, and Liesl asked me if it would be all right for him to stay with us for about a week.

"I guess," I said, with less enthusiasm than I should have displayed.

"I want you to like Alan, Poppa. It's important to me."

"I had to get over a bit of selfishness, Liesl, but just the fact that you like him made me stick with him. He *is* starting to grow on me, a little," I said showing her my thumb and forefinger about an inch apart while winking at her. "You know, any friend of yours—

"I know, 'is a friend of mine,'" she said, not amused.

"Seriously, I'm happy for you, sweetie."

"Thank you, Poppa," she said with a reserved hug, probably indicating she wasn't convinced I was leveling with her. My attitude toward Alan was something I needed to work on.

Alan pulled into the driveway at Four-fourteen the next afternoon in his new vehicle, a six-year-old, Ford pick-up truck.

"What on earth?" Liesl said, wide-eyed.

"What do you think?" Alan asked. "Other than my clothes, an old television, and a cassette player, it's all I own."

"It's really nice," I overstated. "But what do you need a truck for?"

"It's SpadeWorx' first and only piece of equipment," he said.

"So you're taking the plunge into business and you're going to use the name SpadeWorx?" I asked.

"Yes, that is if it's okay with you, Mr. Foley. I really like the name."

"Sure," I said. "Absolutely." Perhaps he was just strategically buttering me up, but I didn't care. I was flattered that he wanted to use the name I had coined.

"Well, I guess congratulations, or maybe condolences, are in order," I said. "Either way, a commemoration is required. Why don't you get settled in, and I'll treat you guys to dinner tonight."

"I was hoping we could do that," Liesl said. "What time?"

"Would seven o'clock give you enough time to refresh and be ready, Alan?" I asked.

"You bet," he said smiling broadly at Liesl.

"I have to run a quick errand," I told them. "I'll be back in about forty-five minutes." I had a spontaneous idea of purchasing a garden spade to commemorate the new business, so I drove to the hardware store, purchased the spade, and hid it in the tool shed after I taped an old green Christmas bow on the handle.

The three of us met in the kitchen after we had showered and dressed. "I would've made plans for El Rascal's tonight," I said, "but I feel like drinking good wine, so I made reservations at the Three-Sixty. I hope that passes muster."

"Perfect," Liesl said. "I love it on the turntable."

"I do too," Alan said. "How about a ride to dinner in the new truck?"

"A pick-up to the Three-Sixty," I mused. "I like it. Hold on for a minute, I said, raising an index finger. "I need to run get something."
I walked to the tool shed where I retrieved the results of my afternoon errand.

"This'll be SpadeWorx' *second* piece of equipment," I said," handing the implement to a surprised Alan. "Don't look so stunned. It's not as if I bought you a backhoe or a cherry-picker."

"What a gracious gift, Mr. Foley. Thank you."

"Poppa, that's so sweet," Liesl said. "It's just like you to come up with something like that."

"I only think of appropriate gifts for those of whom I'm fond," I said, surprised that I'd actually meant it. The sparkle in Liesl's green eyes and the extra-deep dimples formed as she smiled told me she was happy. I was glad I said it.

"Liesl," Alan said. "If I had bought a spade as the first piece of equipment, do you think your grandfather would have gotten me a truck?"

After being seated on the outer edge of the turntable by the tuxedoed maitre d', a white-shirted bus boy clinked ice water into three tall crystal goblets. Intermittent light and shadow were reflecting upon Liesl and Alan's youthful faces, the result of two flickering candles atop the white linen tablecloth. The youngsters' expressions reflected peacefulness, an unmistakable affection for each other. At that moment, I experienced genuine happiness about their relationship for the first time. It was a comforting revelation.

The lights of Louisville's urban landscape appeared as if in a valley below us, providing a soothing sparkle to our gathering. I ordered a bottle of expensive Shiraz, and after the cork-smelling ritual and the sample taste, the waiter filled Liesl's glass, then Alan's, then mine. I waited until the waiter was out of earshot before proposing a toast.

"Here's to the new graduates and the new business. Cheers."

"Cheers," Alan and Liesl responded simultaneously, as our glasses clinked again.

"And here's to you, Poppa," Liesl added, head tilted, gesturing again with her glass. "Thank you for getting me to full-fledged adulthood with most of my wits still about me. Not an easy task with all the distractions and difficulties of the twenty-first century."

"I'll drink to that," Alan said, just in time to help me resist a tear or two. I knew Liesl's appreciation was genuine, and that, coupled with the wine, had me pleasantly abuzz. After the courses of dinner were presented and consumed, and a second bottle of Shiraz was well on its way to emptiness, I asked, "So, Alan, have you decided where to headquarter SpadeWorx?"

"I still think Louisville might be a strategic location," he said, after patting his lips with his white linen napkin.

"Yeah? What's so 'strategic' about Louisville?" I asked, forming quotes with my fingers to surround the word strategic.

"Well, for one thing, it's a very pleasant community, of manageable size, and a guy might leave his mark there more easily than, say, Chicago or Boston. For another, the woman the company's president loves lives there."

"It's hard to fault that reasoning," I said. Then turning to my granddaughter, "I can't believe this is a surprise to you, Liesl. Tell me what you're thinking."

As Liesl spoke, she cast her eyes on the sparkling cityscape below. "I'm thinking SpadeWorx' president's love is returned, and that the woman he's fond of is happy he wants to live in Louisville." Then looking at me. "Near her family."

"Mr. Foley," Alan said.

I interrupted, with the distinct feeling I knew what he was going to say. "I can't help but feeling what you are about to tell me will make me want to forbid you from calling me Mr. Foley after you say it."

Alan continued, unfazed, "Mr. Foley, Liesl and I love each other. With your permission, sir, we'd like to become engaged in the next few months and plan a wedding for next summer."

I stared at Alan. Without turning my head, I moved my eyes to Liesl. I saw her Adam's apple rise and fall. I sent my gaze back to Alan. "My permission?" I asked.

"Yes sir."

I made them wait for a moment or two, then, "I can only assume that you have my granddaughter's permission to ask for *my* permission."

With a smile breaking across his face, Alan said, "I do, sir."

"You two are so young." Again my glance went to Liesl, who widened her eyes to an expression of approval solicitation. She nodded twice, eyes still wide with entreaty.

"You're young, but you're also quite mature," I said. "You're going to wait till next summer?"

"Yes, Poppa, for sure."

I again took my time responding, making sure I didn't say anything in haste I might regret later.

Finally, "In that case, nothing would make me happier." I relished the relief I saw flooding across Liesl's face. "You've always made good judgments and you've always been well grounded," I told her. "So were your parents. They were about the ages of you two when they married and look what they produced," I added, nodding once at my granddaughter.

Then, looking into Alan's eyes, but continuing to speak to Liesl, I said, "I'd also have trepidation if I wasn't sure this was the right guy."

"Poppa," Liesl said as she reached to embrace me at the same time Alan was clasping my hand.

"Thank you, Mr. Foley," he said.

"Well now, what'll it be, Alan?" I said, as I winked at Liesl, but making sure that Alan saw the wink. "Will you be calling me Poppa or David? It can no longer be Mr. Foley."

Alan looked at Liesl. She tilted her head slightly, shrugged her shoulders and her face.

"I think . . . I think, David," he said.

With that pronouncement Alan and Liesl rose and surrounded me, bent downward and embraced me from both sides.

As my inevitable tears began to stream, I set them at ease about the crying.

"It's a lucky man, indeed, who sheds his tears from joy, as I myself mostly have in my lifetime."

As Alan and Liesl settled back into their seats, I said to him, "If, as you said, the only things you own are the truck, a TV, and a CD player, you'll have to make SpadeWorx self-sustaining from its inception, that is, unless you want to let your as-of-the-moment, unemployed wife support you."

"I might need to have a preponderance of grass-cutting jobs to begin with," Alan said, "but I believe I can make it work."

"What if you had an investor?" I asked. "An investor who would front the capital for, say, a year's worth of projected expenses. Wouldn't that take the pressure off having to make your enterprise float from day one?"

"Well, yes," he said.

"What if someone would cough up an investment, or a loan, if you prefer. You could have capital to purchase equipment as it became necessary and still be able to pay yourself a salary. After a year, you could revisit the arrangement and see if it still worked for both of us, I mean, for both *parties*, and then negotiate any changes deemed necessary. I know an investor who could front the equity or float a loan without compromising his financial security."

"Mr. Foley, I don't know what to say," Alan said.

"Begin by saying David, Alan. D-A-V-I–D."

"I'll have to get in the habit," he said. "But I will . . . *David*."

"And don't be so grateful," I said. "If you weren't able to pay yourself a salary, you might have to live with the future in-law, and that might not be such a desirable situation. I'd love for you to be in the same zip code, but not at the same address"

"Thank you regardless, David," Alan said, "but I apologize for being so grateful."

Liesl and Alan found what they considered an ideal apartment for him, and he signed a year's lease for a second-floor duplex in the Crescent Hill section of Louisville, within a couple of miles of Four-fourteen. Alan and I had come to an agreement about SpadeWorx financing. He felt more comfortable floating a loan rather than issuing stock.

The essence of the arrangement was that I'd lend SpadeWorx a total of sixty thousand dollars, of which twenty thousand would be immediately forthcoming. The other forty thousand would come in increments of five thousand on the first day of each of the following eight months. Repayment wouldn't begin until the first anniversary of the loan.

Upon an official, albeit modest, closing of the financial arrangements, Alan found a vacant, twenty-two hundred square-foot, rectangular building in the inner city Old Louisville area, and signed a one-year lease in the name of SpadeWorx. He keyed on large jobs and his low overhead helped facilitate very competitive pricing.

My loan enabled the company to purchase a tractor with attached, trailing mowers. This helped Alan to bid on and secure a contract to mow the massive expanse of grass on the Presbyterian Seminary property. He then parlayed his "expertise" in seminary mowing, competitive bidding, and a likable personality into a contract with the Southern Baptist Theological Seminary.

"Damn," I said, upon learning of the two contracts. "All those Christian dollars rolling in."

Liesl, meanwhile, took permanent employment with the Farnsley Women's Center with no consultation with me. I didn't complain, but it was a kernel of worry with which to contend.

"It doesn't pay that much," she said, "but I like the work. It's very rewarding."

As autumn set in, I felt its tug of melancholy a little less than usual. I surmised this was because of what was in store for the Foleys when spring returned, full courses of wedding festivities and the bittersweet emotion that transformational experiences always served up.

Nevertheless, the annual ritual of the ginkgo's leaf divestiture never occurred without it stoking a passion within me. During the afternoon of the ginkgo's shedding cycle, I stationed a chair in the yard from which I could see the full height of the tree, and watched as the Oriental fans sped to earth.

I thought about Patrick and Kathryn, both of whom I still missed terribly, two decades after their deaths. I contemplated Floyd and Elizabeth Rausch, who in their later years, couldn't enjoy their grandchildren. It would have been better for them, and for the Maddoxes, had Floyd and Elizabeth passed the way these leaves were passing, before they had emaciated.

Late in November, Alan purchased a snowplow and the adaptor necessary to use it on the company pickup, hoping that the revered *Farmers Almanac* was correct in its prediction of "unusually heavy snowfall" for Jefferson County, KY. Whether the Almanac had lucked out, or it had the proper tools and methodology to predict the weather months in advance, was unimportant to Alan. The prediction was accurate and SpadeWorx had another revenue stream.

Deep in December, Liesl and I hosted the traditional, understated Foley Christmas with an additional partaker, Alan. That tripled to six from two, the number of wrapped packages covertly placed under the light-strung, indoor fern that had been serving as the Foley Christmas tree year after year.

Liesl gave Alan a green enamel business card holder with an old-fashioned, rotary-blade lawn mower embossed on the side. For me, she had a tie clasp that was a miniature gold violin and bow.

I had a contemporarily styled purse with brightly colored, violet, blue, and yellow pansies for Liesl. For Alan, I'd purchased a calendar, the images of which were twelve wheelbarrows from different parts of the globe and different points in time.

He presented me with an eight-piece wine kit, complete with a foil cutter, drip stop-ring, and bottle seal, in addition to a foolproof corkscrew. For Liesl, he had a very small, but elegant, diamond engagement ring.

I myself beamed, but Liesl actually shrieked her approval. "Alan, I can't remember ever hearing a similar sound emanating from Liesl in twenty-three years. I think it's safe to assume she likes it."

After the holidays, Alan and Liesl decided to set the wedding date for Friday, June 7 at seven-thirty in the evening. The ceremony would be held outdoors at historic Locust Grove, near Zachary Taylor National Cemetery where Patrick and Kathryn were buried. A reception would follow at the facility's Visitor Center.

Locust Grove was over two hundred-years old, and was the one-time home of William Croghan and his wife Lucy Clark Croghan. Lucy was a sister to William Clark of Lewis and Clark expeditionary fame, and of George Rogers Clark, regarded as the founder of Louisville. The latter Clark lived at Locust Grove for the final years of his life.

I always regretted I wasn't present for the run-up to Liesl's parents' wedding, having at the time resided in Boston, but I had sensed from afar the wonderful crescendo they experienced in the months and weeks before their marriage. I was determined to savor that exhilarating period this time around.

Upon learning of Liesl's betrothal, both Mia Smith and Madonna Maddox were intent upon having an engagement party for the couple. "I think I only want one engagement party," Liesl said. "Maybe an alternative would be a wedding shower."

Madonna agreed to the shower for Liesl closer to the wedding date, while Mia would host the engagement party. I hoped it was obvious to Liesl how much I relished the attention drawn by the wedding plans, and that I'd become very comfortable with the upcoming union.

The initial event of the soon-to-be-Martins' marriage festivities, was the early-February engagement party at the Smiths' house. This was the first opportunity I had to meet Alan's parents. I surprised myself by liking both Phillip and Patricia Martin. My surprise, no doubt, was due to my low expectations, that likely stemmed from learning that the senior Martins were "serious Episcopalians."

I had envisioned them as Floyd and Elizabeth Rausch "lite." Instead, I found both of Liesl's soon-to-be in-laws engaging and charming.

Philip was quick with a smile and seemed content listening rather than expounding. Patricia was conservatively dressed and one of those fiftyish women so attractive one had to wonder just how beautiful she must have been thirty years ago.

"I understand you're retired, David," Philip said, "and that you've been so for quite awhile. You must be good at it."

"Yes, and getting better all the time," I said. Then seriously, "I was fortunate to be able to do it at a relatively young age. It was necessary to be able to raise Liesl."

"I can tell you were good at that, too," said Patricia Martin, as she jestingly hoisted her wine glass toward me, making Liesl blush. "She's so expressive and captivating," Patricia continued, now looking at Liesl. "I've never met a young person so poised. We just love her."

"Thank you," I said, putting an arm around my granddaughter. "She had wonderful expression the day she was born."

Alan and Liesl had invited friends from both Chicago and their days in Bloomington to the party. I tried to meet and speak with each of them. I was reminded of the good feelings I experienced about the friends of Patrick and Kathryn I had met at their wedding, and, sadly, again at their respective funerals.

April in Kentucky was always a prelude for the sporting and social event of the year in the Bluegrass State, the Kentucky Derby, contested for well over a century on the first Saturday in May. This year, however, it also portended the marriage of Miss Liesl Foley to Mr. Alan Phillip Martin.

For the previous twelve years, I'd been extended the opportunity from Churchill Downs to purchase Kentucky Derby tickets due to my membership in the track's Turf Club. Most years I chose to avoid the crowds, but that year, even though I had attended the previous Derby, I thought it would be nice to have Alan and Liesl, along with Madonna and Michael, join Justine and me trackside. It would be a festive way to get the month before the wedding off to a great start.

In the five-million dollar featured Derby, Pony Keg pulled a mild upset by getting up in the final strides to nip Launch Director at the wire for the garland of roses. None of my guests seemed to realize the significance of having seen a record Derby time established, as Pony Keg covered the mile-and-a-quarter distance in one minute, fifty-nine seconds flat, eclipsing Secretariat's decades-old record.

Liesl had a two-dollar win ticket on Pony Keg and when Alan asked her why she had bet on him, she confessed, "He looked so sad in the paddock. I just felt sorry for him."

"That's as good a way to handicap as any," I said.

Madonna's bridal shower for Liesl was the week after Derby, and it was a ladies-only event. Because the out-of-town Maddox daughters couldn't come for the shower and the wedding, it was modestly but genuinely attended by Mia Smith, Heather Cassidy, Justine, Bernadette and Lourdes Maddox, and Patricia Martin. I dropped in unannounced just as coffee and cake were being served, hoping that none of the guests would object to my presence.

"I haven't been to a shower since Liesl was a week old," I said. "I just had to get to one more before my time was up."

I left a few minutes after I finished my beverage and dessert, despite the urgings of the ladies for me to stay.

The wedding rehearsal was on Thursday evening, the night before the wedding, and Alan's parents hosted a dinner after the dry run at the elegant Three-Sixty, atop the Jefferson House. There were about thirty attendees, approximately half of which were Alan's relatives or friends from Chicago. The other half seemed to be of the Maddox clan, all members of which having had descended upon Louisville for the weekend celebrations.

Justine and I sat with Alan's parents, under glass, rotating atop the city, with excellent wines being served by willing waiters. I was somewhat buzzed from the wine, but altogether drunk with the moment. All about me were either people I loved or people I liked. My granddaughter was happy and ready for the new phase that tomorrow's events would launch.

"I'm fortunate to realize how lucky I am," I said to Justine.

"I haven't the foggiest idea what you're talking about," she said, her head tilted and eyes squinting.

"Hell, you know, Justine. So many people don't know how lucky they are. Christ, if you're going to be born, what are the odds of you being born a human on a plush, Goldilocks planet like Earth, in an economically successful country? Think about how many unfortunate simple and complex organisms there are in the cosmos. Somewhere, right now, some poor snake is in the clutches of a mongoose and a mouse is chomping on some unfortunate spider. And that's just here on earth!"

Liesl and Alan came by our table just as I'd gotten my weighty bit of philosophy out in the open. "When you and your father leave tonight, you do the driving," Justine said to Liesl, touching her arm and widening her eyes for emphasis.

So Liesl drove the car back to Four-fourteen after the dinner, with me in tow. "I just can't believe June seventh is here," she said, as we pulled into the driveway. "These last six months have just flown by."

"I can't believe June seventh is here either," I said, pulling the knot out of my bowtie and unfastening the top button of my shirt. "These last twenty-three years have just flown by. I suppose my biggest mistake was to blink."

Liesl took my limp hand in hers and rubbed it on the soft skin of her cheek.

"After tomorrow, I'll be an empty-nester," I said. "I'll be living alone for the first time in nearly a quarter-century."

"That *is* a big deal," she said, putting her hand on my knee. "But at least I'll only be ten minutes away, and not even that far in my heart, Poppa."

I awoke Friday morning feeling rested, hardly a wonder. It was already nine-twenty, and I'd slept for almost ten-and-a half hours. I was grateful to Liesl for insisting that I take a liquid antacid before retiring the previous night. As I made my way down the stairs and into the breakfast room, I could hear her hair blower whirring from her bedroom. I sipped my first cup of coffee and was beginning to contemplate the prior evening's activities when Liesl came down the stairs.

"Good morning," she said, as she breezed into the kitchen. "I'm glad you slept late. We have a big day ahead of us."

"I'll say."

"Wasn't last night just great?" she asked. "I had a ball."

"I did too," I said, buttering the piece of toast she had slipped onto my plate. "The more I'm around the Martins, the more I like them. They seem very genuine and not at all righteous, as many people of their religious ilk are."

"Really, Poppa?" Liesl said, shaking a bottle of orange juice. "I'm so glad you feel that way. It means a lot to Alan and me that our families like each other. He phoned me this morning and told me that his parents enjoyed your company as well. They said they were surprised and delighted that you didn't wear your atheism on your sleeve, as many people of your irreligious ilk do."

"They said that?"

"Uh huh."

"Uh, I'll be darned. Have you heard the weather forecast?" I asked, moving on. "It sure looks cloudy out there now."

"The sun's supposed to pop out late this afternoon and a nice evening is forecast," Liesl said. "I have a few errands to run, Poppa, some last minute things I need for the trip. Can we have lunch together here at about twelve-thirty or so?"

"Sure. Is there anything I can do for you today? I think I'm in pretty good shape as far as being prepared for tonight goes, so I have a little extra time if you need me for anything."

"I don't think so. I have a hair appointment at three-thirty and I'm planning on going straight to Locust Grove from there, but keep your cell phone on just in case."

"What about something to eat before the ceremony?" I asked, refilling my coffee cup.

"Justine was kind enough to offer to bring a few sandwiches to the dressing room for Heather and me and Alan and his dad. She's going to bring one for you too, in case you don't eat something here before you leave."

Heather Cassidy was Liesl's maid of honor and Alan had chosen his dad as best man, the wedding's only groomsman. My role was to escort Liesl up the aisle between the temporary, white-backed chairs to the platform in the front of Locust Grove's East Garden.

Liesl had decided to have live piano music played during the marriage ceremony and Justine had arranged for the Associate Professor of Keyboard Studies at the Phillips Conservatory of Music to play. I myself had never met an Associate Professor of Keyboard Studies, but I was sure he'd have no trouble making me cry like a cloud as I walked my granddaughter up the aisle to give her away.

When I learned Liesl had selected Mozart's "Piano Concerto No. 21" for the march, the most beautiful composition ever, in my opinion, I suspected Justine had a hand in the choice of pieces. She knew how I felt about that composition, and it would be just like her to help inject an overdose of sentiment at "crunch time."

I decided it would be more than I could manage to keep my poise with the notes of that beautiful melody wafting into my ears, rolling through my cerebral cortex, and exiting my eyes in the form of tears. Jesus! I could actually pass out.

Searching my archives of CDs, I came up with an old disk of classical music containing "No. 21." Any time Liesl wasn't in the house that week, I had it blaring. The idea was to get used to it so that its effect on me during the march would be neutralized.

I found that the morning newspaper couldn't divert my attention from the significance of what was going to take place later that evening. I was actually going to escort Liesl in a procession to meet Alan, then, literally and figuratively, hand her over to him in front of about one hundred-twenty witnesses.

Liesl arrived home at twelve-fifteen, all missions accomplished. I had chicken salad sandwiches and vegetable soup ready for the *Last Lunch*.

Afterward, Liesl was busy upstairs as I sat in the front porch swing. The expected breakthrough of the sun had occurred a couple of hours earlier than forecasted, and weather conditions were removed from the worry list.

My eyes lost focus as I thought about Patrick and Kathryn, what a pity it was that they and Liesl had been robbed of this day together. I remembered the many events my granddaughter had celebrated, perhaps endured, without her parents. "Sweet Liesl," I whispered, as I swallowed with difficulty.

I refocused and gazed out over the grounds of Four-fourteen. Alan had taken the foundation I'd given the landscape and added a few professional touches, such as enclosing several small flowerbeds with brick borders and placing a clay birdbath in the back yard. The lot was a source of pride for me, from which I drew immense pleasure.

As I admired the foliage and the privacy of the lot, I hoped Alan and Liesl would choose to live there after my death. I made a mental note to express that wish to them sometime soon.

Shortly after three o'clock, Liesl appeared on the front porch, carrying a huge shopping bag. "I'm heading over to the hairdresser's," she said, dropping the bag and angling her head to attach her earrings.

"What's in the bag?"

"It's my veil. The hairdresser will put it on me as she finishes styling my hair. Justine is bringing my dress"

"Do you mean you'll be driving to the wedding wearing those jeans, that tee shirt, and the veil?"

"Sure," Liesl said. "Most brides do it that way."

"Will the photographer be there?"

"Yes, he's supposed to be there at five o'clock."

"Well, tell him to get a shot of you with the veil over the tee and the jeans. I'm serious."

I could see by Liesl's expression that my stab at levity didn't keep her from realizing I was beginning to have a tough moment.

"Are you going to be okay tonight?"

"Oh yes," I replied. "I've sworn to myself that I'll control my emotions, for the most part anyway."

"So I don't have to worry about you not showing up?" she asked as she hugged me.

That caused me to laugh, easing the fervency of the moment. "I'll be there," I promised. "If I didn't show, it would only temporarily delay this inevitable, torch-passing, guard-changing, mind-altering, fear-striking, goddamned, transformational event."

"Poppa, you're so silly."

"See you there," I said as I shooed her off, flipping the back of my hand at her.

I began my pre-wedding regimen early, so I wouldn't be rushed and so that I could tend to all the extra hygiene/grooming chores a seventy-three-year-old man wouldn't perform on himself every day, but needed on the day of his granddaughter's wedding; details like rinsing my ears with hydrogen peroxide to remove wax, soaking my still hard feet and ever-dangerous toes in Epsom salts long enough for my nails to soften to the degree where they wouldn't bleed or break the toenail clippers when I trimmed them, rubbing my rock-hard calluses with pumice, and using the battery-powered ear/nose hair trimmer Liesl had suggestively bought for me a few years back.

Wanting to look as well as my timeworn countenance would allow, from the neck down, anyway, I had purchased a charcoal-gray, three-piece suit. I still had the yellow tie I had worn to Mia Smith's baby shower when Liesl was about ten days old. I even splashed on a bit of time-honored Old Spice aftershave lotion, but only after checking to see if the bottle didn't bear a twentieth-century expiration date. It bore no such notice and smelled just like it used to, so I gave myself a little extra shot. I thought it might be interesting to see if anyone noticed.

I was tempted to wear my signature argyle socks, but thought better of it, yet not deferring until I had a pair on and had checked them out in the mirror. Hmmm, maybe not, I thought as I raised my pants legs.

I arrived at Locust Grove at six o'clock sharp and was hustled into the visitor center by the photographer's assistant for a few pre-ceremony pictures of various combinations of Justine, Mia, Madonna, Heather, me, and, of course, Liesl.

My granddaughter was statuesque, radiant in her dress and veil. She hadn't allowed me to see her wearing them beforehand. I wasn't going to speak, because saying anything would cause me to begin to cry, perhaps uncontrollably. Knowing that, Liesl put her index finger to her lips and shook her head once. I put my index finger to my lips and nodded once. I was back in control after a few clicks of the shutter.

Alan and Liesl wanted Phillip and me to greet the guests as they arrived, so we positioned ourselves at the entrance to the visitor center a few minutes after seven and began receiving guests and pointing the way to the East Garden.

One of the first to arrive was Sheila Cassidy, who I'd only encountered a few times since the night I ran naked through her house in argyle socks some fourteen years earlier.

"Sheila," I said as we hugged, she somewhat aggressively. "How come I got old and you didn't?"

"Sweet David," she said, fixating on my eyes while holding one of my hands in both of hers, touching it to her midsection. "I've missed you. Will I see you on the dance floor at the reception?"

"How's Ansel?" I asked, pulling our three hands away from her tummy.

She sighed. "He's still out of the country most of the time." Then, with a sparkle in her eyes, "Mmmm, what *is* that fragrance you're wearing?"

I shuffled Sheila along, forcing her to give way to Michael Maddox, his seven grown children, and granddaughter Bernadette.

"Oh dear Maddoxes, thank you for being here," I said. "It'll be a happier evening for Liesl with all of you here."

At that moment, a black Chevy Tahoe pulled into the semi-circle at the entrance to the Visitor Center. An unemotional, thirty-something woman in a dark suit and sunglasses emerged quickly from the right front door. Though surprised, I knew exactly what was happening. Sophie Burnett slid across the back seat and out the door, followed by another Ray-Banned, dark-suited person. With the T-woman at her side, Sophie approached me.

"Sorry, Mr. Foley. It was better for security if I didn't announce I was coming. I can't wait to see Liesl."

"Oh, Sophie. Wait till I tell her you're here. She'll be thrilled."

"My mother said to tell you 'Hello,' Mr. Foley."

As the stoic Secret Service agents escorted Sophie toward the East Garden, Samantha and Idelle McCoy approached me at my post, in the company of a young man, who could have been an agent himself, had he worn the proper shades. I erupted when I saw them.

"Dr. McCoy, and the woman who made that title possible," I said hugging them both at once.

The McCoys had moved to a downtown condominium and we didn't see them much those days. Samantha was poised, stately. As I reflected on how far she'd traveled, I couldn't keep from a degree of sentimentality.

"Mr. Foley, this is my fiancé, Spencer Albright," she said.

"Oh, sweet Samantha, congratulations. And you too, Idelle."

"Spencer's a doctor, too," Idelle said with obvious pride.

"Really?" I reacted. "Do husband/wife physicians ever have time to see each other?"

"I'm a dermatologist, and Spencer's a psychiatrist," Samantha said. "That's about as good as it gets for scheduling if you're in medicine."

"Samantha, you always had things pretty well figured out," I said. "I'm so happy for you. Please let me spend some time with you guys at the reception."

"I'd like that," said Spencer. "I just *have* to analyze the 'piece of work' Samantha has talked about so often."

I froze for an instant until I saw the rascality in Spencer's eyes and Samantha give him a mock shove.

"You had me there for a minute, Spencer," I admitted. "I thought maybe you were looking for a busman's holiday tonight."

It was seven twenty-five, time for Philip and me to join our respective offspring for the start of the ceremony. It would be a short procession, Heather, then Liesl and I. I knocked on the door, walked into the makeshift dressing room set aside for Heather and Liesl. When I entered, Heather said, "Well, it's time for me to line up out there." She gave Liesl an affectionate hug and walked out the door.

"Sophie's here," I said.

"You're kidding," Liesl replied. "That's wonderful."

"You know, there's still time to back out," I teased. "I can improvise some excuse and give you time to clear the grounds."

"Poppa, you're so silly."

Suddenly Liesl began the quietest of sobbing. "I'm just so happy, Poppa."

"I understand, sweet girl, but this is going to be fun. Once you see the faces of all those loved ones out there, you'll be fine." Looking at my watch, "Hey, there's a young guy out there waiting for us. Take a deep breath."

Liesl complied, took another. "Let's go, Poppa."

We emerged from the visitor center and, behind Heather, walked down a path formed by linear rows of dogwoods, baby magnolias, hydrangea, and roses of Sharon, until we came to a square clearing behind the seated guests in the East Garden. At the far side of the clearing, separated from our processional by two sections of fifteen rows of white-draped temporary chairs, stood Alan and Phillip Martin at the left hand of the presiding Justice of the Peace. Four dark green holly trees formed a beautiful backdrop behind the groom and his witness.

I led Liesl to a halt, just in back of the last row of chairs as Heather proceeded up the aisle way. The Associate Professor of Keyboard Studies began to play Mozart's "Piano Concerto No. 21" as I looked at my granddaughter who was beaming at all the happy faces that were turning, looking backward, beaming at her. I myself beamed. Liesl took my arm and we took the first steps between the rows of admirers toward Alan.

Chapter Twelve

"Pity, pity, too late."

— LUDWIG VAN BEETHOVEN

After the wedding and reception, Liesl and Alan spent Friday and Saturday night in their apartment in Crescent Hill. Alan had renewed the lease for another year, and the second-floor duplex was now home for Mr. and Mrs. Alan P. Martin for at least that time frame.

They had asked me to drive them to the airport on Sunday morning, from where they'd fly to Montreal for a couple of days. Following, they were to motor by bus to the Laurentian Mountains, north of Montreal, and honeymoon for a week at the Glacier Lake Inn, a recreational lodge on Lake Ouimet in St. Jovite.

I picked up the newlyweds Sunday morning at six forty-five. "Thanks for chauffeuring us" Alan said, after we loaded their baggage into the trunk. "We hate to make you to get up so early."

"It's okay, I don't mind rolling out to help you guys. Actually, I have to get up early again tomorrow for a physical at St. Anthony. My new internist ordered a complete examination. My old GP, Bill Regan, retired in December, so I have to break in a new physician as to how I like things done."

"What's this lucky fellow's name?" Liesl asked.

"Bridget Tyler."

"A woman, no less," Liesl said. "Did Dr. Regan recommend her?"

"No, Samantha McCoy referred me to her some months ago, but I wanted to wait until after the wedding. I believe they were med school classmates."

"A young person," Liesl said.

"Yes, young medics are easier to indoctrinate than the older ones who get set in their ways, and women understand me much better than men do."

"Poppa, you're so silly."

"She insisted that I submit to a complete physical so she 'can get to know' me, as she put it."

"And you agreed to that?"

"It makes sense at my age, don't you think?"

"Yes, I do. I'm proud of you, Poppa."

I hopped out of the car when we arrived at the outside baggage check-in, and gave a hug to Liesl and Alan at the same time.

"It used not to be so difficult to hug my entire family," I said, "but I'm glad the clan has grown. Have a great time, and give the old man a call or two."

"We will Poppa," Liesl said. "Behave yourself at the physical tomorrow."

The next morning I reported to the West Wing of St. Anthony, where the hospital's testing and diagnostic facility was housed. After registering and signing a few releases that would let any medic off the hook who might accidentally kill or maim me, I was shown to a dressing room where I was instructed to put on a hospital gown and come back to a seat in a waiting room with all the other herded sheep in hospital gowns who were also there to be poked and pricked and probed.

It was only the thought of the look on Liesl's face when I'd have to tell her I'd backed out of the physical, that kept me seated, resigned to the humiliation.

A chest X-ray was the last procedure and, once it was over, I admitted to myself that the two-and-a-half hours weren't nearly as bad as had been my dread of them.

That afternoon, I received a call from Bridget Tyler's nurse saying that the young medic wanted me to come to see her Tuesday, the very next day.

"What's that all about?" I asked.

"I don't know, Mr. Foley," said the nurse. "Dr. Tyler just asked me to make the appointment."

"Something tells me I'll have a great time in that meeting," I said.

It pleased me that Bridget Tyler knocked on the door of the exam room before entering. Most of the old boys, as I termed MDs over fifty, often failed to display such courtesy. They behaved like unaware, spoiled brats who thought they were anointed, and seemed to believe mores of etiquette didn't apply to them; etiquette such as not being chronically late, or at least apologizing when they were.

"Hello Mr. Foley," she said, her white lab coat billowing slightly as she swirled to face me after closing the door

"Hello, Bridget. To what do I owe the honor of this visit?"

"Well, there are several spots on your lung that showed up on the film that bear some follow up. It could be nothing, but we need to confirm that."

"Well, I'll be damned," I said, hesitating a moment before adding, "I'll bet I'm just going to love your confirmation process."

"It's a PET scan, somewhat inconvenient, not painful or anything."

"How inconvenient?" I asked.

"About two hours," she said, focusing her brown eyes on mine over the narrow reading glasses she used to read my charts. "We really need to get this done."

"Yeah, I know. I'm just giving you a hard time. Does everything else look okay?"

"Yes, very much so. Other than that one hitch, you're practically a poster boy."

Ordinarily, hearing that beautiful young woman with the sparkling dark eyes make the poster boy analogy would have made me wish I was thirty, but today it didn't, probably because I was a little concerned about the "spots" on my lung.

"The receptionist will get a few convenient times from you on the way out and schedule something over in the West Wing. Before you leave the diagnostic area that day, I'll drop by to see you."

The receptionist and I overlaid the PET scanner's availability with my schedule and came up with the morning of June 14.

"I'll probably show up," I said as she handed me an appointment card.

I rose early on Friday the fourteenth and drank a cup of hot water, which was all the PET Scan prep sheet allowed me to ingest. I arrived at the West Wing at seven sharp, less crusty than usual because I was a bit concerned with what might result from the diagnostic procedure.

A hospital gown was probably the least desirable of any wardrobe item, unless one considered shackles and manacles wardrobe items, but even the insult of having to wear that gown wasn't enough to elicit any of my usual verbal cynicism. A nurse injected me with a dye, after which I lay in wait, mentally preparing to be intercalated into a cylindrical tube for an ultimate show-all session.

After an hour, I was escorted to the scan room where it was noticeably cold. An aide spread a heated cover over me as I lay face up on an automated slab. I thought of myself in the future, on the ultimate slab, stiff, and wearing a toe tag.

The room was barren, the lighting a languid green. Technicians were courteous when they had to interrupt their conversations to give me instructions, but always quickly resumed talking to each other about extraneous things, as if I weren't there. While not offensive, such treatment made me feel lonely.

As the slab slowly, inexorably dragged me into the cylinder, I felt sorry for myself for having to be mechanically searched for a dreaded malady. An internal section of the cylinder began to turn, gain speed, and spin circuitously, loudly. It sounded like jet engines upon takeoff from inside the cabin. My body was tightly strapped, so I could move only my eyes.

Soon enough, it began to end, the noise and motion abating ever so gradually, at last to a stop. The slab with me on it was extracted from the robotic duct.

"That's it, Mr. Foley," said a tech. "You did great."

After I put my street clothes on, in the prep room, I was surprised when Bridget Tyler knocked on the door, entered. Skipping any perfunctory pleasantries, "Mr. Foley, I see something disturbing on the film, an enlarged lymph node."

"And?"

"And that could indicate some serious problems."

"Problems?"

"Maybe some type of lung disease metastasizing. I don't want to

speculate, but I don't like the way this looks. I want you to have a bronchoscopy."

"More fun, I'm sure," I said.

"Once again, more inconvenient than anything else. It's a scope
with a camera inserted down the throat and threaded to the lungs. We'll
see those spots much better that way and we can take samples with the
attached forceps for a biopsy. It sounds like an ordeal, but there's enough
anesthesia administered to make it painless and unremembered."

"Are we ever going to have a definitive diagnosis, or should I keep
expecting more procedures?"

Tyler squinted, shook her head. "I understand your frustration, but
what you've undergone so far have been diagnostics designed to rule out
certain conditions under most circumstances, not definitively identify a
specific problem. We haven't been able to rule out something serious as
yet, but the bronchoscopy and a biopsy will shed some light for us."

"What's the worst I can expect?"

The young internist didn't hesitate. "Lung cancer."

Oh, fuck, is what I thought. "The damned C-word," I said, surprised at myself for not feeling afraid. It was the dread of telling Liesl
that pressurized my chest as I sat on the padded examining table, legs
hanging in front of me, ankles crossed.

"When do we do the procedure?"

"As soon as possible, the receptionist will schedule it for you."

"How about this Thursday, the twentieth, Mr. Foley?" the receptionist said five minutes later.

I had invited the Martins for a cookout at Four-fourteen on Tuesday, June 18, the day after they returned from Canada. "Come on," I
coaxed. "Let's take advantage of the yard in the summertime. I'll ask Justine."

I prepared the entire meal outdoors, pork tenderloin, fried green
tomatoes, brown rice, and asparagus. After dinner, we all sat in the back
yard enjoying coffee and ice cream. Liesl told us about the seaplane ride
they chartered on Lake Ouimet while Alan had the Martins' honeymoon well documented with dozens of photos.

Justine was first to leave, and Alan and Liesl were helping me get the dishes inside and scraped. I was struggling not to think of my upcoming procedure and to keep the conversation flowing when I dropped a wine glass in front of the sink. It bounced off an area rug, flipping over to impact the side of its bowl on the tile. The glass shattered across the floor, three or four large pieces and scores of tiny, twinkling diamonds.

"Goddamn it," I thundered, after which loss of control, Liesl and Alan were awkwardly silent.

After a time, with Alan outside retrieving the last of the dinnerware, Liesl said, "Is anything bothering you Poppa? You seem a bit preoccupied."

"No, I'm just tired. The last few nights I was tossing a bit and didn't sleep well."

"Any reason?"

"Just some aching in my shoulder. Probably the routine arthritis that visits us old folks."

"You should take ibuprofen or something when that bothers you."

"I will if it happens again tonight. I'm thinking it'll go away, for a while anyway."

"Okay. Good night, Poppa."

Liesl's expression was sad, her eyes searching, telling me I hadn't convinced her everything was hunky-dory.

I called Justine on Monday and misinformed her that I needed to have a precautionary colonoscopy on Thursday and hoped she could drive me to St. Anthony's that morning and pick me up in the afternoon. She agreed to drive me both ways.

When the morning arrived, I complained to Justine on the way downtown. "I'm spending too damn much time in hospitals. First the physical, now the butt probe. Hopefully this will be the last trip for awhile."

"Are you sure you don't want me to go in with you?" Justine asked as she eased the car into the semi-circular drop-off point of the diagnostic wing.

"What do you want to do, watch? Of course not."

"I figured as much, Mr. Big Stuff."

"They told me I'd be out of here about one-thirty. I'll give them your cell number."

"I'll keep the phone with me," she said.

I leaned to her side of the front seat and turned her chin toward me with my index finger. I kissed her on the lips for a few seconds rather than offering my usual peck on the cheek.

"What's that all about?" she said.

"I just appreciate you driving me around today, that's all."

After the familiar routine of signing in, donning the gown, pulse taking, temperature and blood pressure checking, an anesthesiologist came into the prep room and instructed a nurse to begin an intravenous drip.

"I'm going to give you an injection, Mr. Foley. You'll feel a bit of warmth, and wake up in about an hour in the recovery room, procedure over."

"You know, Doc, when I was in college, I had a couple of friends who were trying to become anesthesiologists. All the other guys called them the "gas men." I'll bet you don't use a lot of gas anymore, do you?"

"Actually, some types are still used, usually in combination with an intravenous anesth—"

That's the last I remembered hearing, though later I was sure I recalled being transferred to a gurney and getting pushed down the hall.

"Mr. Foley? Mr. Foley, do you think you can sit up?" a nurse said in the recovery room.

I blinked several times and she came into focus. I didn't answer, but sat up as she had requested. She raised the head of the bed to meet the angle of my back.

"Is that about right?

I nodded. "What time is it?"

"It's ten forty-five. Do you care if I open these curtains?"

I shook my head and then squinted as the sunshine bolted into the room.

"I'll be back in a bit. Just push this button if you need anything," she said, placing a thick cable with a red thumb button next to me. "Dr. Tyler will be in too."

I dozed back off and was awakened by a different nurse. "Mr. Foley, Mr. Foley, will you take this pill for me?"

I retrieved the med from her hand and a glass of water she offered me from a tray next to my bed. I winced as I swallowed.

"That's it. Good job. I know it's a little uncomfortable swallowing with your throat still a bit raw."

A bit raw? It felt like somebody rammed a goddamned inch-and-a-half garden hose down my throat. "What time is it?"

"It's eleven-ten."

"Hello, Mr. Foley," said Bridget Tyler as she entered the room. "Are you doing okay?"

I wanted to shrug, but I nodded.

"I want you to stay here for another hour or so, then come see me in the morning. You'll be able to remember things a little better when the anesthesia has worn off. They'll give you an appointment card when you leave the unit."

"What did you find out?"

"I won't know anything until very late today or first thing in the morning after the biopsy report gets to me. Your appointment will be late morning if that's okay."

"Sure."

"See you then," said the young medic, putting her hand on my shoulder.

"Would you like anything to drink, Mr. Foley?" asked the nurse as Tyler walked out of the room.

"No thanks," I said, frowning and rubbing my throat.

"Is someone meeting you?"

"Oh I forgot. Can you call this number and tell Ms. Colgate that I'm ready to be picked up. She thinks I had a colonoscopy. Let's keep it that way."

"I won't say anything except that you're ready to go," said the nurse. As I waited for Justine in a wheelchair next to the revolving door near the pick-up circle, the young nurse standing behind me, it occurred to

212

me that the anesthesia was wearing off much the same as my marijuana experiences used to wear off. One minute you thought the effects were gone and you'd "landed," the next minute you were surprised to find yourself "tripping" again, mind racing. Then down again, followed by shorter and shorter versions of the pattern.

Though I couldn't quite discern which piece it was, beautiful music was sounding in my head. Holy shit, I remembered it was there while I was anesthetized. Yes, I could remember dominant violins and a robust bass. I hadn't seen the musicians, but there was a man conducting, in a white robe. He had the face of the person I used to envision when I conjured up God's image as a child, prominent nose, white combed-back hair, stoic expression, around fifty-five or sixty.

Wait, it was Pachelbel's "Canon in D." Jesus! If ever I was at the gates of heaven, and had just been admitted, "Canon in D" was the music I'd want played.

I saw Justine pull into the semicircle pickup area and the music was gone. I remembered to remind the nurse. "Don't forget, mum's the word about the procedure."

"Mum's the word?" she asked.

"Yeah, you know. Don't say anything. It's one of those idioms from Shakespeare that stuck around to become part of the language, like 'something's rotten in Denmark,' or 'a rose by any other name.' How old are you?"

"Twenty-three."

"Ask your parents about 'mum's the word.'"

"Here's your appointment card for Dr. Tyler tomorrow," she said.

After the nurse closed the car door, and Justine had the vehicle underway, she asked. "Why do you have to see Dr. Tyler again tomorrow?"

"I don't know. She just said to stop by her office tomorrow."

"Don't you think that's rather irregular?"

"I don't know. Is it?"

"David, are you not telling me something?"

"Of course, Justine. I'm not telling you a lot of things."

"You know what I mean."

"I don't *know* what she wants, Justine. For Christ's sake, ask me after I see her tomorrow. Jesus."

After about twenty seconds of pressurized silence, "I'm sorry, Justine. Hospitals, physicians and procedures just unnerve me. I'll call you when I get back from her office tomorrow afternoon."

She smiled, put her hand on my knee.

The next morning, I was in Tyler's office at the appointed time of ten-thirty. At ten forty-four, I was about to ask the receptionist if it'd be much longer before I'd get in to see the doctor, when a nurse came through the door. "Mr. Foley?" She showed me to an examining room.

"Is your throat tender from yesterday?" she asked.

"Actually it's much better. I'm a little surprised after the way it felt last night."

"She'll be right in," the nurse said, as she closed the door behind her. It was almost eleven o'clock when Tyler knocked on the door, but before I could complain, she said, "I'm sorry I'm late. I had a patient in an emergency situation and I had to be at the hospital longer than I expected."

That pretty well disarmed me, but I quipped anyway. "Come on, Bridget, don't give me that stuff. You've been in the next room practicing your putting, haven't you?"

It took her a half-count to realize I was joking. I enjoyed seeing her eyes soften and her mouth relax as she caught on, but quickly her expression became serious again.

"The news isn't good, Mr. Foley. The tissue samples taken from your lung are cancerous, a cancer of the most serious type. It's what's known as small cell carcinoma and it has metastasized to your lymph nodes which is extremely troubling."

"Extremely troubling?"

"It suggests that it could have spread to other parts of your body."

"What parts?"

"I don't know. Could be the abdomen, the liver, even the brain. I'm suggesting a CT scan of your abdominal area and an MRI of your brain."

"More tests?" I said too loudly, throwing my head back and looking at the ceiling in frustration.

"Yes. If the cancer has spread to any other of your vital organs, an operation to remove those tumors in your lung most likely wouldn't be worth it."

"Okay," I said, looking and sounding like my problem was her fault. "Will the tests be an organ a day, an organ a week? What?"

Quickly, I was ashamed of my boorish sarcasm. "Jesus, I'm sorry, Bridget. It's just—"

"I understand, Mr. Foley. This is difficult to deal with. But the scans we need can all be done in one session."

About a week later, I was back in the West Wing of St. Anthony's, submitting again to the receptionist, the nurses, the hospital gown, the techs, the cylinder, and what I considered the goddamned indignity of having my organs scanned.

Two days after that, I was in Bridget Tyler's office, fifteen minutes early for a pre-scheduled morning appointment. Even though I was early, a nurse called for me before I could cross my legs after dropping into a chair and escorted me to an examination room.

My physician was already in the room when I entered, giving me nervous pause. She, the office staff, and the nurses had usually been punctual, but I was wondering if the accelerated pace of processing me that day was a bad sign.

When the young MD looked at me, her customary broad smile, always exposing perfect white teeth between her beautiful lips, was absent. She wasn't frowning, but she was stoic.

"Bad news?" I asked, suspecting already.

"Mr. Foley, your liver is cancerous. The tumors are of a size that they're inoperable. They're just too far along. This is a terminal illness. I'm sorry."

Above me, the sour yellow light of a dying florescent lamp danced erratically and buzzed within its cylindrical enclosure. I attempted to perceive my liver, to feel and visualize its size and shape, its weight. Of course, I couldn't. Hell, I wasn't even sure exactly where my liver was.

After dropping my head, chin almost to chest, I didn't move or change expression for what seemed like a minute. When I did raise my head, I stared into Tyler's eyes. They were sympathetic but unbowed, strong, indicative of someone up to the task of telling another human he was going to die. I moved my eyes back to the floor, sighed heavily, and looked again at my young caregiver. Her eyes had remained steadfast on me.

"How long?"

"A year at most, probably more like six months."

"Where can I learn about this? Where can I find out what to expect?"

"The American Cancer Society has a website I recommend, and you can speak with me anytime, ask any questions you want. I'll give you the best answers I can."

"Jesus Christ. There are a couple of people close to me who aren't going to deal very well with this."

"I'm sure, but the better you deal with it, the better they'll deal with it."

"What do you want me to do now?" I asked Tyler, but heard the question as if I'd asked it of myself. Funny, I couldn't think of a solitary thing to "do now," to do differently. Nothing had changed, had it? I'd always known I was going to die. Should there be drastic changes just because I was able to put a schedule to it? I couldn't keep from smiling at that thought.

"Mr. Foley, are you okay?" Tyler asked, I suppose confused by my grin.

"Yes, I'm fine. I just had a strange insight. Sorry, Bridget, did you tell me what you wanted me to do now?"

"You can try chemotherapy. That won't eradicate the cancer, but it might slow it down somewhat."

This time I heard what she said, but I was thinking of the task of telling Liesl and Justine about the situation.

"I need some time to think about chemo," I said. "I might not want to 'fight the good fight,' knowing I'm going to lose."

"Yes, I can understand that."

"What can I expect as far as pain is concerned," I asked.

"The lung cancer usually produces a burning sensation in the chest." It can be controlled with medication, but in many instances, the strength of something like morphine renders the patient unconscious. Liver cancer often induces nausea and vomiting, in addition to chronic weakness and fatigue. Pain in the upper abdomen is not uncommon, either, with swelling and bloating."

"It sounds like there's loads of fun ahead," I said to myself more that to Tyler, who didn't react to my sarcasm.

"Call me anytime you'd like, she said. "We can talk some more."

When I reached the parking lot and got into my car, I was facing the centerpiece of the St. Anthony complex, the original hospital structure where I first encountered Liesl, held her, just minutes after her birth. I came out of the vehicle without having made a conscious decision to do so, and walked toward the entrance. The core structure still looked the same. It had merely sprouted wings.

Inside, the lobby had been refurbished, but its early twentieth-century ambiance had been preserved. The marble floors, the powerful, upsurging pillars, the arching ornate ceiling were all as I remembered. Seeing and remembering the interior architecture set me on an emotional errand. Moving through the building, I felt as if I were walking against the grain of time, seeking a precise mid-summer day when, in the course of a few minutes, I lost Kathryn, but found Liesl.

I rode the elevator to the fourth floor, robotically exited walking left before coming to the maternity ward's nursing station. Just beyond was the viewing window into the nursery. I instinctively walked to it.

There they were. I counted sixteen of the youngest people on earth, the blue-blanketed boys outnumbering the pink-covered girls, nine to seven.

It's our turn old guy. You've had your turn.

Yes, my young friends. I guess I have.

I stood motionless, staring at the newborns for several minutes, then turned and walked to the elevators. As I exited the building, I decided to walk the grounds for a while rather than drive home right away with my emotions palpitating with such intensity. Twenty minutes ago, I didn't know what small cell carcinoma was. Suddenly, I owned some of it. Moreover, it was the phrase I'd use going forward to avoid having to say lung cancer or liver cancer.

As I passed the research clinic and the nursing school, I thought again of Liesl. How was I going to tell my granddaughter I was dying and that the run-up to my death would probably be physically painful for me, emotionally so for her?

What about Justine? At least her perspective of death would be tempered by sixty years of life. Liesl's youthful notion of fatality wouldn't have had time to inure, even with death having played so prominently in her short life.

When my circuitous route of the grounds led me around again to the front of the hospital, I saw a thin man wearing plaid pajama bottoms under a flimsy hospital gown. He had on soft indoor slippers and was slowly short-stepping the sixty feet or so from the hospital's automatic glass doors to the sidewalk. He was unnaturally bald and pushed a rolling IV pole, complete with suspended plastic drip bag. When he reached the sidewalk, the man sat on the end of a bus stop bench.

I first thought that he was a deranged, or at least confused, patient who had decided it was time to leave the hospital and go home. I angled toward him, became close enough to see the fear in his sunken eyes, under which were prominent black semicircles. I envisioned the death demon standing next to him, waiting with patience and confidence, smirking.

I smelled tobacco smoke a second or two before the man raised his orange-stained fingers to his mouth and sucked the smoke out of a filterless cigarette.

"Are you okay?" I asked.

"Just burning one here, pal. You can't smoke in the building anymore. They won't even let you light up just outside the goddamned doors."

I was home, my death sentence about an hour old, when I remembered I was supposed to call Justine. There's where it would get difficult. I dialed her number and was relieved to be relegated to her voice mail. "Justine, it's David at about two-thirty. Give me a call."

Knowing I had merely put off the inevitable by an hour or so, I began to ponder how I'd go about informing friends and loved ones. The way Bridget Tyler told me about it was probably best, straightforward, economical, unemotional. No doubt the young internist had been briefed somewhere in her training about the proper way to break the news to a patient that he was dying.

A half-hour later, I was sitting on the toilet when I heard my land-line ring. Goddamn it. Why does the phone inevitably ring when I'm trying to take a dump?

I heard the caller disconnect without recording a message. My cell phone tinkled from the pocket of my pants that were on the floor, draped around my shoes. I found the pocket and retrieved the phone just in time to hear the disconnect signal before I could push the receive button. God*damn* it!

I saw "Justine Colgate" on the display, pushed the "return" button. Two rings later, I heard Justine. "David?"

"Yeah, sorry," I said. "I couldn't get to your first call, and I dropped the second." With the bowl accumulating an overload, I flushed the john.

"For Christ's sake David, are you using the toilet?"

"Well—"

"You could have waited until you were finished to call me back."

"Come on Justine, I'd already missed you twice, and besides, I might be here awhile."

"I don't know why I bother with you. And to think, you're a classical music patron. Anyway, what's up?"

"Can you come over for dinner? I need some good company. About six?"

"Sure, can I bring anything? Is anything wrong?"

"No, just bring yourself, and, no, nothing's wrong. See you at six"

I had some frozen pizza dough and a batch of pizza sauce, so all I needed to do was cut up some vegetables and wait for Justine to arrive. On second thought, to make it seem like I'd gone to at least a little trouble, I prepared a wilted lettuce salad with bacon bits and croutons.

Justine arrived and entered the kitchen. "My God, David, what's that smell? It's terrible."

"Well, it could be the remnants of what I was doing when I called you this afternoon," I said. "You know the line about 'the evil that men do lives after them. The good is oft—'"

"Stop it!" she snapped. "It's something burning." As she opened the oven door, "There's a plastic measuring spoon in there. Hand me the tongs. Turn on the fan."

After she retrieved the bubbling spoon, dropped it into a mixing bowl of water to be deposited outside, I suggested we sit on the front porch while the fan worked to clear the kitchen air. I placed a glass of wine on each twin table aside the swing.

"Thanks for coming," I said.

"Is everything all right? You're usually not so spontaneous."

"Considering the circumstances, yes."

"What circumstances?"

"Drinking wine from a moving swing is something I've gotten good at through the years," I said, trying to delay having to tell Justine her best friend was dying.

"What are you talking about?"

"Justine, I don't know how to tell you this, other than to just tell you. Bridget Tyler has diagnosed me with lung cancer. It has metastasized to my liver and she says I *might* have a year to live. Probably more like six months."

"David—"

"I'm sorry to drop this on you, but I didn't know just how to—"

"David," she said again.

I put my hand on her knee. She picked it up with both of hers, raised it to her mouth, kissed it repeatedly.

Then without breathing between sentences, "Tell me what the doctor said. She could be wrong. She's so young. Have you gotten a second opinion? Surely you will."

"I haven't thought about it."

"The hospital trip wasn't for a colonoscopy."

"No, a bronchoscopy."

There was a tic in Justine's upper lip that I'd never seen before.

220

"What can I do? When did you find out? Does Liesl know?"

"Oh no. I needed to talk with you first. I need some help on how to deal with that."

"Poor Liesl," Justine said. "You can't tell her until you get a second opinion."

"Justine, Bridget talked like it's an open and shut case. Two pathologists looked at the tissue."

"I don't care. You need to—"

"At least Liesl's an adult now," I interrupted, "and she has Alan. If this had happened five years ago—"

"David, I—"

"Let's walk around back," I suggested, trying to diminish the tension of the moment. As we walked back the side driveway, we stepped in unison. She had my arm in both her hands, her head resting on my shoulder. As our path opened to the spacious rear lot, we remained in gentle contact. Her body felt congruous with mine, her softness itself, comforting.

Coming under the ginkgo tree, I stopped our progress, pulled her into my arms. "Hold me for a while," I said. While we embraced, we swayed slowly left and right. Looking up, I saw what I could tell was a not-quite-full moon filtered through the ginkgo's shimmering leaves. Though it wasn't dark yet, the moon was silvery bright, beautiful. I felt as if it belonged only to Justine and me.

Her high forehead and large eyes, sculpted cheekbones, and thick, moist lips flaunted her natural beauty. Her blonde hair was pulled back tightly into a bun. She was lovely without the flourish of full, fluffy hair, one of those people whose intelligence was evident in her handsomeness.

After a substantial but unmeasured time, I suggested, "Let's eat," attempting to diffuse the intense emotion spiraling around us. "How about on the porch?"

"That'll be nice," she said. Tears weren't streaming, but her eyes were glistening.

I wrestled with ideas as to how to tell Liesl what the situation was. Her life was so joyous, so uncomplicated, that I felt guilty about loosing the death demon into her existence again.

Contemplating how best to handle the dilemma had me no closer to an answer two days later. I knew I'd keep it to myself until I was sure I'd arrived at the best alternative, though that would probably wind up being the least dreadful of terrible options.

I decided to solicit Alan's opinion. I called him at SpadeWorx, left a message on the recorder that I wanted to see him and would "be there at one-thirty Friday, unless you call me and tell me that's not a good time."

When I arrived at his office on Friday, Alan's pickup was in one of the building's two parking spaces. I wheeled into the other, walked into the unadorned, cement block building, and moved toward an enclosed office space that Alan had partitioned to deal with the "business of the business."

He spotted me through one of the office's windows and motioned for me to come in.

"Hi, David. Want something to drink?"

"No thanks, I just had lunch."

He was sitting in front of his computer. "Just let me bookmark this website. I'm sort of shopping for equipment. There. What's going on?" he said as he pushed his wheeled chair back from the computer, turning it until he was facing me.

There was no merit in wasting any time. "Well, I've had what you might call a serious health setback and I want your opinion as to how I should deal with Liesl about it."

"Damn, David, what do you mean, a serious setback?"

I smiled, then didn't.

"You're only the second person I've told about this, so I haven't quite hit on the proper words to express that I have small cell carcinoma, lung cancer and liver cancer, put another way, and that it's a terminal situation."

"*What*? How did you find that out?"

"By holding still for a battery of CT scans, a PET scan, a bronchos-copy, and a biopsy. I haven't gotten an official second opinion, but all of those tests point in the same direction, the biopsy very definitively."

"David, I don't know what to say. You seem so healthy. I'm stunned. What can I do? I feel so inadequate."

My bad news seemed to cause its recipients to breathlessly utter sentence after sentence. "Help me tell Liesl," I said.

"David, this'll kill her."

"It'll be difficult, yes. Dealing with how to tell her is the hardest part of this mess."

"I'm sorry, David. I still don't know what to say. Did they give you any time frame?"

"Probably six months."

"God."

"I would very much like for you to be with us when I tell her," I said, "and I think it should be at your apartment rather than my house."

"I'll be there if you want, of course. When?"

"As soon as possible, I think. This weekend?"

"I could ask her if she'd like to have you over for a meal Saturday or Sunday," he suggested. "The answer to that is always 'yes,' so be expecting a call."

"Thanks, Alan. I need to be going now." In actuality, I didn't need to leave, I had nothing to do, nowhere to go. I just wanted to relieve my son-in-law of the intense pressure my extended presence would bring, forcing him to try and figure out how to behave around a dying man. I'd have to get used to people's uneasiness.

We stood up, looked at each other for a moment. He opened his arms and took a step toward me. We each clutched the other, still silent. I drew slowly away, placed my hands on his uppermost arms, squeezed and shook him gently.

"You got here just in time, Alan. The way Liesl feels about you and the wonderful way you treat her are great comforts to me. I trust you. I know her welfare is your priority. Thank you."

"Jesus, David."

Liesl phoned that evening and asked if I'd like to come to their apartment early Sunday afternoon for lunch with her and Alan. Her voice was cheerful which made me all the more dread having to disturb her unfettered existence.

I answered, "You bet. What time?"

"Twelve-thirty or so?"

"Let's see," I said, trying to stay in character, "yes, I should be out of church by then."

"Poppa, you're so silly."

Alan and Liesl always greeted me together whenever they knew I was coming. That Sunday was no different. The fact they both walked down the flight of steps to greet me, always made me feel welcome.

"Hi, Poppa," Liesl said with a hug. "Come on up."

"David," Alan said, nodding once, shaking my hand, and looking me in the eyes.

"What did you guys do last night?" I inquired as I settled, at Alan's insistence, into his easy chair in the living room.

"We went to a party down the street," Liesl said, before moving into the kitchen. "There's a couple we often see strolling their little boy through the neighborhood and they had a few other friends over, mostly people on this block. It was nice to meet some neighbors."

"It's funny," Alan said. "The year I lived here by myself, I'd only get perfunctory waves from the locals. With Liesl here, they seem to have a different attitude."

"I suppose people assume that young bachelors have more stimulating things to do than hang around at neighborhood affairs," I said, "or maybe marriage legitimizes men."

Liesl summoned Alan and me to the small, eat-in kitchen where we lunched on chicken noodle soup, a fresh garden salad and grilled tuna steaks. While Alan cleared the table, Liesl scraped the dishes and put them into the small, antiquated dishwasher. I myself remained seated.

"Would you like some coffee?" Alan offered.

"No thanks, I'm done. That was wonderful."

"It was very simple, Poppa," Liesl said, drying her hands on her apron. "Let's go into the living room where we can be a little more comfortable."

"I'm comfortable anywhere in your home," I said, "but sit with me

224

here on the couch."

She took the middle cushion of three, in contact with me on an end cushion. Alan chose the second-hand, upholstered rocker that was closer to the couch than his easy chair. I began speaking before Liesl had a chance to initiate a conversation.

"Liesl, I have some bad news." I paused to let her process the comment, understand that something unpleasant was coming. She looked at Alan, whose sympathetic expression made her realize he already knew what she was about to be told. She turned to me, fear now on her face.

"The physical Dr. Tyler had me undergo while you were away, turned up a spot on my lungs. It's an aggressive type of cancer, already spreading, inoperable, something I won't be able to recover from. I wish there'd been a better way to tell you, other than just blurting it out."

Her face contorted. She looked straight ahead for a moment before she glared at me with the same expression she would have worn if she were angry with me. She slumped onto my shoulder and slid her arms around me. She squeezed me, seemingly as hard as she could, as if trying to press the demon out of my chest. "Poppa, no. *NOOO!*"

Her eyes were pressed shut. I closed mine, our heads touching. It felt as if I were in a dream, spiraling downward, tumbling. Kathryn, in a hospital gown, and Patrick, in his uniform, were toppling with me. I tried to cling to them, but couldn't.

I opened my eyes as Alan moved onto the empty cushion of the couch, next to Liesl. His patting and stroking her thigh caused her to open her eyes. I put my arms around her shoulders. Her torso was convulsing without vocalizing the pain.

"Liesl, you need to know I feel fine. I'm not sick or in any discomfort."

That assurance did nothing to mitigate her despair. She began to weep audibly, not loud wailing, but a low moan.

The tears tracked down her cheeks, and she had paled. Her forehead was moist as she continued moaning, almost inaudibly. She vomited. On my pants. On the couch.

"It's going to be all right, Liesl," I whispered, ignoring the mess. "Everything will be all right. It's just terribly hard right now."

As Alan tried to clean the results of the upheaval, I stroked my granddaughter's hair, told her to keep her head on my chest. She did, for a long time.

Chapter Thirteen

"I fear I am writing a requiem for myself."
— WOLFGANG AMADEUS MOZART

When *Liesl learned* I had an appointment with Bridget Tyler the following Thursday, she insisted on accompanying me to hear my internist's assessment of my condition for herself. When she picked me up at Four-fourteen, I was wearing a gray sport coat with a lapel pin that she recognized as a ginkgo leaf.

"When did you get that?" she asked.

"I saw it online last week and couldn't resist. It just came yesterday. Do you like it?"

"Of course, it's beautiful. Is it gold?"

"Well, gold plated anyway."

While Liesl drove, we talked about SpadeWorx, the weather, a conference she had recently attended, the Martins' new dishwasher; anything but cancer.

Once in Tyler's office, we were escorted to a conference room. When she made her entrance, before I could introduce Liesl to her, "You have to be Liesl," she said, smiling, taking my granddaughter's hand in both of hers. "I feel like I know you. Your grandfather talks about you a lot."

"Really?" Liesl said, casting a playful glance at me.

Determined to maintain my usual bantering style in spite of the circumstances, I said, "Actually, Bridget, lately I've been talking to Liesl a lot about you, too." Both women showed perfunctory smiles.

"Are you still feeling well?" Tyler asked, as she started moving her stethoscope around my torso.

"Oh yes," I replied. "For a sick man, I feel wonderful." I was pleased when Liesl and Bridget couldn't stifle simultaneous chuckles.

"Have you given any more thought to the chemo?" Tyler asked, notating something on her clipboard, definitely sobering the conversation.

"I'm probably not going to do that, Bridget; too much effort for too little gain."

"Poppa, you didn't tell me chemotherapy was an option. What's your opinion of that, Dr. Tyler? Are we making a mistake?"

The internist pursed her lips, took a breath. Answering Liesl, but looking at me, she said, "If my dad had small cell lung cancer that had spread to his liver, I'd probably advise against chemo. Usually it's just a matter of buying some less-than-quality time, like trading a few weeks of feeling relatively well for a few extra weeks with sickness at the end."

For the rest of the visit we discussed the obvious things, medications and pain management, physical changes to expect, sources of information, even the possibility of entering hospice or moving to a nursing home. "I won't let that happen, Poppa," Liesl said, the sentence fragmented because she had choked up.

After a few more minutes of my physician expounding on my malady and its repercussions from a medical perspective, there came an uncomfortable silence. Bridget broke it by asking, "Do you have any questions?"

"Not at the moment," Liesl said, recomposing. "Thank you, Dr. Tyler."

I had a few but didn't ask. I was glad Liesl had an opportunity to hear the details from Bridget herself, rather than my interpretation. I put my coat on and, as we were moving to leave the conference, Tyler noticed my new jewelry. "That's pretty," she said, nodding at my lapel pin. "Is it a leaf of some kind?"

"It's a ginkgo leaf. Are you familiar with ginkgo trees, Bridget?"

"Actually, I'm not."

"Oh, they're most interesting," I responded with typical confidence. Liesl playfully moved her eyes upward knowing the young physician was in for a condensed dendrology lesson.

"Ginkgos are living fossils, their ancestors dating to the Jurassic period, but the great glaciers of the Ice Age exterminated them everywhere except China. All the ginkgos alive today emanate from those Asian survivors."

"That's really ironic," said Tyler. "Your pin is shaped like a Far-

228

Eastern fan."

"Yes, but the most intriguing aspect of the ginkgo is the way it sheds its leaf," I asserted, "but I know you're busy. Perhaps we can discuss it further on another visit."

On the trip home, I managed to again keep the conversation geared to Alan's and her respective jobs, sparing my granddaughter any painful conversation about my medical situation. "Is Alan's work schedule still running about sixty hours a week? Are you still happy at the Center?"

After she dropped me at Four-fourteen, I wondered if she had extracted any meaning from my words to Bridget Tyler about the cycle of a ginkgo's leaves. I didn't think so.

During a mid-August brunch at the Martins' apartment, Liesl told Alan and me that Nestor's wife and daughter were back on the Center's campus.

"I have to be careful talking about this, but I need to vent. I won't mention last names, and I know neither of you would ever breathe a word. We readmitted Nestor's wife Thursday night. Metro Police brought Joanne and her daughter, Molly, to the campus at about eleven o'clock. Joanne is five-months pregnant by Nestor.

"She'd been treated at Jefferson Emergency Clinic for emotional trauma as well as facial cuts and bruises. When I interviewed her Friday morning, her left eye was swollen shut, surrounded by an inch of purple bruising and her lips looked like pieces of raw liver, twice their normal size. Even little Molly had bruises on her arm that were clearly the imprints of fingers.

"It seems before Nestor beat hell out of Joanne, he grabbed Molly by her arm, and kept squeezing it harder and harder, threatening to kill her if Joanne didn't tell him what was 'going on' between her and a kid downstairs."

"He threatened to kill his daughter?" Alan asked.

"Yes, Joanne had mentioned to him that a teenager who lived on the first floor of their tenement, helped her up the steps with some groceries. Nestor doesn't need much reason to turn violent, and that set him off.

"Joanne didn't have anything to admit. She was screaming for him to let go of Molly when he turned her loose and started punching Joanne in the face."

"For Christ's sake," I said. "Did they lock him up?"

"No, the police didn't see him do it and Nestor was gone by the time they got there. Joanne wouldn't fill out the papers to charge him and that's typical. Abusive husbands are so domineering and their wives so fearful, they feel even the law can't protect them.

"It was a neighbor who heard the screaming and called the police. They took them to the hospital and when Joanne was released, they wanted her to go to the station and file a complaint. She was too frightened to do it. The cops weren't going to take her back to the house, so they brought her to us."

"Jesus," I said. "What's the kid like?"

"She hasn't talked, just clings to her mother. She's four now."

"What'll happen now?" Alan asked.

"Typically, they'll stay with us for a few days, then drift back home. A lot of times, it takes several rounds of a beating, a call to the police, and a trip to the hospital before we can convince them we can help break the cycle. They're usually more willing to let us help them if there's a child involved."

"Anyone who would do that to his family doesn't deserve to draw breath," I said, more to myself than to Liesl.

When I left the Martins' apartment an hour later to make the short trip to Four-fourteen, I was still disturbed from thinking about the family Liesl described. I knew that kind of brutality and misery existed, but until I heard Liesl's involved account of it, spousal and child abuse was something from which I'd been insulated. My granddaughter's proximity to it, coupled with Nestor's earlier threat to her, made it more than just some remote unpleasantness.

To commemorate Alan's twenty-seventh birthday in September, I had the Martins join Justine and me at El Rascal's for a celebratory Sunday lunch.

After the meal, a waiter produced a birthday cake for Alan that had two candles, a two and a seven. Following a rousing variation of "Happy Birthday," Alan closed his eyes with a squint and held up both hands so that everyone could see his crossed fingers. Opening his eyes, he effortlessly extinguished both flames with one puff to a round of applause.

"What did you wish for, Alan?" I asked.

"Aw, I can't tell you that," he said. "It might not come true." Liesl only smiled.

Driving me home after dropping Justine at her condo, Liesl related to Alan and me that Nestor had again assaulted Joanne and Molly.

"The girls are back on our campus," she said. "This time he kneed Joanne in the groin with such force that she miscarried a few hours later. He also apparently backhanded Molly, loosening a tooth and bruising her face.

"He'd been drinking at the bar just down the street from their duplex, and when it closed at two in the morning, he came home staggering. Joanne says he's in a place called Pat's Taproom just about every night."

"Still no arrest?" I asked.

"Actually, they did detain Nestor outside his house a few hours later with a 'suspicion of justification,'" Liesl said, framing the words suspicion of with two fingers from each hand, "but they couldn't hold him or charge him since Joanne wouldn't sign a complaint. He was only in custody for a few hours."

"Somebody needs to help those girls," I mumbled.

"Joanne will eventually help herself if Nestor doesn't kill her first, Poppa. Every day we're trying to convince her to take legal action, but so far she won't."

"Somebody needs to do something about that guy," I reiterated.

"Joanne also told the social worker that Nestor again threatened to get anyone who helps or encourages her to keep Molly away from him. He said he didn't care if that were lawyers, police, counselors, or whoever, he'd make them pay."

"Damn," Alan said. "That's twice he's threatened you."

"You have to take that seriously, Liesl," I said, putting my hand on her shoulder from the back seat.

"Don't worry, Poppa," she said, patting my hand. "It was basically a generic threat. Remember, Joanne doesn't know any of our last names. The Center's security protocol dictates that we keep our names from clients for that very reason."

"Do the police know about this?" I asked.

"The Center's attorney told us that, in the past, the police have said they're powerless to do anything about non-specific threats garnered from a third-party. Since they couldn't do anything anyway, and because Nestor's already on the cops' radar, the Center didn't notify the police about what Joanne said."

"I would think another visit from uniformed officers would at least put the guy on notice they were paying attention, maybe deterring him," Alan said.

"It's hard to say," Liesl said. "Sometimes a police visit exacerbates the situation and the abuser wreaks a kind of vengeance on the wife for telling someone about the violence."

"But she's staying at the Center," I said. "Isn't she safe there?"

"For now at least, Poppa. It's hard to understand, but these poor women all too often leave us and return home. Joanne's done it a couple of times. In a way, they're similar to addicts."

"Jesus Christ," I said. "I don't like a goon like that threatening you, generically or otherwise."

"Try not to worry about it, Poppa. The Center has a professional and experienced staff of advisors."

"I suppose," I said, "but it still seems like somebody should do something about him."

"I know, Poppa, but what can you do?"

I stayed silent for the remainder of the trip home, while Liesl and Alan admired and talked about some of the houses along the route. "Look what a nice enclosed yard that one has, Alan," Liesl said.

After I was dropped off, I sat in the front porch rocker. I couldn't keep from thinking of Joanne and Molly, and now Liesl was possibly at risk. Contemplating Nestor's threat, I worked myself into a near furor just thinking about some brute bringing harm to my granddaughter. I tried not to allow a remote long shot to morph into a definite possibility, but—

As I was shaking my head at the situation, I noticed a cat walking across the yard with a chipmunk dangling by the nape of its neck, suspended lifelessly in the clench of the predator's teeth.

When the cat spotted me, it stopped, stared at me. It was as if the feline had been caught in a crime and was waiting to see what I was going to do about it. Suddenly, the cat scurried away with the furry carcass swinging from its mouth.

I assumed the chippie was either too slow or not intelligent enough to have avoided the cat's clutches, maybe both, sluggish *and* dumb. Too bad there wasn't a predator to dispose of a sluggish and dumb lowbrow by the name of Nestor.

"Now that's a thought," I heard myself say.

I decided to take a nap, a replenishment that had become more frequent and necessary in recent weeks. As I lay in bed, I began to drift between consciousness and repose, shifting between intended contemplation and dreaming. My thoughts were the same in both states; it would be right and just for this guy, Nestor, to be eradicated, a man who apparently neither loved nor was loved, a man who inflicted terrible pain and fear upon a vulnerable woman and an innocent child.

After an hour of dozing, the good riddance of Nestor was still resonating in my thoughts. Suddenly awake, those ruminations crystallized. Wouldn't it be a grand gesture before moving to my own nothingness, my own weightless black hole, to escort Nestor to nothingness?

That scenario so intrigued me, I began to calculate how one might execute such a contingency. Poisoning? That would be logistically difficult, too slow, too painful, even for a worthless lout like this Nestor guy. A fire? I realized quickly that would be too dangerous to those around him, not to mention putting responders at risk. What about blows from a blunt instrument? Nah, I was no longer up to a physical skirmish. Besides, bludgeoning would be so gory.

The best solution, I deduced, would be a bullet delivered by a long-barreled firearm from relatively afar. Could I hire someone to do it? No, again, it'd be too risky with another person in on the scheme. If I wanted it to happen, I'd have to do it myself.

Suddenly I retreated from my felonious thoughts. What in the hell was I thinking? Why was I wasting my limited time on such goddamned cowboy nonsense?

I decided to read for a while, but before I could choose from among books on a den shelf, the murderous contemplation returned, unsolicited, unwilling to concede its eerie priority in my consciousness. I found that it even relieved me, more than other activity or thoughts, of pondering my own impending doom, so I allowed my consideration of the inconsiderable to continue, to accelerate.

I remembered Pat's Taproom.

Looking in the phone book, I found Pat's Taproom listed at 2301 Kerry Street, and I knew that address to be in the city's West End, near the Portland neighborhood. After dialing the *67 code to keep my number from being displayed, I dialed the listing, waited.

"This is Pat's," said a man's voice, raised over the obvious din of a loud television set.

After a brief hesitation, I said, "Hey yeah, is, uh, Nestor in there today?"

"Cahill?"

"Uh, yeah. Nestor Cahill."

"Anybody seen Nestor today?" I heard the man's hand-muffled voice ask. After a moment, now without the muffling, "Nah, he ain't here, pal."

"Okay, thanks, I'll catch him later." I said, as I disconnected.

Nestor Cahill.

I went back to the city directory. Let's see, Cahill, Cahill. *Shit*, no Nestor Cahill. Wait.

Cahill Loraine | 2305 Kerry Street.................778-6103

Two doors from Pat's Tap Room, I thought. No doubt, the piece of shit couldn't get phone service in his own sorry-ass name, and Loraine was probably his mother or sister, but no matter, I knew his name and address.

As a young teenager, I did some small game hunting with my father. I owned a twenty-two-caliber rifle, and my dad let me fire a shot-gun on a few outings. That was the extent of my knowledge of guns, but it was enough for me to realize operating a long-barreled firearm was in no way akin to nuclear physics.

I felt certain a high-powered rifle, commonly used for deer hunting, could be easily obtained, and that such a weapon would have the preci-sion and the range to fell a human from a relatively far distance.

That such thoughts stirred my blood was astonishing to me. I was actually relishing the concept of ridding the earth of a bestial human be-ing. The more I reflected on it, the more at ease I became with the idea of myself, a condemned man, condemning a guy like Nestor Cahill. Wielding the power of judge, jury, and executioner appealed to me in a lurid, but fascinating way; so much for the Fifth Commandment.

I began researching rifles on the Internet to refamiliarize myself with them. Many arms manufacturers were old-line companies and that gave me a sense of security as I whittled down the possibilities of a weap-on of choice. Historic names such as Remington, Winchester and Browning had centuries of combined existence in the firearms business. I figured if I'd purchase a model that had survived a few years in any of those companies' catalogs, I'd have myself a quality product.

On its website, White's Firearms boasted of being the largest gun retailer in Kentucky. White's carried all three of my preferred manufac-turers' lines of rifles in its Hopkinsville store that was about a two-and-a-half hour drive from Louisville. I decided Sunday night to make a trip to Hopkinsville Monday morning. It seemed more prudent to buy a mur-der weapon somewhere other than my hometown.

When I awoke Monday morning, the idea of executing Nestor Ca-hill had lost a little luster, but two cups of coffee and thoughts of a threat to Liesl rekindled my enthusiasm. I was on the road before eight, cruis-ing south on Interstate 65. After forty-five minutes, I came to the exit for Elizabethtown, the small city near Fort Knox where Patrick and Kathryn had their first home just after they were married. Liesl was con-ceived there. I exhaled a deep breath.

My beautiful Liesl. What would she think of this plan? I knew the answer and the resulting emotional turbulence gave me thoughts of turning around, abandoning my bizarre scheme, heading back to Four-fourteen. Conjuring an image of Nestor Cahill stalking Joanne and Molly Cahill, or Liesl, for that matter, squeezed sentimentality aside and I continued my business-like mission to find the right weapon with which to slay Nestor Cahill. I was becoming more and more comfortable with the idea of executing a person who didn't deserve to live.

As I traversed the aisles of White's Firearms in Hopkinsville, I was amazed at the weaponry on display. I shouldn't have been surprised at guns being sold in the venue of a mega-store, every other commodity was. Why not firearms?

A tall, thin man, wearing blue jeans seemingly several sizes too large in the waist, was writing on a clipboard in one of the aisles. His pants were tucked into boots, and only a pair of red suspenders kept them from collapsing and folding around his ankles. His shoulders were barely wide enough to support the suspender straps. Even his head was tall, and it was topped by an obvious toupee. The "rug" looked like a skunk pelt without the stripe, black as coal, and silky. The hairpiece ended abruptly just above the man's ears and he hadn't the slightest trace of sideburns.

I noticed an ID badge pinned to his flannel shirt that had the name "SLIM" set in large, all capital lettering that dominated the White's Firearms logo beneath it.

"Can I help you find something?" he asked.

"Yeah, maybe. I haven't fooled with guns since I had a small rifle as a kid and squirrel hunted, but my grandson loves to hunt, so I thought I'd get him a deer rifle for his birthday."

"How old is he?"

"He'll be twenty on Friday."

"You know this gun'll have to be in your name and if anything bad happens with it, you'll have responsibility," Slim informed me, using his thumb to adjust the latitude of his left suspender with a snap, as if to make sure I was paying attention.

"Oh, he's a responsible young fellow," I said.

"Did you have any clue as to what you might be looking for?"

"If I remember, a thirty-aught-six or a thirty-thirty were the basic deer rifles. Is that still the case?"

"Those are definitely the 'go to' rifles. You can't go wrong with either."

"Which has the greater range and accuracy?"

"Definitely the thirty-aught-six."

"Do the big names make a thirty-aught-six? Remington? Winchester? Browning?"

"Definitely, I like the Winchester Model-70 myself," Slim said.

"Do you have one I could see?"

"Yes sir, definitely!"

You sure do say 'definitely' a lot, skunk head, is what I thought. "Great."

Slim led me two aisles to the right and, without having to search, he pulled down a Winchester Model-70, 30.06-caliber, bolt-action rifle. "Here it is. From this model on up, you can pay more and get a little more, but you won't be getting your money's worth. This one's the best value on the market."

"What about a scope?"

"I recommend a Bushnell Model-3200, which is a three by nine variable. It's two-hundred-twenty dollars."

"A three by nine variable?" I asked.

"Yeah, it's adjustable from magnifying something from three times to nine times closer than it is. It'll bring a deer up close and personal from a hundred-and-fifty yards, for sure."

"How about a silencer?"

"Silencers are illegal for hunting. You can only use one on a licensed weapon, which this one ain't."

"Shows how much I don't know. I'll bet my grandson's aware of that."

"A lot of guys use them anyway when they need to take out varmints. You know, coyotes and the like," Slim said, his tall face falling into a frown. "If you don't have a silencer, you can only pick off one before the other little bastards scatter."

"Where do the varmint hunters get their silencers?"

"They make them themselves or they buy them privately. If you're dead set on having one, here's a guy who'll sell you a nice silencer for fifty bucks, cash only. Name's Cam." Pulling Cam's hand-written card from his wallet, Slim said, "Tell him Slim sent you."

"What about ammo?" I inquired. "Is there a standard?"

"Once again, it's just personal preference, but I like the hundred-and-fifty-grain shells. They're lighter and I believe they come out of that barrel a tad hotter."

"Hotter?"

"Yeah, you know, faster, more velocity," he said, smiling as if he thought I should have known that.

After running a two-minute background check using my social security number, Slim swiped my credit card for just over a thousand dollars. Upon approval, he placed the Winchester rifle, complete with a mounted Bushnell scope, into a white box that could have been used to house a dozen long-stemmed roses. Then he handed me an unopened box of SuperX 150-grain, hollow-point cartridges.

"Those are on the house. Happy hunting. Don't forget to tell Cam that Slim sent you. And tell all those critters your grand boy scopes and shoots that Slim sent *him*, too."

"Thanks," I said. Then I couldn't resist. "Slim, let me ask you something. If you took all the guns in this store and fired them all at once, do you reckon the concussion alone might level all of downtown Hopkinsville?"

"It just might, friend," Slim said without hesitating or smiling. "It just might."

After having a quick burger in my car at a drive-through restaurant, I realized I was tired. I pulled the car to the rear of the lot, lowered the back of my car seat, and quickly fell into a heavy nap. Sleeping deeply, I dreamed I was in a police lineup with four other suspects. I myself was a black man, but the other four guys were white. A Caucasian woman pointed at me and shouted, "That's him! That's the one! The nig—, I mean, the colored guy!"

"Wait a minute!" I yelled, as a man wearing black tights, a medieval tunic top, and a black hood over his head approached me, wielding a double-edged, medieval executioner's axe.

"Hold on, goddamn it! How could they *not* pick me? Look at these other guys." Just before I awoke, the hooded man cocked his head and shrugged.

Coming to and perspiring, I raised the back of the my seat to a vertical position, "Jesus Christ!" I looked in the mirror, raised my chin, and stroked my neck with my fingers.

After that dream, it took a few minutes to decide whether to call Cam or call it off, head home. Once I made the decision, I dialed the number and said, "Hello, is Cam there?" when a man with a country accent answered the phone.

"You're talking to him."

Only after saying, "Slim sent me," could I coax Cam into discussing silencers.

"What kind of gun you shooting?" he asked.

"A Winchester thirty-aught-six."

"That's easy. Come on over and ask for me, but when you get here, don't parade in with that 'raffle' like a soldier. Put it in a bag or something."

I followed Cam's directions to an auto repair shop outside of town, and also followed his directions as to how to walk in, with my unobtrusive box of roses.

"Is Cam around?" I asked of a man behind some display cases.

"You're looking at him."

Cam was about thirty-five. He was short and rotund with oily, but neatly combed brown hair, except for a pronounced cowlick. He had a red face and a redder neck. It occurred to me that he looked a lot like the guy on *Hee Haw* back in the seventies who used to say, "The number to call is BR-549." Junior something or other.

"I talked to you on the phone, Cam. Here's the gun I want equipped."

"You're one of those city fellas, ain't you?"

"Well—"

"You got the sixty bucks?"

"Sixty? Slim said fifty!"

"Sorry, city boy, had a price increase."

"Mother mercy," I said, reaching for my wallet. "Here."

"All I have to do is thread the barrel of your 'raffle,'" Cam said, as he palmed my three twenties, wadded them into his pocket. "I always keep a couple thirty-aught-six suppressors made up, beings they's the most popular 'raffles.'"

Cam turned around, bent over to open the bottommost drawer of the cabinets that lined the back wall of the shop. As he did, his shrunken and faded red tee shirt separated from his beltless blue jeans, exposing a good three inches of his gluteal cleft. I looked the other way and faked a cough to disguise a burst of laughter.

He took the Winchester and the object he had fetched out of the cabinet drawer and told me to have a seat in the waiting room. He went through a door toward the back of the building, returning less than five minutes later carrying the Winchester.

"Come here," he said. Holding a six-inch by one-inch PVC cylinder with a half-inch, hollow, metal adapter on one end, he said, "This's your silencer. You just screw this adapter into the barrel like this. You know, this unit'll keep the flash down too. Now don't try to take it off just after firing the 'raffle', it'll melt your goddamned hand."

As I was leaving, with my rifle and silencer in the flower box, I couldn't help asking my new weapons technician a question.

"Tell this city fellow, Cam, have you ever heard of plumber's butt?"

"What?"

I arrived at the outskirts of Louisville at five-thirty, just in time to meet the day's rush-hour traffic. The trip had fatigued me and my chest was uncomfortable with what felt like severe indigestion. The last fifteen miles took almost an hour, and, thanks to the bumper-to-bumper stupidity, ignorance and thoughtlessness of other drivers, it seemed like three hours.

When I pulled into the driveway at Four-fourteen, I retrieved the flower box from the trunk and carried it inside. I turned on the television to watch the evening news, but fell asleep before the lead story was over. The need to nap was becoming more frequent. When I awoke, it was dark in the house except for the gray light of the television screen dancing about the den as the scenes of a moronic quiz show changed.

I hadn't eaten since lunch, but the discomfort still burning in my chest kept me from being hungry. Switching off the picture to the television, I picked up the flower box, walked upstairs in the dark. Entering my bedroom, I sat on my bed and turned on the nightstand lamp, then pulled the gun out of its white cardboard enclosure.

Its stock was indeed elegant, solid walnut. For a moment, I understood how gun aficionados could speak of the "beauty" of such a death instrument. I turned off the light, carried the weapon to the window, where I pointed its barrel outward to nothing in particular, and squinted one-eyed into its scope.

I adjusted the Bushnell to focus on an upstairs window of the house the McCoys used to live in. The clarity of the magnification astounded me. Through a bedroom and into its adjoining bath, I could see the young woman of the house blow-drying her hair, wearing only a black thong. "Whoo! Slim sent me, ma'am."

My sense of honor eventually won out, albeit belatedly, after I'd examined my neighbor's physique from thighs to shoulders, slowly and with great admiration.

"Angels and saints," I muttered as I dropped the rifle to my lap.

I closed the window shutters, and placed the Model-70 back into its box, slid it onto the top shelf of the closet. After removing my pants, shirt, shoes and argyle socks, I appreciated the luxury of my down comforter for about thirty seconds before again falling asleep.

Chapter Fourteen

"Suddenly a mist fell from my eyes and I knew the way I had to take."
—EDVARD GRIEG

I *awoke Tuesday morning*, the discomfort in my chest mitigated, but lingering. The burning sensation in the mornings meant it no longer took a few minutes when I came conscious for me to remember the adjacency of my approaching demise. It helped to get out of bed quickly, not lie and contemplate what was coming.

Even the most routine occupational tasks, rinsing my face, brushing my teeth, or making coffee, occupied a part of my sentience that, in turn, kept the specter of death out of a proportional segment of my consciousness.

Less mundane undertakings, such as planning the death of Nestor Cahill, were even more of a diversion, and I could sometimes completely remove my impending quietus from my thoughts. More often, however, I couldn't.

In times when I failed to avoid contemplating my end-of-life, I took comfort in believing my death would be no different than the death of Fielder, no different than the death of a single, unrevealed microbe on some distant planet, no different than a supernova, the violent expiration of an enormous star in some unknown, undetected solar system. In the totality of existence, all death was inconsequential.

I wished I could derive as much solace from that conviction as Christians, Muslims, Jews and other adherents found in the life-after-death nonsense they embraced, but I couldn't. Though I felt a smugness in believing I was merely going to be plunging into nothingness, there were occasions when that egocentricity did nothing to help ward off the dread of death, the fear of the unknown. What if I had the whole goddamned thing wrong? What if I *should* be worried whether or not I'd pissed Jesus off?

That morning, however, after a cup of coffee and an English muffin, I was anxious to return my attention to Nestor. I had the weapon, now I needed a plan. I decided to take a ride to the west end of town and get my first look at Nestor's home. It took about fifteen minutes to get to the head of Kerry Street, where I proceeded west. I'd donned a baseball cap and my out-of-fashion aviator sunglasses to disguise my appearance.

Real cloak and dagger shit, I thought, catching my image in the rearview.

At the corner of 23rd and Kerry, I was happy to catch that intersection's red light so I could study 2305, the third structure on the left. It sat two doors west of Pat's Tap Room, where Nestor spent his evenings loading up before heading home, often to abuse his wife and daughter. Twenty-three-oh-five was a large, two-story frame structure, the double front doors of which made it obvious that it had been duplexed. White paint was curling and peeling from the east exposure and the small front yard was dirt, no grass, no shrubs, no flowers, just dirt and a few weeds, enclosed by a rusting, chain-link fence and gate.

When the light turned green and I drove forward, three pre-teen kids came out the door on the right side of the porch. I pulled the car to the curb across from 2305, retrieved a map from the console, and held it fully opened as I eyed the front porch from behind my Ray-Bans.

Through the glass storm of the left front door, I saw that it opened onto an upward stairway. I deduced those steps led up to the Cahills' second-floor apartment since the three kids had come out of the other door. I glanced upward to see three, large, side-by-side bay windows on the second level. Refolding my map, I decided that I'd seen enough for one day and pulled away from the curb, turning left two consecutive times which put me in the easterly direction of St. Matthews.

After an afternoon nap and a makeshift dinner, I settled into the first-floor den, anxious to put the segments of my plan together. I would need a different car than my Civic when I drove to Kerry Street on "E-night," the term I'd given to the night I'd execute Nestor. If anyone later described to police a car they'd seen in the vicinity that night, it should be a description of another very common, generic vehicle and one with bogus tags, not my Civic.

I set the date of "E-night" for Friday, Oct. 11 with back-up dates of Oct. 18 and Oct. 25. I figured Nestor was likely to be in Pat's Taproom on any given Friday night, right up until its two a.m. closing.

I recalled Michael Maddox telling me he had a friend who hunted deer near Brandenburg, KY, which was west of Louisville about forty miles and on the Ohio River. I needed a spot where I could practice firing my Model 70. As I remembered Michael's account, there was a large area of woodlands just west of Brandenburg, the depth of which ran six or eight miles between the main highway and the river, with a width of about twenty miles. I figured I could easily find a practice range to test my marksmanship in that roughly hundred forty square miles of wooded terrain.

I fell asleep that night strangely exhilarated by the process of plotting the death of Nestor Cahill.

Liesl phoned me on Sept. 23, the first full day of fall. "Hi, Poppa. How are you feeling today?"

"Pretty well," I responded. "I have a few things to keep me occupied and that's always good. What are the Martins up to?"

"Not much, actually. Alan has been swamped with SpadeWorx stuff and the Center always keeps me busy."

"Well, tell Alan his father-in-law said the key to capitalistic success is to make sure his income is parallel and proportional to the degree of his busyness. Then being swamped is more tolerable. Anything new with the Molly and Joanne?"

"No, they're still with us. Joanne is afraid to go home, but also afraid to file a criminal complaint against Nestor, sort of in limbo."

"What do *you* know about limbo?" I asked.

"What do you mean?" Liesl said. "Limbo is a state of uncertainty, betwixt and between, if you know what I mean."

Liesl's generic definition got me started. "In Catholic theology, which delineates and defines the rules and results of what happens in just about every conceivable circumstance, limbo is somewhere below heaven, but above purgatory and hell. It's the place one resides if one dies

244

as an infant before being baptized. There is no pain, but no joy, because limbo dwellers can't see God. I think my early teachers stated that when the end of the world occurs, those in limbo get to go to heaven rather that remain in a state of suspense. Or was that the souls in purgatory? I get confused. At any rate, if Catholics only believed that everyone went to, and forever remained in limbo, they'd be infallibly correct."

"Poppa, we were talking about Joanne and Molly."

"Oh yeah, sorry. There are certain words and phrases that always set me off, limbo, plenary indulgence, venial sin, Holy Ghost, extreme unction—"

"I know," Liesl said. "It's okay."

"Does Nestor have a job?" I asked.

"No. Joanne says he draws unemployment. Why do you ask?"

"Oh, just curious to learn what makes someone like him tick. Have you ever seen a case like this one have a happy ending?"

"No. That is unless the perpetrator is locked up. The most you can hope for is that the woman eventually summons the courage to file a complaint against the abuser and that the law keeps him away from her. I've never seen a total conversion of the abuser, if that's what you mean."

"That's what I thought," I said.

"Alan and I would like you to come over for dinner on Sunday, Oct. 6, Poppa. Can you make it at six?"

"Sounds good."

After the phone conversation with Liesl, I was anxious to resume developing my plan of seeing Nestor into limbo. I wished I could send him to hell, or at least purgatory.

I had decided to rent the car I'd use for transportation on "E-night" at an out-of-town location, so I reserved a car online with Circle City Car Rental in Indianapolis from Oct. 10 to Oct. 12. I put ten a.m. as the flight arrival time, and got a kick out of checking both "Business" and "Pleasure" in answer to the "Purpose of Travel" question.

After submitting my reservation, I drove to Gold's Medical Supply just west of St. Matthews, and bought a dispenser box of twelve ultra-thin latex gloves. I couldn't leave any fingerprints at the scene and wanted my hands void of the traces of gunpowder residue inevitably transferred to the hands of one who discharges a firearm.

On Sunday, Oct. 6, I kept my dinner date with the Martins and brought a bottle of Cabernet Sauvignon as my contribution to the meal. Liesl wanted to be brought up-to-date on my health issues.

"Bridget called me two days ago to tell me the scans I had last Wednesday indicated my abdomen and brain are still cancer-free and that the lung and liver tumors haven't grown," I said. "She also prescribed hydrocodone if I should need it to relieve any pain."

"That's good, Poppa."

On Monday morning, I awoke early, retrieved the Winchester, its silencer, and the SuperX shells from the top of the closet. I scratched through a kitchen cabinet drawer until I found six thumbtacks that I secured in an empty pill vial. I tore a few sheets of yellow, legal-size paper from a notepad. After placing everything into the trunk of my car, I drove west on US 60 toward Fort Knox, turned right onto KY 1638 toward Brandenburg. I was looking for the wooded area where Michael Maddox's friend hunted deer.

Just west of Brandenburg, I took another right onto an unnamed road, heading north in the direction of the Ohio River. After about three miles, I came to a clearing on the left side that had a sign with two dictates, "Hunters, park with all four wheels off the pavement. No littering." I wheeled the car into the clearing, cut the engine, and removed my rifle and accessories from the trunk. I began walking into the woods along a defined path toward the river. When I felt far enough into the timberland to have lost contact with the road, I stopped and took stock of the surroundings.

In front of me, the forest floor began to break abruptly downward, toward a swift-running stream that I knew was rushing toward the Ohio. Following the descending contour of the path down to the creek's edge, I noticed four stones sitting high enough in the creek to force the rippling water around them.

I flipped the rifle across the stream, did the same with the shells. With my arms outstretched from my sides at seventy-degree angles, I stepped across the miniature causeway, alighting on the other side next to my weapon.

I was tired, breathing laboriously after hiking and fording the brook. My condition had weakened me and I was forced to stop and rest. Easing myself to the ground using the Winchester for leverage, I braced my back against a large hickory tree. The sounds of the forest, its rhythm, melody, and harmony, were beautiful, unenhanced music. Closing my eyes, I could hear the cleeks and caws of dozens of birds, beautifully staccato over the continuous chord of the stream's purl.

I hadn't been to these places often enough, I thought. After a few minutes, I was rested, respiring normally. I rose from the forest floor and ascended the slope for about forty yards, then looked back across the water's excavation to a spot the same altitude as where I was standing. Seventy yards, I guessed. Not far enough. I walked another twenty yards up the hill and again stopped to assess the distance to a spot of equal height on the other side of the stream. I concluded it was about a hundred yards, more than the distance my 150-grain slug would have to travel to make contact with Nestor Cahill.

I took three sheets of the yellow legal paper from my jacket pocket, unfolded them to their full size, and refolded each to seven by eight-and-a-half inches, roughly equivalent to the size of a human head. With two thumbtacks, I affixed a paper target to each of three trees that were about five feet apart. I printed the letters R-O-T-S-E-N on each of them with a black marker, the letters facing back across the creek. Reversing path, I walked down to the four stones in the water, tossed the gun and ammunition across the creek, and stepped myself over to the original side of the stream. With some difficulty, I trekked the sixty yards up the rise until I was the same height as the three sheets of yellow paper.

I was eager to see the targets across the way through the Bushnell scope's refracted light, but I was once again in need of rest. I lay on my back for ten minutes or so, rehearing the symphony of the forest. I smiled. None of Bach's six Brandenburg Concertos was more vital than the music I was hearing. I thought of it as the debut of the Kentucky Movement.

I rolled from my back to my side, preparing to push myself to a sitting position, when I heard the rustling of leaves surrounding the snap of a cracking twig echoing up the slope from the stream. Moving nothing but my eyes, I scanned the creek bed until I spotted them.

A doe and her fawn were at water's edge, motionless, assessing the safety of taking drink. Each had its ears pricked to full extent. The youngster was about half the stature of its mother, but already its ears were as large as hers. The fawn had white camouflage marks dappling its coat, its face infused with innocence. After another minute of caution, the animals lowered their heads, and began to lap at the water.

As I lay inert, eyes fixed upon the pair, I wondered if it was legal during hunting season to kill a doe with a fawn at her side, or did hunters have a code among themselves wherein it was disdainful to slay a doe with accompanying offspring. Or was the hunting season timed so that fawns were weaned and most could survive without their mothers, as Patrick and Liesl had to do? I wondered.

Considering the eons-old template of the relationship of doe and fawn to each other and to their environment, I marveled at the beauty, the righteousness of that pattern. I realized I might well strike down a disordered Nestor Cahill, but I knew I could never slay either of those two orderly and beautiful beings. I didn't understand how anyone could.

When they finished drinking, the doe walked downstream for a few strides, the fawn in close contact. Mother then veered right and, with no light coming between them, they climbed the hill away from the creek, sometimes walking, sometimes pushing upward off their hind legs and hopping, until distance and camouflage absorbed them into the pattern of the forest.

I remained motionless for another five minutes, wanting the deer to be out of range of sensing me before I sat up to continue my business. After the interlude, I sat facing the paper targets, my knees bent, rifle in hands. Placing my left hand under the weapon's forestock and my right hand just behind the trigger guard, I put my left elbow onto my left knee for support and stability.

Closing my left eye, I leaned my right one into the scope. I adjusted the power to 9X, and a twinge of excitement rushed over me as I saw R-O-T-S-E-N through the lens so clearly that I recognized my own printing.

I retreated from firing position and pulled the box of ammunition from my jacket pocket, set it next to me. I took five shells from the box, and, after unbolting the rifle, pushed them into the magazine. I returned the bolt to firing position, forcing a shell into the chamber. Again I closed my left eye and refocused through the scope.

I pushed off the safety, slid my finger onto the trigger. I remembered my father's words from so long ago: "Don't pull the trigger, David, squeeze it, ever so slowly." When I had the scope's crosshairs on the center of the 'O,' in R-O-T-S-E-N, I began to squeeze.

The powerful recoil of the rifle, coinciding with its ear-piercing crack, surprised me, knocked me from my sitting position onto my back. *Jesus!*

As I regained my composure and sat up, I looked through the scope at the target to see that I'd hit the "O" on its topmost part, the spot where one begins and ends that formation when printing. I duplicated the feat on a different sheet of paper two more times, but was then prepared for the kick of the weapon. I pulled the silencer from another jacket pocket.

After threading it onto the barrel, I focused on another sheet of paper, looking for the spot where the cross stroke and the down stroke of the capital T met. The sound of the shot was effectively muted. Geez, that wouldn't wake anyone up on Kerry Street, I thought.

When I checked the accuracy of my fourth shot, it was the best yet. I took another muted shot at one of the papers, and again, came within a half-inch of the target center.

I stood, looked for my ejected, spent cartridges. "One, two, three, four, five," I counted, finding them all within two feet of my firing position.

Traipsing out of the woods, I felt more alive than in weeks. I was tired but exhilarated with the aggregation of the forest, the colors, the sounds, the earthy, pungent smell. Then I remembered how numbered sensual experiences such as those had become.

I drove to Indianapolis the morning of Oct. 10, parked my Civic at one of the airport lots, and boarded a shuttle to the terminal. I carried a tote bag and an empty suitcase to appear as an ordinary traveler. That charade called to mind, and made me grin about, the time I overacted by waving an empty briefcase at the guard at the Cassidys' mansion. *Jesus!*

Once inside the terminal, I had a cup of coffee at a Starbucks, then walked out of the building to the Circle City Car Rental shuttle stop, where I boarded a bus to transport me to the that agency's lot. There I picked up a non-descript Chevrolet Malibu.

Two hours later, I was back in Louisville at the huge parking lot of the St. Matthews Mall shopping center. I parked next to an old, rusty, brown Geo Prizm, as far away from the buildings as I could get and still have other cars around me.

Pulling a screwdriver from my tote bag, I removed the license plate from the old Prizm and replaced it with one I took from a Mustang in the south end of town a few days earlier. I drove the rented Malibu to the other side of the parking lot, took off its Indiana tags and affixed the Prizm's plate in its place.

Having decided not to chance having the Malibu at Four-fourteen, I pulled the rental close to the shopping center buildings, disembarked, and walked through the mall's center concourse to the opposite end. Exiting the building, I walked the six blocks to Four-fourteen. That exercise was fatiguing, and I was exhausted by the time I arrived home. I didn't bother to undress before lying across the bed for some needed sleep.

After awakening late that afternoon, I walked to the Derbytown Car Rental office, a distance of about a half-mile, and rented a blue Ford Taurus, then headed back to western Louisville and the Cahill house. I didn't want my own car in that vicinity again and I didn't want the rented Malibu at the scene except on "E-night."

Kerry Street ran from the downtown sector to the Portland area of the city that was the extreme northwestern point of Louisville. Portland was the neighborhood near the rapids of the Ohio River where the city first germinated. It was heavily Irish-American and had maintained its distinct Caucasian identity even through the years when Louisville's African-American population was abjectly herded into the city's west end, thanks to Urban Renewal and blatant discrimination.

Portland's historical significance, coupled with the steadfast diligence of some proud, sixth and seventh generation residents, kept local tax dollars flowing into the community, allowing that neighborhood to buck the trend of diminution other blue collar areas were experiencing. The downtown area, for obvious reasons, had no problem attracting the attention of local legislators and the funds that followed such attention.

Kerry Street and its surrounding district were caught between the rock of Portland and the hard spot of Downtown. The sector had no identity. It wasn't even named, other than the "area between Portland and Downtown." Unemployment was common and the crime rate was high, as could be expected in an area that was off the radar of much in the way of governmental assistance. Such was the venue in which Nestor Cahill operated, wreaking hell on his wife and daughter.

I drove west on Kerry Street, and at the intersection of 23rd, I again saw Pat's Taproom, where I knew Nestor spent a preponderance of his evenings, probably shooting pool and drinking beer. My gaze moved to the duplex tenement that was the home of the dysfunctional Cahill family.

I parked the Taurus just short of 23rd Street where I had a clear view of the entrance to Pat's and also of the front of 2305. It was dark, and I felt some apprehension sitting alone in a car in that area. Two men walking on the sidewalk passed the door of my car. One of them looked in my direction. I knew he saw me but they didn't stop. One flipped a cigarette over my car into the street. After that, I slouched down and adjusted all three rear-view mirrors downward to angles from which I could see anyone approaching the car from behind.

After about twenty minutes, a large man came out of the left front door of 2305. He was wearing a baseball cap and a sweatshirt, the sleeves of which had been removed. After he descended the four steps from the yard to the sidewalk, he stopped, lit a cigarette.

As he walked east on Kerry, headed toward my car, but on the opposite side of the street, I knew the man I was observing was Nestor Cahill. Raising his arm to take a drag of his cigarette and caught in the glow of a street light and Pat's Taproom's backlit sign, Nestor exposed the milky white flab of his breast through the extra-large hole created when the sleeves had been cut away from his sweatshirt.

He was pretty much the way I had him pictured, lowbrow and crude, mean looking, with a mouth that made it appear he was snarling.

After my quarry had disappeared into Pat's, I started the Taurus and headed west on Kerry. The houses, on the opposite side of the street from 2305, backed up to the switching yards of the Kentucky & Indiana Terminal Railroad Company. Only an alley behind those dwellings separated them from a steep, grassy slope that ascended to a chain-link security fence that kept potential interlopers out of the K&I yards.

I turned right onto 24th Street, which discontinued after about fifty yards due to the fence-enclosed railroad property. Again to the right I swung the Taurus, entering the alley behind the houses across Kerry Street from Nestor's house. I slowed down between the back yards of 2306 and 2304.

From that vantage point, I could see the front bay windows of the second-floor Cahill apartment. It was obvious that if I'd climb the slope to the K&I's fence from where I was, I'd have a clear line of fire into the unadorned, second-floor front windows of Nestor's place. That distance, I estimated, was a little less than a hundred yards.

I made a mental note to pick up some athletic cleats for "E-night" to help me negotiate the steep grade leading up to the railroad yard's fence. After scoping the alley, I wanted to get back onto Kerry Street and hoped Nestor would be home from Pat's before long.

I circled the Taurus around the block until I was headed west on Kerry. Again, I pulled to the curb just short of 23rd where I could see Pat's and the Cahills' house. After about forty-five minutes, during a few of which I dozed, Nestor strolled out of the tavern toting a six-pack and began walking the short distance to his house.

As I watched, he unlocked and entered the porch door to his upstairs apartment. Within a few seconds, the upstairs front room with the bay windows illuminated, and I saw Nestor standing still, very near the middle window. He seemed to be looking at something in the room, maybe a television. The center bay window symmetrically framed him, making it appear as if he himself was on TV. If he followed that pattern on Friday night, he'd be an easy target.

Nestor took a swig from a bottle of beer, continued looking at whatever it was that had his attention. Just seconds after he walked out of my view, the lights in the room went dim but the gray, darting light of a TV was still jumping around the room. I figured Nestor must have turned out the lights, sat down to watch the tube.

"You need to be sure and turn that light on Friday night, Nestor, then stand still for a minute," I whispered.

Figuring I shouldn't push my luck, I decided I'd made enough progress for the night and headed back to St. Matthews.

The next morning I drove to Rick's Sporting Goods and purchased a pair of size 11-D rubber baseball cleats to assure proper traction when scaling the hill. They were on sale at that off-season date.

"Are you still playing, old-timer?" asked the middle-aged clerk.

"Nah, these are for my grandson. I don't have any whip in my bat anymore."

I smiled when I thought of expensing the cleats' cost on my tax return as a business expense, but frowned when I remembered that I'd probably filed my last tax return.

I awoke at six-fifteen on Friday morning, Oct. 11, and that was earlier than I wanted. I'd have to take a longer than usual nap, maybe even two, since I wanted to be as fresh and rested as possible around midnight.

Liesl phoned me at ten o'clock to ask if I'd like to come for a meal either Saturday or Sunday.

"Sunday would be better for me," I said.

"Can you come for dinner? About six?"

"Yes, that'll be nice. Let me bring a bottle of wine. We'll celebrate."

"Celebrating anything in particular, Poppa?"

You bet, the death of Nestor Cahill, I thought. "No, just the present, just the present."

When we disconnected, I contemplated my approaching death, knowing I'd soon have to choose either a cognizance permeated with pain, a concluding narcosis, or another, less passive way out. In any event, my relationship with Liesl would soon be drastically altered, or ended.

I placed my new pair of cleats and a pair of the recently acquired latex gloves into the white box with the Remington Model 70 that I'd loaded with three 150-grain, hollow-point shells. I'd set the bolt so that one of the three shells was in the chamber of the rifle, a bullet's final resting point before its trajectory down the barrel and out, toward its target.

After driving the Taurus to the Mall, I parked a few spaces behind and to the left of the rented Malibu and pulled the white box out of the trunk, then walked toward the shopping center's buildings.

About halfway to the stores, I feigned forgetting something, using the gestures of an angry, forward snap of my head, pursed lips and a simultaneous grimace. I executed a one-eighty turn, heading back to the vicinity of my two rentals. Comfortable that anyone who might have seen me exit the Taurus had moved on, I approached the Malibu and popped its trunk with the remote key. After placing the white box into the trunk, I again walked toward the buildings and headed straight to an El Rascal's franchise in the center of the complex.

Eating at El Rascal's always put me in mind of Liesl as a toddler. El Rascal's had been "our place" in much simpler, happier times. I grieved the loss of that era, the loss of my granddaughter as a little one.

As I waited for my lunch, I noticed a young mom and her youngster in a booth against the wall. I smiled at the little girl, then to her mother, who smiled back at me. I experienced a brief onset of self-pity before remembering that Liesl never had such a common experience as lunch out with her mother *or* her father. I felt shame for having felt sorry for myself before I did my granddaughter.

After my traditional taco salad, I walked back through the mall and exited by the same door I had entered. I went straight to the Taurus and drove home.

Justine and I had a date for a matinee IMAX film about the Titanic that afternoon, after which we enjoyed a quiet, early dinner at a trendy little Spanish restaurant on the eastern edge of the downtown district called *La Nieta,* which meant The Granddaughter. I told Justine my car was in the shop and asked if she'd mind driving.

After dining, she invited me up to her condo but I, quite truthfully, told her I was too tired and needed some sleep. She dropped me at Four-

fourteen about seven forty-five and said she'd call me in a couple of days. After setting the alarm for eleven-fifteen, I stretched out across my bed.

I slept soundly until the loud, intrusive series of three electronic tones from my alarm clock jolted me to consciousness. After turning the alarm off, I lay back down, wanting more sleep. If ever a time was right for calling off my felonious plan, it was at that moment.

If I continued to lie prostrate much longer, sleep would overtake me, and my efforts of buying a rifle and silencer, practicing shooting in the woods, and renting dual cars would all have been a waste. Did I want to go through with this? Even if my actions broke Joanne's chains to Nestor, would she follow the routine of countless other abused women and gravitate to another abuser? Might Liesl and the Center convince and empower Joanne to leave Nestor on her own? Perhaps, but Nestor would no doubt find others to abuse and he'd be left unpunished and unfettered.

I forced myself to a sitting position, opened my eyes widely and shook my head a couple of times. Coffee. Yes, caffeine. I fumbled in the cabinet for a filter, measured a portion of grounds into it, and added water.

I had severe discomfort in my lower spine, so I retrieved the hydrocodone tablets from the bathroom cabinet, and took two with a gulp of water. Five minutes later, the coffee had served its purpose. Thirty minutes later, the hydrocodone had too. I was wide awake and feeling no pain.

I pulled the Taurus out of the garage and drove to the Mall, parking a few rows behind the Malibu. After opening its trunk to assure myself the box was still there, I drove the Malibu out of the huge, deserted lot and headed for Kerry Street.

As I was headed west on one-way Main Street, a police car pulled behind me from a side street, and followed along, a few car-lengths back. My inclination was to turn onto a side street, but I was terrified that the black and white would turn behind me. Main Street was deserted and it was after midnight. Might the officer run a routine check on the Malibu's plate?

That thought made my heart hammer to where I thought my temples would explode. If the cop ran the plate through his on-board computer, it would come back as belonging on an older model Geo Prizm. *Fuck.*

The trailing cruiser pulled into the left lane. As it went by my Malibu, I could see the guy talking and laughing into a cell phone. The relief felt similar to emptying my bladder after holding it for hours.

I proceeded to Kerry Street and, catching the red signal of the traffic light at 23rd, pulled the Malibu to a stop. Pat's Taproom was like an oasis of white light in the darkness of Nestor's neighborhood. I could only hope he was among its revelers.

When the signal turned green, I pulled slowly by the bar and glanced in to see a crowd of patrons. Two doors west, 2305 was dark on the second floor but a few lights were on in the first-floor unit.

I turned the vehicle right onto 24th Street, heading toward the K&I's yards, turned out the headlights, and made a U-turn, facing the car back toward Kerry Street. Pulling to a stop, I surveyed the only three houses from which someone could see the Malibu. They were all dark, lifeless. It was twelve thirty-five a.m.

At one o'clock, I opened the door after moving the interior light switch to the off position. I moved to the trunk, opened it, and pulled the cleats out of the white box. I slipped off my loafers, slid an athletic shoe onto each foot, and laced them tightly.

I pulled a latex glove onto each hand and picked up the loaded weapon. There was no streetlight on the corner of 24th and Kerry and my dark pants and coat were unreflective as I walked up the alley past the rear of seven residences. Looking between the seventh and eighth houses, I could see 2305, the first floor of which was still lighted. It was five after one.

Aided by the cleats, I ascended the slope to the fence that bounded the K&I's tracks. When I reached the top, I turned and sat with my back against a fence pole. All I could do then was wait and hope that Nestor was among the evening's patrons at Pat's.

I heard the diesel of a K&I switching engine accelerate on one of the many tracks behind me. A few seconds later, an uncoupled boxcar slammed into another train, probably one of several a switching crew was assembling to roll to distant destinations.

At one-nineteen, the lights on the first floor of 2305 went out. The only illumination by then was the reflection of the bright lights of Pat's along both sides of Kerry Street.

One-twenty, one forty-five, one fifty-five, two o'clock.

At four minutes past two, the lights outside Pat's dimmed, and I could hear voices. One of them was loud enough to wake neighbors. Shut the hell up, I thought, and was happy to hear a few admonishers on the street. "*Shhhhh!*"

The crowd was quieting, dispersing, the surrounding houses and their residents undisturbed it seemed. I saw a group of three people walking west on Kerry past Nestor's house, and heard them close three doors of a car. A few seconds later, I heard the car pull off.

It was quiet, and all activity associated with Pat's seemed to have subsided.

Goddamn, no Nestor.

Just then, I heard a man's voice. "Take it easy, Cahill."

"Catch you later, Pat."

My heart accelerated. Would I be too excited to hit a target at a hundred yards?

Nestor appeared, slowly ambling west on the sidewalk, sucking smoke from a cigarette.

I watched, my temples throbbing again, as he made his way up the porch steps to the left front door of 2305. He fumbled with the key to his door for a moment or two before unlocking it. Seconds later, the overhead lights of the second-floor front room illuminated. Nestor walked to the center window and raised it so that only a screen and a hundred yards separated him from the cartridge in the chamber of my Winchester. He turned around, disappeared from the window. The overhead lights went out, but the TV reflection continued to bounce around the room.

To be prepared, I raised my weapon, braced my back against the fence pole, drew my feet closer to my butt, so that my knees elevated. I steadied my left arm on my knee. Nestor reappeared in the center bay window. He was apparently looking at the television.

With my head pushed forward, my right eye was at the back end of the Bushnell-3200 scope. I closed my left eye and saw Nestor, larger than life. I watched my target raise a half-gallon milk container to his mouth and tilt his head backward, pouring a portion of the carton's contents down his throat. He lowered the container, leveled his head. His face was flickering in the grey reflections of the TV screen.

I pushed the rifle's safety off, moved my index finger to the front of the trigger. With the center of Nestor's forehead in the crosshairs, I whispered, "Hey Nestor, Slim sent me." I gently squeezed the trigger of the Model-70. The explosion of powder, muffled by Cam's silencer, created but a whisper.

Through the scope, I saw Nestor's head flip backward, then snap forward. As it recoiled to an upright position, I could see a small red circle in the center of his brow. Nestor didn't fall over, he crumpled, his torso disappearing downward, still clutching the milk container. The wall immediately behind where he had stood was spattered with blood and splotched with gray matter turned red matter.

I knew Nestor was dead when he hit the floor. I lowered the rifle, raised my head and straightened my legs. I sat motionless for a few seconds, straining to detect any sounds. Hearing none, I rose, hurried down the slope to the alley, and walked briskly to the Malibu parked on 24th Street.

After putting the rifle and latex gloves into the trunk, I keyed the Malibu's engine and, without turning on its headlights, crossed Kerry Street headed south on 24th. I rolled my eyes when I realized I still had on my cleats. *Jesus!*

As I veered east onto Duffy Avenue, the next street past and parallel to Kerry, I turned on the vehicle's lights, and proceeded at the assigned speed limits to the Mall. When there, I stopped the Malibu about ten parking spots to the right of the Taurus and sat still. When I was sure there was no one in the area, I walked to the Taurus, got into the driver's seat, started the engine, and drove the six blocks to Four-fourteen.

I went immediately to the laundry room, put every item I was wearing, except the cleats, into the washer. I put the cleats in with the wet garbage. Slipping on my pajamas and robe, I decided to sit on the front porch swing, even though it was a bit chilly. I speculated about what the reactions of those who knew Nestor would be when they learned he was no longer among us. Molly? Liesl? Pat?

After a short time, I went inside, poured myself a glass of Pinot Noir and began reading former president Hanford Burnett's autobiography, "To The Mountain and Back." Wine and reading always helped me to relax and ease off to sleep. Despite having effected Nestor's nothingness, that night was no exception.

Chapter Fifteen

"Time is a great teacher, but unfortunately it kills all its pupils."
—HECTOR BERLIOZ

Awakening at 7:45 Saturday morning, I turned on the radio, listened to the eight o'clock local news. There was no mention of Nestor's untimely passing.

After coffee and toast, I took a shower and a hydrocodone tablet. I wasn't feeling any discomfort, but I wanted to preempt any that might occur during the drive to and from Indianapolis to return the Malibu and pick my car up at the airport.

I drove the Taurus to Derbytown Car Rental, settled up with the attendant, then walked the short distance to the St. Matthews Mall. Many of the stores weren't open yet, but in the second-floor food court, a couple of restaurants were serving coffee. I bought a small cup of decaf and sat at a table in the common seating area of the restaurants, reflecting on the previous night.

I couldn't believe I had killed that son of a bitch. Oddly, I hadn't the slightest remorse. The only sensation I was experiencing was fear, more like apprehension, that I might somehow be found out. Upon finishing the brew, I walked outside to the Malibu and popped its trunk. I needed to tidy the compartment a bit. Keeping all items below eye level of any passing pedestrians, I placed the Winchester into the white box along with the cleats and latex gloves. Then I removed the bogus Kentucky plate and reattached the Malibu's Indiana tag.

The two-hour trip to Indianapolis International passed quickly, every minute of which, I replayed the prior night's events. Reaching the airport, I drove the Malibu to the remote lot and pulled into a spot just behind my Civic. I removed the white box, along with the bogus Kentucky tag, from the Malibu's trunk and put both into the trunk of my car. I looked at the Malibu's trunk one last time and was comfortable it looked undisturbed. There was certainly no indication it had transported any tools of murder.

I drove the Malibu to the Circle City rental return, checked through the express lane, and boarded a shuttle back to the remote lot. I was home in St. Matthews at one-fifteen and decided the extreme tension of the past fourteen hours merited a nap.

I awoke at four-twenty p.m. and lay motionless in bed for five minutes or so. Realizing I was hungry, I pulled myself up and descended to the kitchen, where I baked a frozen tuna casserole.

I watched the six o'clock evening news on WLVL to see if Nestor's carcass had been discovered, but there was no mention of it.

On Sunday, I arrived at the Martins' Crescent Hill apartment for dinner at the appointed time of six o'clock. As usual, Alan and Liesl were at the door to greet me, usher me up the steps, into the apartment.

"What did you do this weekend?" Liesl asked.

Well, let's see, I *did* kill Nestor Cahill with a high-powered rifle, I thought. "Oh, not much, really."

"I figured you had some things on the agenda for Saturday since you said today would work better for you to come to dinner," she said.

"Oh, you know, I just had Saturday marked for shutting down the yard for the winter."

During dinner, I asked about Joanne and Molly. "Is anything different?"

"Not really," Liesl said. "We explained to Joanne that if she'd prosecute Nestor and testify that he kneed her in the groin just before she miscarried, he'd probably have to spend a lot of time behind bars. But she's convinced that once he was out, even years later, he'd come after her. We had a lawyer and a criminologist counsel her, and the criminologist told her that most often, substantial incarceration time cools the revenge passion of spousal abusers. She wouldn't buy it."

"For some reason, I tend to think there's only one thing that would cool Nestor's penchant for wreaking pain on his family," I said. "That would be croaking."

"You might be right," Liesl said. "Is the medication Dr. Tyler gave you helping?"

"Yes, as a matter of fact, it is. I get through most days feeling reasonably well. All the yard work yesterday tired me out, but for the most part, I feel pretty well. How's business?" I asked Alan.

"It's been good, David. It's the middle of October and I haven't had to lay off any of the seasonal help we took on in the spring."

"You've really hit a niche."

"We've been pretty lucky."

A few minutes after nine o'clock, with a delicious meal and several Limoncellos consumed, I yawned in earnest and told my hosts I needed to get home and get some sleep. During the short drive to Four-fourteen, I speculated as to how Liesl would react if she knew what I had done to Nestor. I realized that any disturbance to our relationship was something I didn't even want to think about, so I tuned in an oldies station on the car radio and smiled when I heard,

As I walk through this world
Nothing can stop the Duke of Earl
And you, you are my girl
And no one can hurt you, oh no

When I arrived home, I fought sleep until ten o'clock, when the first evening television news aired. There was no mention of Nestor Cahill's death.

I didn't sleep well. One reason for my restlessness was a growing apprehension about somehow being linked to the slaying. I was also experiencing pain in my back and chest despite the hydrocodone.

My discomfort and temperament were no better through Monday. I was still on edge about the possibility of some investigator inserting me as a dot of connectivity in the puzzle of Nestor's murder.

Before the fact, I had convinced myself there would be nothing to lead police to consider me a suspect, but my certainty of that had waned. Would the grandfather of a counselor to the wife and daughter of the deceased be too far removed for consideration? If I ever were to be investigated, they'd nail me easily.

The rifle, the gloves, the stolen license plate, and the shoes were still in the tool shed near the garage, where I put them upon returning from Indianapolis. Until now, I'd felt no compulsion to unload the evidence, thinking that haste in executing a disposal plan might lead to a mistake, but now, it was time to get rid of that stuff. That goddamned gun was pointing right at me.

I had purchased a quantity of epoxy flooring resin and the accompanying hardener for the purpose of concealing the contents of the flower box. Cement would have been easier to work with, but the weight of a slab of concrete the size of the flower box would have been difficult for me to lift. A rectangular prism of cured epoxy, however, would be quite manageable.

That afternoon in the tool shed, I poured the resin into a five-gallon pail and, with a mixing drill, stirred the epoxy, while I added the hardener. Once the compound was mixed, I added the contents of a sixteen-ounce container of a lamp black pigment solution that would hide my finished product's contents.

Feeling the compounded solution beginning to heat as the curing process began, I placed the open flower box and its contents onto a sheet of plastic on the floor of the workspace. With much effort, I lifted the five-gallon pail by its handle and, with yard gloves and a red rag for protection against the heat, gripped the bottom of the pail and tipped it so that the coal black solution flowed like black cake batter into the box, encapsulating the contents while taking the shape of their white cardboard container.

I stayed with my project for a few more minutes, making sure that the oozing ebony solution was firming and wouldn't exceed the constraints of the flower box. When convinced, I walked back into the house and turned on the local evening television news. There was still no story of the misfortune that had befallen Nestor.

Jesus, it'd been three days. Someone would surely begin to smell him before too long.

After dinner, I walked back out to the tool shed to check on my concoction. It was harder than a rock and had lost its elevated temperature. I lifted it from the floor onto the workbench and peeled away most of the white cardboard.

I returned again an hour later and carried the slab outside into the fading sunlight, looked intently at the creation. No light was perceptively penetrating the monolith, its sordid contents invisible.

As I was about to put the sealed evidence back into the tool shed, "What's that, Poppa?"

I jerked to a defensive position and, at the same time, emitted a prolonged, multi-vowel syllable of panicked fear, before I could process that my granddaughter was paying me an unusual surprise visit.

"Jesus Christ, Liesl. You scared the buh-jeebies out of me."

"I'm sorry, Poppa. I could hear you from the driveway and figured you heard my car. I was going to the store and thought I'd stop by. I feel terrible."

"Don't, sweetie. It's okay now," I said with a weak smile, the hefty black rectangular prism still in my arms. I felt like I was naked.

"What on earth *is* that, Poppa?"

There was nothing to do but ad lib. "What, *this?*" I said with what I knew was a dumb look on my face. "You know, I'm not sure. I found it at the curb in front of the house. I was going to put it into the tool shed. Do you have you any idea what it might be?"

"No, I've never seen anything like it. I wonder if it fell off a truck or a work machine. Maybe you should prop it up in the front yard so people can see it from the street. You know, in case someone comes looking for it."

"Yeah, that's a great idea. I'll put it out there in the morning."

"I'd do it now, Poppa. Someone might already be looking for it."

"You think? Well, maybe you're right. Go on in while I put it out there."

"No, I can't stay. I was just close and thought I'd pop in. Do you need anything from Walgreen's?"

Just a couple of fucking tranquilizers, I thought. "No thanks, Sweetie. I think I'm all set."

"Can I help you carry that thing to the front yard?"

"Oh no, it's not heavy."

"Okay then, I'll call you in a day or two. I'll tell Alan what it looks like. He might have some clue."

"Yeah, you bet. Bye."

As Liesl backed out of the driveway, I followed her car, carrying what I was almost willing to pray didn't become state's evidence. When I got to the front yard, I walked under an oak as if I were going to set the blackened evidence on display there. As soon as her car cleared my sight, I scurried back to the tool shed with it. *Jesus!*

I went inside and set my alarm clock for midnight, located Hanford Burnett's book, and continued my reading of the ex-President's autobiography. I began dozing at about eight forty-five and, just before nine, I put down the book, gave in to slumber.

When the alarm sounded, I hit the snooze button twice before sitting up on the edge of my bed at twelve-twenty a.m. I was tired, but figured a cup of coffee would invigorate me enough to get my weapons-disposal plan executed. I prepared the coffeemaker to brew a single cup, dressed while it percolated.

After downing the coffee, I walked to the tool shed, retrieved the black monolith, and toted it to my car where I placed it into the trunk. I drove off the property, heading to Interstate-64. When I came to that expressway, I took the on-ramp leading to the westbound lanes and saw the lights of downtown Louisville as I leveled my speed at fifty-nine miles-per-hour and set the cruise control.

From St. Matthews, I-64 West ran between the heart of the downtown area and the Ohio River, shortly thereafter traversing the Sherman Minton Bridge that led out of both Louisville and Kentucky, into Indiana. As I crossed the river on the westbound upper deck of the bridge, I tried to glance at the gleaming Ohio River as much as possible and still maintain control of the vehicle.

I still enjoyed viewing the river at night when the reflections of city lights made the big stream come alive from bank to bank, made it shimmer as if it were rushing to get somewhere.

I took the second Indiana exit off I-64 and turned left, heading back under the superstructure. Then I wheeled the car left again, heading up the ramp that was marked *I-64 East: Louisville*. Soon I was on the eastbound, three-lane, lower deck of the bridge.

One aspect that had helped me to determine the Minton Bridge's suitability for my mission that night was from the lower deck, the reflection of an approaching car's headlights could be seen well before the car itself came into view and, conversely, well before a car stopped on the bridge would come into the view of any approaching car's driver.

With that confidence, I slowed the vehicle to a stop at a spot on the bridge I perceived was roughly above the middle of the river's forty-five hundred foot width. I sat for a moment searching my mirror for any detectable approaching light. Seeing none, I exited the driver's seat, retrieved the flower box turned black box from the trunk, and carried it to the side of the steel frame of the bridge. I extended the sealed evidence outward, past the rusting steel barriers of the bridge's sides, and released it.

I pushed my head and shoulders between the riveted girders and looked down. The bridge lights helped me to see the rifle, gloves and shoes, encapsulated in their black tomb, floating downward in silence and grace until they were visually absorbed by the darkness of the water. Seconds later, a small, circular, white explosion of surface water, along with the muffled splashing sound of impact, ended their journey. I stood motionless, looking downward, a prisoner of the sheer enormity of all that had transpired since Friday night. I thought of Patrick, of Kathryn, wondered while looking into the water's blackness, what they might think of my plotting, executing a murder.

I envisioned myself jumping from the bridge, falling into the liquid ebony canvass, causing a similar explosion of white water, feeling the devastating shock of impact, maybe even the coldness of the river. That reflection was at once exhilarating and frightening.

To allow oneself the contemplation of death for the seven or eight seconds between jumping from a bridge and impacting the water, to have that much time to think while floating into mortality's abyss, seemed more courageous, more intellectually proper, more graceful, than acquiescing to the thoughtless millisecond that separated the squeeze of a trigger from the resultant piercing of one's brain by a piece of lead.

Suddenly, a reflection of light flashed on the steel beams of the bridge, ending my philosophical exploration of suicide methodology. A car was approaching. I hurried around the Civic, got into the driver's seat, and cranked the motor. I turned on the headlights and remained in the right lane of three across the bridge. I leveled the car's speed, awaited with apprehension the oncoming vehicle. When it rolled by me at about eighty mph, I decompressed, exhaled deeply, frowned.

"They ought to lock that criminal son of a bitch up."

When I opened my eyes the next morning, I was surprised when I saw the digits of the clock reading 11:04, my early morning expedition to the Sherman Minton Bridge notwithstanding. I couldn't remember the last time I'd slept until such an hour.

I brewed coffee, retrieved the newspaper from its front-porch landing place. I scanned the Metro section where on page six, in the lower portion of the right-hand column, was a fourteen-line article headlined:

BODY FOUND IN WEST END APARTMENT

The body of a man was found Monday afternoon in an apartment at 2305 Kerry Street in the city's West End. The remains of Nestor D. Cahill were discovered by police, who were called to the scene after a downstairs neighbor detected a stench from the front porch of the duplex and couldn't raise anyone in the apartment. Carlene McWilliams told reporters she called police after her children noticed the odor while playing on the front porch and stairs leading to Cahill's second-floor apartment. "The cops said he was shot," McWilliams said. Lt. Jennifer Blalock, spokeswoman for the Metro Police Department, refused to confirm that. "Details are sketchy at this moment and I can't comment on the cause or the timing of Mr. Cahill's death," she said.

Nestor found at last, I thought. Let us pray for the repose of his soul.

The midday television news was a mere rehash of what the newspaper had reported in its morning edition. There was still no mention of details. Carlene, however, was on the newscast and seemed pleased with her newly found celebrity, as she talked with excitement to WLVL's on-the-scene reporter.

"The police said he was shot," she said. "You just can't imagine the smell. I don't know. He seemed like such a nice man."

I wondered whether Carlene felt Nestor was too nice a man to have been shot, or too nice a man to have stunk so much.

The phone rang just after noon and I recognized the Martins' number on the caller ID.

"Have you read the paper or seen the news?" Liesl asked. "The police found Nestor Cahill dead in his apartment. They told Joanne that it was 'a sniper-like' shooting."

"My god," I said. "What happened? How did Joanne seem?"

"She's upset but stable. I'm not sure she's had a chance to process everything. I know it's hard to understand, but she loved Nestor"

More like she was addicted to him, I thought. "Unbelievable," I said. "Did the police tell her anything else?"

"I don't think they actually know much," Liesl said. "other than the shooter wasn't in the house but shot him from somewhere across the street, probably with a rifle."

"Jesus! Let me know if you hear anything else."

I awoke the next morning at five-fifty when I heard the newspaper bounce off the front door and onto the porch. I retrieved it, went into the kitchen, and perused it for any news of Nestor. An even smaller article than the previous day's was on page seven and headed, "Police Treating Man's Death as Homicide."

There was nothing new in the article, and I thought that might even be the last mention of the incident, unless and until the perpetrator was caught. Turning to the obituaries, I moved my eyes down the columnar listings of the recently departed to the Cs, stopping at:

CAHILL, NESTOR DELBERT, 31

Nestor Cahill of Louisville died unexpectedly on Oct. 11 at his home. He was the devoted husband of Joanne Cahill and loving father of Molly Cahill. He is also survived by his mother, Loraine Cahill, and a sister, Beulah Cano-

va, of Jupiter, FL. Cardwell and Sons is in charge of arrangements.

For the first time, I wondered about Nestor's upbringing. Had his
father beaten Nestor's mother and sister? Had he beaten Nestor? I wondered, but I didn't care. One can rationalize anything, even brutal behavior. Nestor was now where he needed to be, nowhere.

Chapter Sixteen

"Now is my final agony. No more."

—FREDERIC CHOPIN

ny reference to the word baseball would often send me spiraling back to my first visit to Fenway Park, home of the Boston Red Sox. I was six years old and that evening with my father was one of my earliest, truly vivid recollections, indelibly inscribed. I was fond of saying that life never got any better than it was on that uncomplicated, mid-summer, Friday night.

"Our seats are really close to third base," my father told me as we made our way through a dim, tunnel-like structure. When we at last broke free of the entrance ramp's colorless drear, and I stepped onto the concourse separating sections of seats, I was mesmerized by the light flooding onto the bright green grass and perfectly manicured orange-brown dirt. It looked like a huge, brilliant painting, still wet.

A member of the grounds crew was walking behind and pushing a wheel, laying a rigid line of white powder from home plate to the out-field fence. The enormity of the green wall in left field was accentuated by the dwarfed, uniformed players warming up in front of it, talking, spitting, and occasionally scratching themselves.

In the bottom of the third inning, a Boston batter couldn't get out of the way of an inside fastball and was hit in the right shoulder, jolting him to the ground. After a few seconds, he arose grimacing, and talked with the team's trainer who had come out of the dugout to tend him.

"Watch, David," my father said, "he won't rub his shoulder."

"Why not?"

"Baseball players never rub the spot where they've been hit."

"Even if it really hurts?"

"That's right, even if it really hurts."

In the four weeks since Nestor's death, my back and chest pain had become more frequent, more intense. Bridget Tyler had prescribed a larger dose of hydrocodone and suggested that I might want to try wearing a Fentanyl patch as a supplement to the pills.

"The patch is a powerful analgesic narcotic and prolonged use will lead to addiction," she said, "but chemical dependence shouldn't be a consideration, unless you have religious or ethical constraints."

"Those I lack," I said.

"You'll know when you're ready for that step," she said. "Just let me know."

The shock of Nestor Cahill's murder had subsided for Liesl and other workers at the Farnsley Women's Center. They couldn't help being glad he was gone, happy that Joanne was responding to counseling. She planned to enroll in a business school and seek an associate degree in Medical Assisting.

The police interviewed Liesl and a few others who were involved with Joanne's case at the Center. I was feeling more confident about remaining undetected.

"An officer told me the shooter fired a rifle from a slope behind the houses across the street from Nestor's," Liesl told me. "Since he was hit squarely in the forehead, they've discounted a random, drive-by shooting. More likely, it was someone lying in wait. There were a lot of people who didn't like Nestor, but the detectives said they had no firm leads."

"Geez, they might not ever catch the guy," I said. "When will Joanne and Molly be ready to leave the Center and start over?"

"We're trying to line up some housing assistance for them now. There's no hurry on our part to see them go, but as you can imagine, Joanne's anxious to live more of a normal life with Molly. It'll be our job to make sure she continues to be counseled and to make her understand what it takes to remain free of any abusive relationships."

"Yes, I can imagine," I said. "Oh, by the way, the ginkgo's leaves are almost completely gold. They'll be falling soon."

"That always seems so *sad* to me," Liesl lamented. "I want to say, 'Wait! Stay where I can see you and appreciate your beautiful climax for a while longer.'"

"It definitely evokes the blues," I said. "Just try to think of it as nature's renewal, a phase of recycling."

I had seen the wonderful pattern of the ginkgo tree for a quarter century, and I knew that fall would be my last turn to observe the onset of its recycling. The November leaf shedding always seemed like the beginning of the pattern to me, rather than the end. I decided to commemorate the last phase I'd get to see. When the leaves fell in early November, I gathered a few, and took them to a studio to have them encapsulated under glass in a diorama-like display, as a gift for the Martins. I directed the stems be adhered to a black felt background, making the yellow-orange fans appear to be suspended under glass.

Madonna invited Liesl, Alan, and Justine and me to the Maddoxes for Thanksgiving dinner just as had been her custom. That year, due to my physical discomfort, I wasn't sure about participating in a twenty-person meal and celebration, so I declined. I encouraged the Martins to go, but they wouldn't consider leaving Justine and me alone on a family holiday. They invited us to Thanksgiving dinner at a restaurant, but again, I thought myself not up to the effort.

"What if we bring dinner to Four-fourteen for the four of us?" Liesl suggested.

"I'd like that," I said.

When the Martins arrived on Thanksgiving, dinner in hand, I gave the display to Liesl, "Something I had made for your winter holidays."

"Aw, it's so sweet, Poppa. Just beautiful."

Increasing pain forced me to schedule an appointment with Bridget Tyler in early December. Moreover, there was another issue I wanted to discuss with her.

"Can I get a larger dose of the hydrocodone? I'd like to try that before going to the patch."

"Why are you hesitant to try the Fentanyl patch, Mr. Foley?"

"I don't know, Bridget; I guess I'm just a traditionalist."

"I don't know whether to laugh or just roll my eyes," she said. "Look, there's a new drug, new in the marketplace anyway, that the FDA has just approved for people who need round-the-clock opioid treatment, and for whom regular hydrocodone doesn't work. It's called

Zohydro ER and it's a much purer form of hydrocodone, five to ten times the strength of what you've been taking. There's a bit of controversy surrounding it because of its extreme potency. You'll have to follow dosages precisely, but if you want, I'll write it up for you."

"Yeah, sure," I said. "Let's give it a try."

As she looked at me with an expression seemingly wondering if there was anything else, I asked, "Bridget, is there not an uncomplicated way of ending this? An easy way of just shutting myself down, before the real suffering starts?"

"Not as far as I'm concerned," she snapped. "Assisted suicide, if that's what you're referring to, is illegal in this state. It's illegal in all states except Oregon, Washington and, I believe, Montana."

"Perhaps I should go there."

"I'm pretty sure there are residency requirements you don't have time to fulfill, Mr. Foley."

"So there's nothing I can do to avoid what's coming, except maybe put a gun to my temple or jump off some bridge?"

"I'm uncomfortable talking about suicide, Mr. Foley."

"I am too. I'm uncomfortable talking about my death, period. I just don't want to have to endure, don't want Liesl to be *forced* to endure, the grotesque results of this damned cancer."

Tyler winced, shook her head, looked at me with an expression of empathy.

"Sorry, Bridget, it's just a tough time. I shouldn't have put you on the spot."

"Don't worry about it," she said. "I know it's hard."

We were silent for some moments before the young physician said, "Look, I'm going to write that prescription for a thirty-day supply of the ten-milligram Zohydro ER capsules. I must caution you, however, take no more than the dosage on the label, which will be one unit per twelve-hour interval. I can't overstress the danger of taking too many, or dissolving them. This med is designed for extended release, and they're just too potent to ingest in altered form, you know, crushed or melted in a liquid.

"You shouldn't consume any alcohol while you're taking this drug, either. That would dangerously increase the opioid level in your blood. If you get up to as little as double the prescribed amount you could pass out, perhaps die. If you triple the amount, you *will* die. People lose consciousness ingesting such excess amounts or altering the extended release pattern. They suffer respiratory depression and their breathing systems just shut down. Do you understand what I'm telling you?"

I *did* understand, as I looked into the young medic's eyes. They were intense but not angry, unmistakably kind. Her expression was that of a person who had conceded an issue, but it also indicated a person reconciled to the concession.

"Thank you, Dr. Tyler," I said, my eyes still fixed on hers. "You are a noble caregiver."

After the visit, I was anxious to be at Four-fourteen with a bottle of red wine, but on the way home, I stopped to pick up the prescription Tyler had phoned in. Once home, I poured a glass of Pinot Noir, took it into the den.

Now that I had a reasonably antiseptic method of effecting my death, I needed to decide how I wanted to say goodbye to each person on my brief list of loved ones, Madonna, Mia, Samantha, Justine, and, of course, Liesl.

It was important that I express to each of these women why I loved them. I began to think of appropriate gifts, final tokens of thanks, meaningful symbols of my affection. Necklaces were intimate and personal. Yes.

Any gift for Madonna should be reflective of motherhood, I thought. It would also be a worthwhile gesture if the gift somehow relegated our disagreement over religion to its current and proper place of unimportance. I believed an artistic but genuine interpretation of the Sistine Madonna would satisfy both criteria.

A token for Mia needed to portray her gentleness, her compassionate concern for the fragile. I didn't have to ponder long for an idea to occur, a delicate butterfly.

I knew any gift for Samantha would demand acknowledgment of the beautiful metamorphosis she had undergone. Though an abstraction, a swan would epitomize her journey and I knew Samantha would understand its metaphoric meaning.

Justine's present would have to be musical. I thought an instrument too obvious, too predictable. I decided that a literal symbol might best show my appreciation to my partner, my dearest friend. Looking at a piece of sheet music, I quickly gravitated to the artistic lines, curves, and circles of a bass clef on a staff.

There was but one choice for Liesl's necklace. My token for my granddaughter would be a ginkgo leaf.

The next morning, I drove to a downtown jewelry shop where I reviewed my ideas with the owner and asked him to have pieces cast in gold in the form of the five symbols. Using images we found on the Internet, I gave specific direction as to what I wanted created.

The jeweler was enthusiastic about the assignment, and I sensed that he believed the resulting pieces would indeed be beautiful and precious. I ordered five necklaces, each consisting of a fine gold chain and one of the five golden amulets. He assured me the merchandise would be ready the week before Christmas.

Over the next few weeks, it seemed that every day, Liesl, Alan, Madonna, or Justine would phone and ask if they could drop by for a while. I got the distinct impression they'd confabulated about a routine and had secretly agreed to an alternating regimen. It seemed a bit premature, but I didn't mind, since each of them was more than pleasant company.

The Zohydro ER proved to be much more effective in controlling the pain in my back, chest, and abdomen than the regular hydrocodone had been. A continuous discomfort still identified where my afflicted areas were, but it was much easier to tolerate, for the present anyway. I was hoping I could experience my last holiday season feeling relatively well.

When I was notified the necklaces I ordered were ready, I drove to the downtown store and was pleased when the owner showed me the gifts.

"I think there will be five ladies who'll think themselves very lucky when they receive these," he said.

"I sure hope so," I said. *I sure hope so,* I repeated in my mind.

Upon arriving home, I penned a last note to three of my loved ones, sealed each transcription inside a box with the appropriate necklace.

> For Madonna, the consummate mother, from whom I learned so much about fostering children. You have my respect and admiration for so unselfishly adapting your precepts to quench the need that your children have for your approval and encouragement. Liesl needs you and your family.

> For Mia, the first and gentlest of Liesl's caregivers, who changed and immeasurably enriched my life when she placed a minutes-old orphan in my lap at St. Anthony a quarter-century ago. Thank you for being there for us. Please stay close to Liesl.

> For Samantha, who loved Liesl from the first day she met us, and who overcame many obstacles to become a beautiful woman and an accomplished person of medicine. You will always be special to Liesl.

There would be no note for Liesl or Justine. I'd present their necklaces personally, as well as have a conversation about what was coming. I needed the understanding and approval of these two special people. I mailed the other three packages the morning of December 24.

The Martins and Justine agreed to come to Four-fourteen for the traditional Foley, night-before-Christmas gift exchange in front of the modestly lighted indoor fern.

Liesl brought a batch of springerle cookies she had baked, and I served another Foley tradition, homemade eggnog.

Justine opened her gifts first. Liesl and Alan had gotten her a Galileo thermometer, a device composed of a sealed glass cylinder containing a clear liquid, and six or eight different-colored glass floats. Galileo's device showed the temp to be seventy-two degrees, a mere degree off the digital thermometer reading of seventy-one.

"I've never seen anything like it," Justine said. "It's not only functional, it's beautiful. Thank you, Martins, it's so original."

"Alan picked it out," Liesl said, "but I approved wholeheartedly."

When the mini-furor over the thermometer subsided a bit, I handed Justine the small package I'd wrapped in my signature canine paper. "How do you find this paper year after year?" she asked.

"Poppa found it about fifteen years ago," Liesl said. "I think he bought the store's entire supply. I've never gotten a Christmas gift wrapped in anything else since he found it."

"We still had Fielder then, and it was on sale a couple of days after Christmas," I said. "It seemed like a natural."

It didn't take Justine long to get the paper off the small package. "Jewelry?" she asked after seeing the obvious jewelry case. Lifting the top, she said, "David, I can't believe it, a bass clef necklace." Holding a chain end in each hand, she displayed it just below the neckline of her emerald green dress, turning to Liesl and Alan. It was only the second time I'd seen Justine cry.

"Poppa, it's so beautiful and delicate," Liesl said.

"Wear it now?" I asked Justine.

"Yes, yes, I want to," she said. "Let me give you a wet hug first."

After clasping Justine's necklace for her from behind, Liesl picked up a package with a tag marked "*To:* The Martins *From:* Justine." It turned out to be an espresso and cappuccino maker, an item Alan told me that both he and Liesl would like when I asked him for some gift ideas. "You must have been talking to a little birdie, Justine," Liesl said, as I tried not to look like the canary swallowed by the cat.

Justine's tiny package for me contained a set of cufflinks in the shape of the iconic socks that serve as the Boston Red Sox logo. "Terrific," I said, "and I have the perfect red bowtie and suspenders to wear with them."

When it was the Martins' turn to open my gift, I picked up the parcel, sat it on Liesl's lap. It was flat, about thirty-six inches by twenty-four. "I took the lazy way out this year and have but a single gift you'll have to share," I said. "But at least, it's a good-size package."

Liesl removed the bow, untied the ribbon, and began to tear away the paper. It was an oil painting on canvas of Four-fourteen, produced from a photograph taken years ago in obvious springtime. The dogwoods were abloom and the annuals had been set. The nandinas were thriving, reaching skyward, while the ginkgo was unfurling its beautiful fans.

On the front porch, the rocker and the swing were authentic and detailed. In front of the screen door, on the soft porch mat was Fielder, having been procured from an older photo and imposed into the painting, with his gentle face beautifully captured.

Liesl began to cry, the swirling emotion keeping her for a moment from looking at me.

"This house will be yours soon," I said. "I want you to live in it. For me."

"Poppa," Liesl said, as she knelt at the front of my chair putting her head on my knees. "Dear Poppa."

"Be happy here with Liesl for a long time," I said to my son-in-law.

"I don't know what to say." Alan said.

"How wonderful," Justine said softly. "It's just like you to think of something like that, David. Very moving."

We sat in silence for the next few moments until I said, stroking Liesl's hair, "Crying is a revival of sorts, but now it's time to stop. It's a deep-breath moment."

Liesl laughed through her tears, raised her head. "Okay, one, two, three," she said, trying to emulate the tone and inflection I'd used for those instructions so many times in the past. Justine and Alan could only watch Liesl and me as we inhaled dramatically and laughed heartily as we released the air.

"We took the lazy way out too, Poppa," Liesl said. "We only have one gift for you from both of us."

She handed the present to me. I held it to my ear and shook it.

"This feels like another something framed." I stretched the red and green ribbons over the corner of the white tissue-papered package and held it up to the light.

"Open it, Poppa."

As I did, and I looked at the framed image, I was unsure of what I was seeing for a moment. Then I saw the inscription attached to the silver frame's bottom brace, below the ultrasound image and read it aloud. "David Alan Martin – Nineteen Weeks Along – Christmas, 2014."

"Oh my God," Justine shrieked.

I looked at Liesl, then Alan, then back at Liesl. I widened my eyes to their fullest extent, nodded quickly several times, knowing by then that the answer to my unspoken question was yes.

"That's your great grandson, Poppa," Liesl said. "What do you think?"

I wanted to answer, but knew if I did, my burst of crying would make anything I had to say unintelligible. After a few deep breaths, I blurted, "He's beautiful, and by God, he looks *just* like me."

"Oh my God," Justine repeated, much quieter this time. Liesl and Alan both stood over me for a minute or two, respectively stroking my hair, rubbing my shoulder, until I dispatched Alan to retrieve a bottle of wine and glasses for a toast.

"After all this emotion, I probably don't need a wine buzz, but we should have a toast to the four of us. I mean the five of us."

Justine joined Alan to help retrieve the wine and stemware. While they were in the kitchen looking for the bottle and gathering glasses, Liesl said, "I wanted you to see him, Poppa. I needed you to see him."

"Oh, sweet girl, now I have." After a pause, "Just in time."

"Poppa?" Liesl implored, squinting at me. "Poppa, what?"

Head down, I pursed my lips, then looked into her eyes and nodded twice, as if acknowledging an appreciative audience.

"Poppa?" Liesl said, anxiety in her features.

"My goodness," I diverged as Alan and Justine returned with a full bottle and a tray of glasses. "How far along are you, Liesl?"

"Nineteen weeks and two days," Liesl said, allowing me to change the subject. "That picture was just taken the day before yesterday."

"When does that make you due?"

"The middle of May."

"I can't believe you're over four months along," Justine said. "You're not showing at all."

"I *do* have a distinct bump, but I've been wearing loose clothing to hide it. We didn't want to tell Poppa until we knew whether we had a boy or a girl coming. Actually, we haven't told anyone except Alan's parents."

Learning my great-grandson was coming was nirvanic, as if my existence had been consummated. The warmth of the tears rushing on my face was sensuous, and spread over my body. I was grateful, still not knowing to whom or what, for realizing I was experiencing one of my happiest moments, while the moment was occurring.

After several proper toasts and the bottle of wine had been drained, Liesl said, "Alan, I know you're tired, but I'd like to stay here with Poppa for a while longer. Why don't you take the car on home? I'll just drive Poppa's Civic and be there in a little while."

"Is that okay?" Alan said, looking to me for permission. "I really am bushed."

"Sure," I said. "You go ahead and I'll send Liesl home soon, after we talk for a while longer."

"Okay. Good night, David. Good night, Justine," Alan said, giving Liesl a quick kiss on the cheek.

Then again to me, "Now promise you'll call us tomorrow if you need anything or just want some Christmas company."

Not wanting my last promise to be a broken one, I merely said, "Thanks, Alan, I'll be fine tomorrow."

"I should be running along, too," Justine said.

"What's the hurry?" I asked, squinting and curling my lips downward. "I'd like to talk to you and Liesl for awhile."

"Yeah, sure, David. I can stay," Justine said. "I just thought you two might need a little privacy."

It was necessary for Liesl and Justine to both understand my intentions. They were the precise people I couldn't leave in shock and bewilderment about my forthcoming termination and I needed no less than their tacit approval. Liesl, I thought, would also be better off hearing what I had to say with a loved one like Justine there for support, moreover, as a counterweight to her youthful perspective.

As we heard Alan's car accelerate down Ascension Road, the three of us remained in the living room with the lighted fern and the opened gifts.

"Does anyone want another glass of wine?" I asked.

Justine declined with a shake of her head. Her eyes betrayed a degree of anxiety, an uncertainty with which, she was not comfortable. Liesl asked the question I knew she'd need to ask, even if Justine was there.

"Poppa, what did you mean when you said you got to see little David 'just in time?'"

I'd rehearsed this moment, but was still unsure whether I could convincingly make my case. Liesl would be anguished whether or not she understood my feelings or agreed with my choice. I had more confidence in Justine understanding my decision.

The specter of death had visited my granddaughter far too often, but had never broken her strength, affected her attitude toward life. Now I needed her to see my choice as triumph over an appalling death, much nobler than passive surrender to a disease's stated conditions. Now I needed her to be brave.

"Liesl, for a long time I've believed the key to a happy life was to *feel* well on the day you die."

"I've heard you say that," Liesl said. Justine was silent, motionless, her hands clasped in her lap

"Well, this disease isn't going to let me do that. It wants to ravage me first."

I sensed Liesl's body tensing, as her eyes darted to Justine, back to me. "What are you saying, Poppa?"

"I'm saying that I feel fairly well tonight and I'm saying there's a better solution to this problem than withering and decaying, enduring either pain or pharmaceutical stupefaction until enough of my body is destroyed that the remainder of it can't live any longer. I'm saying there's a better solution than forcing you, and Alan, and Justine, and the

Maddoxes, to watch me ingloriously linger, die an undignified, painful death, no doubt begging for morphine, while all of you suffer as much, if not more."

Liesl again knelt in front of me, rested the side of her face on my thighs, closed her eyes. She locked her arms around my knees. I felt her chest convulsing.

"I can't talk about this, Poppa. It hurts too much. I'm not strong. I want to hear what you're saying, I just can't talk about it," she said, trying not to bawl.

Justine pulled her chair close to mine and put one hand on my forearm while stroking Liesl's shoulder with the other.

"I understand, Liesl," I said.

After a moment, I continued. "I've always been captivated by the way the ginkgo tree doesn't suffer its leaves to wither on the branch at the end of their cycle. After they change color, before they lose their radiance, they fall to earth, still of substance. A ginkgo leaf's descent is admirably efficient. Because it's still robust and heavy with moisture, there's no uncontrollable wafting, swirling, no blowing in the wind. The leaf falls quickly, on its own terms and not under the dictates of other elements. That's the way I need to fall, Liesl. On my own terms."

What I meant by "my own terms" apparently exploded within my granddaughter, seemingly spread like white heat through her body, her mind. She panted. She trembled.

"Poppa, no. *NO!*"

Justine remained calm, almost stoic as I continued. "I need you with me on this one, Liesl. I don't *want* to suffer. Or *cause* suffering. I need you to tell me you understand this, that you respect and accept my wishes."

Liesl moaned, hesitated, then she cried, lifting her red-streaked eyes to me. "Poppa, I'm so selfish and weak."

After a moment, she uttered words the three of us knew she couldn't take back.

"But it's okay, Poppa. I *do* understand."

Immediately after uttering that phrase, she wailed in a shrill pitch. Still clinging to me, she began panting irrepressibly.

"Take a deep breath," I whispered to her, looking at Justine, whose tense expression was one of painful resignation. "Now another, sweet girl." Doing so, Liesl regained a measure of composure, though we all remained in our emotional cluster for some moments.

"Poppa, I have to say something," Liesl said, raising her head from my knees to look up at me. "It's going to make me cry some more, but I have to get it out. It's just that I've never known how to thank you. I still don't, but I need you to know that I realize what you sacrificed to be my keeper, my guardian, my mother, my father, my best friend. And you're still so wonderful to me in all of those roles. I've always loved being close to you, loved you more than I could ever express."

"Sweet Liesl," Justine whispered, eyes glistening, the three of us motionless. When Justine looked at me, she merely said, "David." I knew that to be her consent.

We continued to cling to each other, no one speaking. Liesl trembled, wept aloud. Justine, too, began to sob. My tears were streaming, but silently. I continued to feel the warmth, the exhilaration of that earlier moment, that happiest moment, when I learned of my great-grandson's existence. What a wondrous comfort.

I disengaged from my loved-ones' embraces and, though my face was tear-streaked, I said with sarcastic assuredness to Liesl, "You're welcome."

That was enough misdirection to make all three of us spurt a laugh, Justine actually spraying a bit of spit, which helped break the grip of the overwhelming emotion that had become almost too intense. Then Liesl said, smiling, "Poppa, you're so silly."

"You know," I said, "learning about the little guy you're carrying makes my circumstance much easier to deal with. It allows me to see it not as an end, but as an inevitable and grand recycling. 'Life goes on' is such a wonderful truism."

Again, we were huddled in silence for several minutes before I asked, "Shouldn't you two be getting home now? It's late."

"Not yet, Poppa."

"No, David," Justine added.

"Okay."

For a time, Liesl knelt silently in front of my chair, her head back in my lap. Justine had risen to stand behind my chair, her hands stroking the tops of my arms. I remembered the joy of having Fielder, the pain of losing him. I recalled my first reluctant, then whole-hearted acceptance of Alan, and what a wonderful wedding he and Liesl had.

I thought of Liesl on my lap in our first meeting at St. Anthony's, her face frowning with her liquid ebony eyes seemingly focused on and assessing her Poppa. I, for some strange reason, also thought of the day I walked in on her as a teenager, in bed with a boy whose name I was glad I couldn't recall. I was still proud of myself for the way I handled her terrible indiscretion, not scolding or punishing her, just understanding.

I remembered the surge of excitement I felt when I first saw Justine, stately and elegant on stage in her chair, waiting with her beautiful dignity for the conductor's call to attention. I thought of my exhilaration when I realized that she liked me too.

After a while, Liesl interrupted my interludes. "I suppose I should be getting on home, Alan's expecting me."

"I'll drop you off, Liesl," Justine offered. "It's on my way."

Once my final guests had donned their coats and gloves, Liesl said. "I love you, Poppa."

"I love you too, Liesl." With a diversionary wink and extended arms, I said, "Here, I need one last hug." As my granddaughter embraced me, I felt again her childlike willingness to press herself to me. How fortunate I was to have always known the unconditional embraces of a person I loved so deeply, without condition.

"You know I love you too, Justine." I said, tilting my head, raising my eyebrows.

"Yes, I do know that, David. And I love you . . . differently, but more than I've ever loved anyone."

"Oh, Justine, my noble patrician who tolerated my plebian tendencies and kept me happy."

Justine's mouth contorted, and with her tears tracking again, she said, "Liesl, I need you to tell me that I'm going to be the embedded babysitter for that new little David you have coming."

"Oh yes, Justine," Liesl said, shaking her head slowly, affirming that there was no doubt about that coming relationship.

"You and I will be together every time I'm with him, David," Justine said, eyes moist and beseeching. The three of us stood in tight union, each holding the other two, and remaining silent for some unmeasured moments.

"Alright," I said. "Run along now, you two."

"Okay, Poppa. I'll see you tomorrow."

"Goodbye, David," Justine said, knowing, I thought, that she and Liesl wouldn't be seeing me tomorrow. I watched from a front window as Justine's car pulled out of the driveway onto the street. I saw the car's tail lights diminish and then disappear into darkness.

I poured myself another full glass of wine, took it upstairs to my bathroom where I pulled the plastic container of Zohydro ER from the medicine cabinet. Counting out eight capsules, I clipped one end of each with a pair of nail trimmers and poured the contents into the brimming wine glass. I stirred it with the only instrument I could find, my toothbrush, and carried the compound into my bedroom, took a swig. How appropriately sweet it tasted despite the deadly additive.

Damn, hold on.

I descended the stairway to the lighted fern and retrieved the framed image of the very young David Alan Martin. I moved to a cabinet drawer and found the golden retriever-wrapped ginkgo necklace tagged "For Liesl." I returned to my bedroom and began taking steady drinks from the wineglass, until my self-prescribed overdose was fulfilled.

I had cued a disc of Mozart's *Requiem* to play the "Dies Irae" segment of the piece's third movement. The haunting chorus, flamboyant tympani, and the dramatic swings in tempo of "Dies Irae" made it the most compelling music of the composition. It also contained the only lyrics I knew of the entire piece.

What then shall I say, wretch that I am,
What advocate entreat to speak for me
When even the righteous
May hardly be secure?

I fluffed my pillow, lay on the bed, and pulled the comforter to just below my shoulders. I clutched my final Christmas gifts to my chest, one I had received, the other I was giving. Closing my eyes, I could feel Mozart's music surging within me like liquid, warm and comfortable, merging with me utterly, lending courage as I embraced the ultimate transformational moment.

— END —

CPSIA information can be obtained
at www.ICGtesting.com
Printed in the USA
BVOW03s1732071216
470071BV00008B/163/P

9 781938 462238